Development and Use of the MMPI-2 Content Scales

Development and Use of the MMPI-2 Content Scales

James N. Butcher
John R. Graham
Carolyn L. Williams
Yossef S. Ben-Porath

University of Minnesota Press   •   Minneapolis

Published by the University of Minnesota Press
2037 University Avenue Southeast, Minneapolis MN 55414.

Printed in the United States of America.

Library of Congress Cataloging-in-Publication Data

Development and use of the MMPI-2 content scales / James N.
Butcher . . . [et al.].
    p.   cm. — (MMPI-2 monograph series)
  Includes bibliographical references.
  ISBN 0-8166-1817-8
  1. Minnesota Multiphasic Personality Inventory. I. Butcher, James
Neal, 1933–   . II. Series
RC473.M5D48 1990   89-20297
155.2'83 — dc20   CIP

Contents

Foreword

MMPI-2 is finally here, and it is difficult to exaggerate the personal and professional significance of this fact for the assessment community at large. This is a happy occasion on which to anticipate the excitement of new generations of clinicians and researchers who will be cutting their teeth on MMPI-2. It is also a time to pay tribute to those past workers who grew long in the tooth developing the original instrument and waiting for its ultimate revision. Some members of the latter group may well recall the historic Fifth Annual Symposium on the MMPI held in Minneapolis in 1972, in honor of Starke Hathaway. That conference was concerned with the possible revision of the MMPI and with the problems that would be encountered in such a revision. To some a revision seemed unwise and to many the problems seemed insurmountable. Given this atmosphere, the achievements described in this book seem all the more remarkable.

Most readers are well aware that earlier contributions of the MMPI to our discipline were not confined to strictly clinical applications. In his recounting of the history of personality research methods, Kenneth Craik (1986) underscored the pivotal role of the MMPI, in the post-World War II era and thereafter, in providing a context for discussion and investigation of the major methodological and conceptual issues of that period. These issues ranged widely over topics such as clinical vs. statistical prediction, profile interpretation, strategies of scale construction, and base rates (to name a few). In critical discussions of these issues, the MMPI was sometimes cited as a paticularly good example (e.g., actuarial prediction) and other times as a particularly bad one (e.g., response styles). But the point is that one cannot conceive of the conceptual and methodological advances (and retreats) of this period as having occurred in the absence of the MMPI. The MMPI has always attracted, and will continue to attract, individuals who, like its developers, are hard-nosed-scientist-practitioners in the best sense of that role.

Of the many issues that have centered around the MMPI, *item content* is probably the one that is closest to home (Minneapolis) and the research described in this book constitutes a milestone in the lengthy history of that issue. Paul Meehl's (1945) forceful statement of the radical-empirical position on the meaning and significance of test responses provided both a manifesto for future development of the MMPI and a caveat regarding the dangers inherent in an uncritical acceptance of the "content" of item responses. The manifesto for development turned out to be extraordinarily productive; the suggestion to ignore the apparent content of a patient's responses turned out to be less so.

The seeds of an alternative and coherent view of the meaning of item responses may be found in Timothy Leary's (1957) seminal work on the *Interpersonal Diagnosis of Personality*. Leary considered self-reports to items reflecting interpersonal dispositions as conscious communications reflecting the manner in which patients choose to present themselves to others. The veridicality of such communications is not an issue. Robert Carson (1969), another seminal interpersonalist, provided a conceptual perspective for MMPI interpretation that also views the testing situation as an opportunity for the communication of messages which serve the function of strategic impression management. Again, the veridicality of such communications is not assumed. Carson also felt that the MMPI clinical scales provided an organizing scheme that relates self-presentations to behavior classifications familiar to the clinician (e.g., hysteria).

Whether item responses are regarded as strategic self-presentations or as less oblique self-disclosures (another possibility), it must be recognized that the MMPI clinical scales provide less than adequate channels of communication between patient and clinician. The message sent by the patient (e.g., "I do not tease animals") is decoded within a frame of reference of which the patient is unaware (e.g., "This patient may be depressed"). The heterogeneous content within most of the clinical scales makes this kind of miscommunication fairly commonplace.

Although the self-presentational and empirical-correlate views call for substantially different strategies of scale construction, the adoption of one perspective need not preclude consideration of the other. The MMPI has become a multi-purpose personality assessment device and, although its defining feature and probably its greatest utility lies in the empirically derived clinical scales, the possibility of supplemental content scales has been considered for many years, as the historical review in this book makes clear. For the most part, the major proponents of the MMPI empirical approach have been sympathetic to the idea of content scales. My own efforts to develop MMPI content scales were encouraged from their inception by such luminaries as James Butcher, Grant Dahlstrom, David Nichols, and Auke Tellegen; John Graham (1987) has described these scales favorably and the Master himself has seen some virtues in this approach (Meehl, 1971). Given this long-standing support and the improved climate that content approaches have enjoyed in recent years, it is not surprising that content scales were accorded a prominent position in the development of MMPI-2.

The development and validation of a new set of content scales that are representative of previously established dimensions and the extension of the universe of content to include dimensions of more recent concern in clinical practice are themselves challenging goals. But to do so while simultaneously correcting the well-known deficiencies of the original items, restandardizing on contemporary representative samples, and above all preserving the continuity of the original clinical scales is a feat that staggers the imagination. The manner in which this ambitious enterprise was carried off and the way in which state-of-the-art procedures for constructing content scales were implemented provide a fascinating chapter in the recent history of personality assessment. The preliminary evidence on the validity of the resultant content scales provides the icing on the cake.

One becomes attached to useful psychological tests over time and I must admit that in reading this excellent treatment of MMPI-2 and the new content scales, I could not help but think of the test (and the old content scales) it replaces. In a sense, this book could be thought of as an owner's guide for a brand new model (Mark II) of a prestigious line of automobiles. Perusing this guide, one is reassured that MMPI-2 retains the distinctive qualities that have attracted discriminating consumers for 50 years; there is no question that this is an MMPI. Yet there are many new features and accessories that promise improved reliability and performance. One can hardly wait to test drive it.

Trading in the older model is a bittersweet experience. The old classic gave many years of faithful service and its ownership bestowed a sense of kinship with a select group of like-minded enthusiasts. True, one had to endure the jibes of owners of competitive brands, who valued technology over tradition. One also had to ignore certain features that appeared objectionable or quaint to almost everyone. But it was worth every minute of it and I'll miss that beauty. Good-bye, old friend.

March 15, 1989   Jerry S. Wiggins

Preface

With the publication of MMPI-2, the first major revision of the most widely used clinical personality instrument, a new chapter in objective personality assessment is underway. Given the broad application of the original MMPI in clinical practice and research, and the goals of the MMPI Restandardization Committee to improve and expand the instrument's utility, we anticipate that the MMPI-2 will be quickly incorporated into contemporary clinical settings. The MMPI-2 provides continuity with the original MMPI by retaining the empirically derived clinical and validity scales that have pervaded clinical practice for the past half-century. The MMPI-2 also will incorporate new ways of viewing personality characteristics and clinical problems — through the themes or content dimensions reported by the client. Personality inventory scale-construction theory and methodology has advanced considerably since the early days of the MMPI. No longer is "blind empiricism" considered to be the most important or the only effective means of developing useful personality scales. Rational strategies have had their "honor" restored in recent years, and as we shall see in this volume they can serve as the starting point for new scale development.

We believe that the approach followed in the development of the MMPI-2 Content Scales incorporates the best of several methods of scale construction. Our purpose in developing these scales was to provide a psychometrically sound and effective way of assessing the client's standing on the major content dimensions in the MMPI-2. We believe the scales meet that goal, thus facilitating more direct communication between client and clinician, subject and researcher. Our hope is that researchers and practitioners will find these new scales useful in personality description and prediction.

This book describes the rationale for the new MMPI-2 Content Scales, including an overview of the content approach to scale construction and MMPI interpretation. The methods employed for the development of the content scales are described in detail, along with the psychometric properties of the new scales. In later chapters of the book, validity and interpretative information and case illustrations are presented.

We would like to express our appreciation to a number of individuals who have contributed substantially to the success of this project:

Dr. Laura Keller has been a project research assistant since the MMPI-2 restandardization study began. She served as a general coordinator for the Minnesota and Washington normative data collections and was involved in every phase of the studies including subject recruitment, proctoring for Minnesota adult and college samples, data processing, and preparation of written materials. She assumed the major responsibility for the chronic pain study cited frequently in this book.

Karen Gayda, our project coordinator and secretary, was involved in the project from the beginning to the end. She participated in such varied tasks as subject recruitment, general organizing of the normative data collection for Minnesota, Washington, and California adult community samples, helped manage the military data collection, the inpatient psychiatric data collection, and the chronic pain study. Throughout the project she assisted in organizing data for processing and preparing tables for publication. Chris Elwell, faced with the difficult task of replacing Karen toward the end of the project, did so admirably.

Wendy Slutske assisted in data processing and analysis. Steven Hjemboe assisted in the normative data collection and assumed a major role in the distressed couples study. Nathan Weed assisted in data collection, data analysis, and review of materials. Kyunghee Han and Noriko Shiota assisted in the data processing and table preparation.

Drs. Linda Roberts and Fred Ninonuevo were key research assistants in the psychiatric inpatient data collection for the Minnesota inpatient samples. Dr. Thomas McKenna organized and supervised the data collection at the Hazelden Alcohol Treatment Program. Mary Alice Schumacher reviewed drafts of most of the chapters and made valuable comments on them.

The following individuals collaborated in the military data collection: Dr. Timothy Jeffrey, Department of Psychology, University of Nebraska Medical Center, Omaha, Nebraska; Dr. Tommie G. Cayton, Lackland Air Force Base, San Antonio, Texas; Dr. Susan Colligan, Naval Hospital Oakland, California; Dr. Jerry R. DeVore, Dwight David Eisenhower Army Medical Center, Augusta, Georgia; and Dr. Rahn Minegawa, United States Marine Corps. Drs. W. Grant Dahlstrom and Eric Bowman, U.S. Naval Academy, collaborated in the college student study.

We are grateful to several clinical facilities that cooperated with us in data collection on the MMPI-2: Anoka Metro Regional Treatment Center (Anoka, Minnesota); Hennepin County Medical Center (Minneapolis, Minnesota); Sister Kenny Rehabilitation Hospital (Minneapolis, Minnesota); Hazelden Treatment Center (Center City, Minnesota); and Falls View Hospital (Cuyahoga Falls, Ohio).

Finally, the cooperation and assistance of Dr. W. Grant Dahlstrom, Dr. Auke Tellegen, and Beverly Kaemmer, members of the University of Minnesota Press's MMPI Restandardization Project made a substantial contribution to the development of the MMPI-2 Content Scales.

Minneapolis, Minnesota   J. N. B.
June 16, 1989   J. R. G.
                                                         C. L. W.
                                                         Y.S. B-P.

Chapter 1
Content Approaches to MMPI Scale Construction and Interpretation

I cry easily—TRUE

I am happy most of the time—FALSE

I believe I am being followed—TRUE

Someone has been trying to poison me—TRUE

Minimal psychological sophistication is needed to conclude that the first two items above are most likely to appear on a personality scale measuring depressive symptoms and that the last two are part of a scale measuring paranoid or suspiciousness symptoms. What may surprise those unfamiliar with personality scale construction is that in addition to the first two items appearing on Scale 2 (Depression) of the Minnesota Multiphasic Personality Inventory (MMPI), all four also appear on Scale 6 (Paranoia) of the MMPI. Such heterogeneity of item content on the basic MMPI scales is the result of the empirical approach to personality inventory construction, the approach most often used in the early work on the MMPI.

The empirical approach was not related to theories about the structure of personality or to the nature of psychopathology. It evolved because of problems with earlier inventories developed according to a content approach:

> It was the sheer frustration of the need for a more practical if not more valid test to use in clinical applications of psychology which led to the development of the first thoroughly empirical personality inventory (Hathaway, 1965, p. 461).

MMPI scales were made up of items that discriminated between normal subjects and clinical groups on the basis of the Kraepelin-derived nosology in wide use at the time. All four items listed above appeared on Scale 6 because the response frequencies of those items in Hathaway's paranoid patient sample differed from the response frequencies of the normal subjects. Likewise, the first two items appeared on Scale 2 because the response frequencies differentiated normals and depressed patients:

> derivation of the items for a scale did not appreciably depend upon the manifest content of the item. The break from the face validity approach to item selection for a scale was the result of a conscious decision. No item was ever eliminated from a scale because its manifest content seemed to have no relation to the syndrome in question, conversely no item was arbitrarily accepted if the validating evidence for the item was not strong (Hathaway, 1956, p. 106).

Although Hathaway (1956) eliminated some of the overlapping items, others were left in the scales because of the assumed overlap in the clinical syndromes themselves.

Almost 30 years elapsed before much attention was directed to the item content of the MMPI, perhaps because of the initial frustration of MMPI researchers with content approaches to scale construction and the success of their empirical methods. As Jackson noted, "while there were some important exceptions, among many adherents it was almost considered unscientific or mystical to investigate categories of content" (1971, p. 231). However, many began suggesting that item content was important to consider in scale development (e.g., Burisch, 1984; Jackson, 1971; Koss, 1979; Wiggins, 1969). As Wrobel and Lachar (1982, p. 470) said: "Content validity is a necessary, although not sufficient, condition for criterion validity."

The inclusion of new content scales in the MMPI-2 (Appendix A) demonstrates that views of personality scale construction have changed considerably since the original MMPI was developed. (See Table 1 for a list of the standard MMPI scales, the most frequently used MMPI content scales, and the new MMPI-2 Content Scales, along with their abbreviations.)

Comparison of Personality-Scale-Construction Approaches

Classification of Scale-Construction Approaches

Burisch (1984) classified the major approaches to personality-scale construction into three categories: (1) the external or empirical approach (the method used in constructing the original MMPI); (2) the inductive or factor analytic approach; and (3) the deductive approach, including theoretical, rational, and construct-oriented methods (the approach followed in developing the MMPI-2 Content Scales). These procedures have been described in detail elsewhere (e.g., Anastasi, 1988; Graham & Lilly, 1984; Wiggins, 1973).

Hase and Goldberg (1967) were among the first to compare the different approaches to scale construction; they used the California Psychological Inventory (CPI), an objective personality measure similar to the MMPI. Six scale-construction strategies were examined: factor-analytic (inductive), empirical group discriminative (external), intuitive-theoretical (deductive), intuitive-rational (deductive), stylistic-psychometric (control procedure), and random (control procedure). The validity of scales developed for the CPI using these procedures was compared in a sample of approximately 200 college women. Criterion measures included peer ratings, as well as other behavioral data. Their results demonstrated that the strategies based on inductive, deductive, and external approaches all produced valid measures that were significantly more valid than scales developed using the two control procedures.

TABLE 1. MMPI Scale Names and Abbreviations

I. BASIC VALIDITY AND CLINICAL SCALES

L	Lie
F	Infrequency
K	Defensivenss
1 (Hs)	Hypochondriasis
2 (D)	Depression
3 (Hy)	Hysteria
4 (Pd)	Psychopathic Deviate
5 (Mf)	Masculinity/femininity
6 (Pa)	Paranoia
7 (Pt)	Psychasthenia
8 (Sc)	Schizophrenia
9 (Ma)	Hypomania
0 (Si)	Social Introversion

II. HARRIS LINGOES SUBSCALES

D_1	Subjective Depression
D_2	Psychomotor Retardation
D_3	Physical Malfunctioning
D_4	Mental Dullness
D_5	Brooding
Hy_1	Denial of Social Anxiety
Hy_2	Need for Affection
Hy_3	Lassitude-Malaise
Hy_4	Somatic Complaints
Hy_5	Inhibition of Aggression
Pd_1	Familial Discord
Pd_2	Authority Problems
Pd_3	Social Imperturbability
Pd_4	Social Alienation
Pd_5	Self-Alienation
Pa_1	Persecutory Ideas
Pa_2	Poignancy
Pa_3	Naivete
Sc_1	Social Alienation
Sc_2	Emotional Alienation
Sc_3	Lack of Ego Mastery, Cognitive
Sc_4	Lack of Ego Mastery, Conative
Sc_5	Lack of Ego Mastery, Defective Inhibition
Sc_6	Bizarre Sensory Experiences
Ma_1	Amorality
Ma_2	Psychomotor Acceleration
Ma_3	Imperturbability
Ma_4	Ego Inflation

III. WIGGINS CONTENT SCALES

SOC	Social Maladjustment
DEP	Depression
FEM	Feminine Interests
MOR	Poor Morale

REL	Religious Fundamentalism
AUT	Authority Conflict
PSY	Psychoticism
ORG	Organic Symptoms
FAM	Family Problems
HOS	Manifest Hostility
PHO	Phobias
HYP	Hypomania
HEA	Poor Health

IV. MMPI-2 CONTENT SCALES

ANX	Anxiety
FRS	Fears
OBS	Obsessiveness
DEP	Depression
HEA	Health Concerns
BIZ	Bizarre Mentation
ANG	Anger
CYN	Cynicism
ASP	Antisocial Practices
TPA	Type A
LSE	Low Self-Esteem
SOD	Social Discomfort
FAM	Family Problems
WRK	Work Interference
TRT	Negative Treatment Indicators

Validity, Communicability, and Economy

Burisch (1984) examined the literature since Hase and Goldberg's (1967) study and compared the three scale-construction approaches on three important attributes of personality scales: validity, communicability, and economy. Hase and Goldberg's (1967) original conclusions were verified by subsequent research: all three approaches yielded valid personality measures. However, the approaches produced different results on the other two important dimensions of communicability and economy (Burisch, 1984).

Communicability refers to an instrument's ability to present comprehensible information about an individual on the basis of his or her responses to items on the scale (Burisch, 1984). It overlaps with "content validity" and "homogeneity" of items. Burisch (1984) concluded that the deductive approach usually leads to scales that are much easier to communicate or interpret than either of the other two approaches. However, it is important to note that the deductive approach does not guarantee high communicability; it depends upon the developers' abilities to define clearly the underlying constructs of the scales.

Communicability is a problem with the standard MMPI scales. Although the empirical approach generated a number of valid MMPI scales that have stood the test of 50 years of use, "blind" empiricism also meant the inclusion on the scales of some items that do not seem related to the construct being measured. This decreases the ability to communicate the meaning of scales (especially to clients) and may adversely affect interpretation of MMPI scales as well. Many of the purely empirically derived MMPI scales contain some heterogeneous items whose appearance on the scale makes little theoretical sense. For example, there is no theoretical explanation for the appearance of the item "I am neither gaining nor losing weight" and the scored direction, False, on MMPI Scale 4, a measure of anti-social tendencies. That same item and response also appear on Scale 1, Hypochondriasis, and Scale 2, Depression, where they fit theoretically.

There are several sources of economy for personality scales (Burisch, 1984). The first has to do with construction economy; Burisch suggests that scale construction using empirical and inductive procedures takes much longer, without an added gain in validity to warrant the additional expense. Another source of scale economy has to do with redundancy or high interscale correlations within an inventory, which can lead to problems with the discriminant validity of the scales. As Burisch points out, empirically developed scales tend to be the most redundant since their developers accept item overlap when it enhances the ability of the scales to predict different criterion groups.

The final source of scale economy pertains to administration and subjects' time. Although they do not have to be longer, empirical and inductive scales tend to be much longer than deductively derived ones (Burisch, 1984). This can lead to subject fatigue and boredom. Another administrative advantage of deductive scales relates to a recent development in personality test construction, adaptive testing. Adaptive testing of personality measures refers to computerized administration of a subset of scale items needed to determine accurately the subject's scale score. For example, in adaptive testing with the MMPI, rather than administering the entire MMPI item pool to get scale scores, only a subset of items, determined by computer algorithms, is needed. Recent studies indicate that the deductively derived MMPI-2 content scales are more efficient than the empirically derived clinical scales in an adaptive testing format (Ben-Porath, Waller, Slutske, & Butcher, 1988). The relevance of this to the future of MMPI-2 is discussed in Chapter 7.

Previous Content Approaches to the MMPI

The view that patients were able and willing to discuss their problems and accurately report their feelings through personality-item responses led to the development of several interpretive strategies for evaluating MMPI content. Perhaps the simplest of these approaches did not involve scale construction, but, rather, consideration of responses to single items, originally called "critical" or "starred" items by Woodworth (1920) on his Personal Data Sheet. Responses to certain items were considered so pathological as to require special attention by the test interpreter.

Critical Items

This tradition was originally adapted for the MMPI by Grayson (1951), who used a rational construction strategy and listed 38 "critical items" thought to have special significance for clinical assessment. The Grayson items had considerable overlap with Scales F (Infrequency) and 8 (Schizophrenia) of the MMPI and dealt primarily with severe psychotic symptoms. Caldwell (1969) used a similar strategy to extend the Grayson item list to make it more useful in clinical appraisal. When using the critical items, clinicians were instructed to ask follow-up interview questions if any of the critical items were endorsed. However, no empirical verification of the importance of these items was presented. As later research showed (Koss & Butcher, 1973; Koss, Butcher, & Hoffman, 1976), both the Grayson and Caldwell items covered a limited range of problems and did not perform well as indexes of crises.

Koss and Butcher (1973) and Lachar and Wrobel (1974) conducted empirical research to identify items associated with common crises or problems encountered by psychiatric patients. For example, Koss and Butcher (1973) asked clinicians to identify items related to six crisis states (i.e., acute anxiety, depressed/suicidal ideation, threatened assault, situational stress due to alcoholism, mental confusion, persecutory ideas). The suggested items were then compared with criterion measures of the various crisis states, resulting in a list of 73 critical items. Using similar procedures, Lachar and Wrobel (1979) identified 111 critical items related to 14 problem areas of patients.

There is considerable item overlap in the various sets of critical items, although only the Koss and Butcher (1973) and Lachar and Wrobel (1979) item sets are empirically based. Like the earlier lists, the newer lists overlap with Scales F and 8, indicating that these items may be associated with an exaggeration of symptoms or severe psychopathology. However, as Koss (1979) and Graham (1987) indicate, these lists are not scales and should not be scored by summing up the number of endorsed items. They are best used as suggestions for further areas of exploration in a clinical assessment, rather than as a source of interpretive statements. Appendix B presents the Koss & Butcher (1973) Critical Items, which have been revised and expanded to include two new item groupings from the content added to MMPI-2. Appendix B also contains the Lachar and Wrobel (1979) Critical Items. Both lists are presented as they appear in the MMPI-2 booklet.

Inductively Derived Content Scales

Several investigators factor-analyzed subsets of the MMPI item pool, but the only significant effort to develop content homogeneous scales based on factor-analytic results was that of Tryon and his colleagues (Chu, 1966; Stein, 1968; Tryon, 1966; Tryon & Bailey, 1965). Based on cluster analyses of item data for psychiatric patients and normal subjects, seven clusters of MMPI items were identified that were judged to be homogeneous both statistically and in content meaning. The following scales were developed by selecting items with high loadings on the clusters: Introversion, Body Symptoms, Suspicion, Depression, Resentment, Autism, and Tension. Although initial research suggested that they might add significantly to the interpretation of the standard validity and clinical scales, the cluster scales, because of the item-selection procedures, were largely from the first factor of the MMPI, and thus not representative of the entire item pool. Since there has been little subsequent research with the scales, they have not been widely used clinically, and they have not been maintained in MMPI-2.

Subscales of the Basic MMPI Scales

One of the earliest attempts to group MMPI items into homogeneous scales based on content was made by Harris and Lingoes (1955; 1968). Because of the communicability problems noted above that are characteristic of some of the basic MMPI scales, Harris and Lingoes developed subscales of Scales 2 (Depression), 3 (Hysteria), 4 (Psychopathic Deviate), 6 (Paranoia), 8 (Schizophrenia), and 9 (Hypomania) by rationally grouping similar items into homogeneous content subsets. These subsets, or subscales, allowed clinicians to determine which of the item subsets contributed most to the elevation on a particular basic MMPI scale.

The assumption was that a score on a particular MMPI scale, for example, Scale 4, would mean one thing if it were made up of high response rates to the Harris-Lingoes Subscale of Familial Discord, and another if it were made up of items from the Authority Conflict or Social Alienation subscales. Thus the interpretation of MMPI scale elevations could be clarified by examining the patterns of responses on the homogeneous Harris-Lingoes subscales.

The interpretation of the Harris-Lingoes Subscales proved to be a valuable supplement to clinical interpretation of the basic MMPI scales, since clinicians were able to focus more directly on particular themes or attitudes being expressed by the patient. The subscales can be used with the MMPI-2; see Appendix C for scoring direction and MMPI-2 booklet numbers for these subscales.

There are some limitations to the Harris-Lingoes Subscales that require consideration since they are relevant for use with the MMPI-2. One of the most serious limitations to the Harris-Lingoes subscales is that they, for the most part, are not effective psychometric measures. Many of them contain too few items to operate as reliable scales. Furthermore, the item lists originally provided by Harris-Lingoes included some items that did not appear on the final form of the original basic MMPI scales. This is a particular issue for Scale 4. The Harris-Lingoes items that are not contained on the parent scale are not listed on the subscales in the MMPI-2 materials. This results in even shorter subscales, which may reduce their utility.

Harris and Lingoes did not provide subscales for Scale 1 (Hypochondriasis) because its item content, focusing on somatic symptoms, was homogeneous, nor for Scale 7 (Psychasthenia) because of its strong relationship to the anxiety factor of the MMPI and its relatively homogeneous content. In addition, Scale 5 (Masculinity/femininity) and Scale 0 (Social Introversion) were not sub-categorized. Later, through item-factor analysis, Serkownek (1975) provided a set of subscales for Scales 5 and 0. However, because of some ambiguity concerning the scored direction of the items and the deletion of some items on the Serkownek subscales in MMPI-2, their usefulness is limited.

The Prototypal Wiggins Content Scales

Wiggins and his colleagues offered an original approach to MMPI scale construction and interpretation with the development of psychometrically sound scales for assessing the content dimensions of the MMPI (Wiggins, 1966; 1969; Wiggins, Goldberg, & Appelbaum, 1971; Wiggins & Vollmar, 1959). Their work represented the most complete investigation of the item content of the MMPI (Graham, 1987). Beginning with the 26 content categories provided by Hathaway and McKinley (1940) to classify MMPI items, they ended up with 13 homogeneous scales. These scales were to be used as supplements for interpretation of the standard MMPI clinical scales. Wiggins's combination of rational and statistical scale-construction techniques was truly innovative.

The Hathaway and McKinley (1940) 26 content categories were used initially as provisional content scales (Wiggins, 1969). To evaluate the psychometric properties of these provisional scales, their internal consistencies were determined with a sample of 500 college students. The obtained internal consistencies ranged from near zero correlations to coefficients in the 80s, which resulted in the collapsing of some categories into one (e.g., several somatic item categories became a single measure of poor health), the reassignment of some items to different categories, and the addition of categories. The internal consistencies of these new provisional scales were obtained from several different samples, which resulted in the elimination of scales that were heterogeneous. This series of revisions led to a final set of

13 content scales (Table 1) that were mutually exclusive, internally consistent, moderately independent, and representative of the major content dimensions of the MMPI.

The Wiggins Content Scales required few theoretical assumptions or complicated interpretive schemata. Wiggins (1969) concluded that they provided a "Woodworthian simplicity" in psychological assessment: individuals who scored high on a particular scale were claiming an unusual amount of the substantive dimension involved and those scoring low claimed only a small amount. Subsequent studies provided normative data for the Wiggins scales, summarized by Graham (1987) and including conversion tables to transform raw scores into T scores.

Initially, Wiggins (1966) demonstrated that there were content scale differences between groups of normal and psychiatric samples that would be "expected" based upon the substantive dimensions assessed by his scales. Payne and Wiggins (1972) found that several content scales differentiated well with five out of six profile types categorized by the Gilberstadt and Duker (1965) actuarial system. Lachar and Alexander (1978) found substantial agreement between patients' self-reported symptoms, as measured by the Wiggins Content Scales, and external ratings made by clinicians in a sample of 384 high-scoring and low-scoring males from an Air Force medical facility. More recently, Lachar, Dahlstrom, and Moreland (1986) demonstrated the external validity of both the Wiggins Content Scales and the standard clinical scales for both black and white psychiatric patients.

A number of studies have reported significant relationships between Wiggins scale scores and other relevant measures. Derogatis, Rickels, and Rock (1976) found the Wiggins Depression (DEP) score to be correlated .75 with the SCL-90. Wiggins, Goldberg, and Appelbaum (1971) found that DEP correlated -.45 (males) and -.38 (females) with Personal Adjustment. Loper, Kammeier, and Hoffman (1973) found that scores on Authority Conflict (AUT) and Poor Health (HEA) significantly discriminated prealcoholic college students from their classmates. Mezzich, Damarin, and Erickson (1974) reported a significant positive association between DEP and a diagnosed depressed state and a significant negative association on Hypomania (HYP) in depressed patients. Gray-Little (1974) reported significant differences between high dogmatic and low dogmatic subjects in the favorability they attributed to AUT items. Hoffman and Jackson (1976) reported high convergence between the Wiggins Content Scales (except Feminine Interests — FEM) and scores on Jackson and Messick's Differential Personality Inventory Scales (Jackson & Carlson, 1973). Overall, the early validation efforts with the Wiggins scales were highly supportive of the content interpretation approach, with most research demonstrating that the Content Scale scores were meaningfully associated with external measures of similar constructs.

Changes in MMPI Content Dimensions with MMPI-2

The Wiggins Content Scales provided a psychometrically sound and valid approach to content interpretation for the MMPI. However, as we will see in Chapter 2, as part of the restandardization of the MMPI, existing items were rewritten or eliminated, and new items were introduced in the MMPI-2. As a result, the Wiggins Content Scales lost numerous items, and owing to the introduction of new content, they were no longer representative of the entire MMPI-2 content domain. This situation could have been remedied in one of two ways. One, to use the items that remained in the MMPI-2 as a basis for updating the Wiggins Scales—which would not have incorporated the new content domains. The second, to develop a new set of content scales using data from the Restandardization Project and other research projects using the experimental form of the MMPI. The second course was followed, and this book describes the development, psychometric properties, and interpretation procedures for the new content scales.

Chapter 2

The MMPI Restandardization Project: The Development of MMPI-2

The MMPI Restandardization Project began in the summer of 1982 when the University of Minnesota Press asked Drs. James Butcher of the University of Minnesota and W. Grant Dahlstrom of the University of North Carolina to serve as consultants to the Press in the restandardization of the MMPI. Shortly thereafter, Dr. John Graham of Kent State University joined the committee, followed by Dr. Auke Tellegen of the University of Minnesota. All work on the revision and restandardization was to include at least one of these committee members, joined, as on the Content Scale project, by other researchers.

The MMPI restandardization was to accomplish several major goals: (a) obtaining a contemporary, representative normative sample; (b) maintaining the continuity of the instrument, thus preserving the vast amount of empirical research on the existing clinical and validity scales; and (c) generating additional item content to address areas of behavior not covered by the original MMPI. Although it was the committee's intent to preserve the existing validity and clinical scales, it was recognized that some items were outdated and in need of revision and that some would probably be eliminated.

The MMPI Experimental Test Booklets

All 550 items (some in modified form) that make up the original MMPI were included in the experimental booklets, with the fate of individual items to be determined by analysis of the data collected during the restandardization. The MMPI Restandardization Committee considered it important to develop two experimental booklets, one for adults (AX) and the other for adolescents (TX). Each booket contained the 550 original MMPI items, some new items relevant to contemporary problems and clinical practices, and items reflective of age-specific issues—a total of 704 items. A total of 154 new items were incorporated into each experimental form, the two forms having about 600 items in common.

Criticisms of the Original MMPI Item Pool

Criticisms of the item pool focused on: narrowness of content coverage, datedness, awkwardness of item wording (Butcher, 1972; Butcher & Owen, 1978), and inclusion of objectionable content (Butcher and Tellegen, 1966). Because the MMPI had not been revised since its publication in 1943, significant contemporary issues of interest to clinicians and researchers (e.g., Type A behavior, prediction of treatment compliance, drug use) were not included in the item content (Butcher, 1972).

The MMPI items were not edited before they became part of the booklet, and awkward wording led to some ambiguous, confusing, or difficult-to-answer items. Some items using the masculine pronoun exclusively were considered to be "sexist" in terms of contemporary language practice and were offensive to many individuals taking the test. Other items were culturally inappropriate for broad use. For example, the religion items referred almost exclusively to Christianity.

The 16 repeated items, originally included in the booklet to facilitate machine scoring, were problematic for several reasons. Confusion existed among users about which appearance of the item should be scored on a particular scale (see Dahlstrom, Welsh & Dahlstrom, 1972). Companies distributing scoring templates contributed to this confusion by publishing scoring keys in which the second appearance of the item was scored rather than the first, as recommended (Dahlstrom, Welsh, & Dahlstrom, 1972). Another problem was that many individuals taking the inventory incorrectly inferred that the repeated items were included in order to trick them, sometimes creating an oppositional reaction to the test itself.

Changes in Item Content for Form AX

The experimental Form AX of the MMPI, the experimental booklet with which we are concerned in this book, was developed through an editorial process by which outdated and poorly worded items were identified and modified, and through a process of item generation designed to increase the content coverage of the MMPI. The first step involved editing the 82 items from the basic scales exhibiting the problems described above. Fifteen of these items were reworded to eliminate reference to a specific gender. For example, "Any man who is willing to work hard has a good chance of succeeding" was changed to "Anyone who is able and willing to work hard has a good chance of succeeding." In many other items, outdated idiomatic expressions were replaced with more contemporary wording. For example, "irritable" was substituted for "cross," "bad behavior" for "cutting up," "often" for "commonly," etc.

A number of MMPI items had become dated and meaningless owing to shifts in language usage or in cultural practices. These items were reworded to substitute current usage and practices. Other items were revised to improve grammar, to define words that might not be understood by all potential test takers, to address cultural bias, and to clarify the time frame covered by an item. Most of these item changes were slight, all aimed at preserving the original content while using more contemporary, acceptable language. In some cases, for example with the outdated and infamous "drop the handkerchief" item, potential substitute items were incorporated in the experimental booklet.

The effect of these item changes on endorsement patterns was studied by

Ben-Porath & Butcher (1989). They administered Form AX and the original group form to 178 college men and 199 college women. These subjects' responses to the original and reworded items were compared to the responses of a second group of 200 college students who took the original form twice and served as a baseline for comparing response change. Of the 82 reworded items, endorsement percentages changed significantly when Form AX was used in only nine items, and in all nine items in only one gender. For these nine items, however, item-scale correlations remained unchanged despite the change in endorsement frequency. Thus, Ben-Porath and Butcher concluded that the goal of improving the face validity of the reworded items without altering their psychometric properties had been accomplished.

In keeping with the plan to broaden MMPI item content, the Restandardization Committee sought to include new, promising items covering content dimensions not adequately addressed in the original item pool. In generating the pool of new items to be included in Form AX, the Committee reviewed the existing content areas in the MMPI and sought the opinions of experts in personality measurement and clinical assessment about item domains or specific item content that would augment the MMPI's coverage. The Committee then wrote items to reflect these content areas. Some content domains thought to be inadequately represented in the original MMPI were: drug abuse, suicidal ideation, Type A behaviors, prediction of change, assessment of treatment compliance, and work and marital relationships.

The number of new items to be incorporated into the experimental booklet was dictated by space available on the scannable answer sheet. Once this maximum length (704 items) had been determined, Butcher, Dahlstrom, and Graham culled the items for those that seemed most interesting, relevant to contemporary clinical practice, and potentially valuable as new content for the item pool. When the final set of 154 items was agreed upon, it was submitted to editorial review and revision by the Committee, including Beverly Kaemmer, coordinator of the Restandardization Project for the University of Minnesota Press. Sixteen new items replaced the second occurrence of the 16 repeated items from the MMPI Group Form; the remaining 138 were printed after the 550 original and slightly rewritten items from the MMPI, bringing the total length of the adult experimental booklet (Form AX) to 704 items.

Form AX was printed in booklet form with separate machine-scorable answer sheets allowing a response of "True" or "False" for each item. The instructions on the booklet were identical to those on the MMPI Group Form, which allow the subject to leave some items blank, but strongly encourage responding to every statement. Identifying information on the answer sheets included subject number, age, sex, and date of testing.

Other Instruments Used in the Restandardization

Biographical Information Form

This form (see Appendix D) was designed to collect background information such as age, sex, marital status, length of marriage, level of education, occupational group, financial status, size of family, ethnic background, current physical and emotional health, legal troubles, alcohol and drug use, and family history of mental-health or chemical-dependency treatment. Questions were multiple choice and the subject was instructed to leave an item blank if none of the choices applied to him or her. The forms were identified with the same subject number used on the MMPI answer sheet and the other forms described below.

Life Events Form

This single-page, machine-scorable questionnaire (see Appendix E) was a slight modification of the Schedule of Recent Experiences (Holmes & Rahe, 1967).

Marital Adjustment Forms

Two rating forms (Appendixes F and G) were developed to obtain information on the married couples included in the sample. These forms were used to determine how each member of the marital pair viewed the relationship and his or her spouse's adjustment in the relationship, and to obtain objective ratings on each member of the pair by the spouse. These behavioral ratings covered a wide range of interpersonal, health, and other characteristics. The Relationship Form, a modification of the Spanier Dyadic Adjustment Scale (Spanier, 1976; Spanier & Filsinger, 1983), was developed to assess the marital adjustment of a subset of the normative sample. The information requested includes financial, religious, affectional, sexual, and leisure-time matters. The individual's overall level of satisfaction in the relationship is evaluated, along with satisfaction in specific areas of the relationship (See Appendix F).

The carefully developed Katz Adjustment Scales (KAS scales) (Katz & Lyerly, 1963), which had been used by one of the authors in previous research (Graham, Lilly, Paolino, Friedman, & Konick, 1973), were used as a base from which to model the structure and content of the Couple's Rating Form (Appendix G). The KAS had been developed to assess interpersonal behavior and covered a broad range of information judged to be relevant to this assessment. The KAS scales were reviewed and relevant item content was incorporated in the Couple's Rating Form. In addition the form included information about the rater (such as education level, relationship to ratee, and an appraisal of "closeness" to the ratee).

The MMPI-2 Normative Sample

This section provides a summary of the sample. Readers interested in a more detailed discussion should consult the *MMPI-2 Manual for Administration and Scoring* (1989). A total of 2,600 subjects (1,138 males and 1,462 females) participated in the study. The sample, in general, matched well the 1980 census data reported by Bogue (1985). The geographic distribution of the sample drawn from diverse regions of the United States, is presented in Table 2. The sample matched, reasonably well, the current ethnic-group representation in the United States today (See Table 3). Age distributions are presented in Table 4.

TABLE 2. Geographic Distribution of Subjects in the Restandardization Sample

Location	Males freq.	Males %	Females freq.	Females %
California	112	9.8	132	9.0
Minnesota	266	23.4	296	20.3
North Carolina	181	15.9	307	21.0
Ohio	196	17.2	254	17.4
Pennsylvania	123	10.8	182	12.5
Virginia	109	9.6	144	9.9
Washington	106	9.3	111	7.6
Military[a]	18	1.6	6	0.4
Indian reservation[b]	27	2.4	30	2.1
Total	1,138	100.0	1,462	100.2

(Source: *MMPI-2 Manual*, 1989)

[a]Active duty personnel tested on several U.S. military bases.

[b]Native American adults residing on a federal reservation in the state of Washington.

One demographic variable, education level, fell somewhat short of a desired match (see Table 5). The original MMPI normative sample was composed of individuals with about an eighth-grade education, close to the mean education of the United States population in the 1930s. Table 5 shows that the MMPI-2 normative group is skewed toward higher levels of education, with about 19% having an undergraduate degree or post-undergraduate education, probably reflecting the fact that the United States population is, on average, much better educated today than it was in the 1930s.

TABLE 3. Ethnic Origins of Subjects in the Restandardization Sample Compared to the 1980 Census

Ethnic Group	Males				Females			
	freq.	%	adj.%	Census	freq.	%	adj.%	Census
Asian	6	0.5	0.5	1.5	13	0.9	0.9	1.5
Black	126	11.1	11.1	10.1	188	12.9	12.9	10.9
Hispanic	35	3.1	*	*	38	2.6	*	*
Native American	38	3.3	3.3	0.5	39	2.7	2.7	0.5
White	933	82.0	83.7	85.2	1184	81.0	82.4	84.7
Other	0	0.0	1.3	2.7	0	0.0	1.1	2.3
Total	1,138	100.0	99.9	100.0	1,462	100. 1	100.0	99.9

(Source: *MMPI-2 Manual*, 1989)
*Adjusted to conform to U.S. Census categories (Hispanic individuals classified as follows: 56% "White," 44% "Other").

TABLE 4. Age Distribution of Subjects in the Restandardization Sample Compared to the 1980 Census

Age Ranges	Males			Females		
	freq.	%	Census	freq.	%	Census
18-19	20	1.8	5.7	30	2.1	5.1
20-29	268	23.6	26.4	373	25.5	24.1
30-39	331	29.1	20.1	438	30.0	18.7
40-49	177	15.6	14.4	224	15.3	13.7
50-59	144	12.7	14.3	177	12.1	14.3
60-69	134	11.8	11.0	143	9.8	12.0
70-79	55	4.8	6.0	65	4.5	9.0
80-84	9	0.8	2.2	12	0.8	4.0
Total	1,138	98.4	100.1	1,462	100.1	100.9

(Source: *MMPI-2 Manual*, 1989)

TABLE 5. Years of Education Completed by Subjects in the Restandardization Sample Compared to the 1980 Census

Education	Males			Females		
	freq.	%	Census	freq.	%	Census
Part high school	61	5.4	32.7	68	4.7	34.2
High school grad.	242	21.3	31.1	398	27.2	37.7
Part college	272	23.9	16.1	379	25.9	15.3
College grad.	310	27.2	9.8	390	26.7	7.5
Post-graduate	253	22.2	10.3	227	15.5	5.3
Total	1,138	100.0	100.0	1,462	100.0	100.0

[a]U.S. Census data are based on adults 25 years of age and older.
(Source: *MMPI-2 Manual*, 1989)

Other Samples

A number of other samples were studied to provide data on specific normal populations or on particular clinical groups for use in developing the MMPI-2 scales. Following are descriptions of several additional samples employed in the development or validation of the MMPI-2 Content Scales. Further information on these samples may be obtained by consulting the initial publication cited.

Military Personnel

The subjects in the general military sample (Butcher, Jeffrey, Cayton, Devore, Colligan, & Minnegawa, in press) were active duty personnel from four branches of the military service: the United States Army (901), Navy (85), Marines (256), and Air Force (220). Subjects were obtained in collaboration with several psychologists on active duty in the military service.

College Samples

A major application of the MMPI over the years has been in the assessment of college students. The sample in this study was 797 women and 515 men. (Butcher, Graham, Dahlstrom, & Bowman, in press).

Airline Pilot Applicants

A sample of applicants for air crew positions for a major air carrier (271) were administered Form AX of the MMPI, the Life Events Form, and Biographical Information Form as part of their medical-psychological screening battery (Butcher, 1987).

Inpatient Psychiatric Sample

Several samples of psychiatric patients were included in the MMPI-2 study (Graham & Butcher, 1988). Testing programs were initiated at three inpatient facilities in Minnesota and Ohio. Patients were tested during their initial stages of hospitalization (after a period of adjustment) at two of the facilities. Patients at one facility, housing more chronic patients, were tested at various stages of their hospitalization. The Life Events Form and Biographical Information Form were administered to the Minnesota hospital samples. A total of 423 patients were included in the study. They were given the MMPI as part of their diagnostic work-up at most facilities; however, some patients at the state mental hospital in Minnesota were paid a small amount ($4.00) for their participation.

Chronic Pain Patients

A total of 502 patients (268 males and 234 females) who were being treated for chronic pain were evaluated in a study by Keller and Butcher (1990). These patients were administered Form AX of the MMPI, the Biographical Information Form, and the Life Events Form as part of their initial treatment evaluation. Information concerning their symptoms, presenting problems, behavior in the facility, illness behavior, medication and other treatment approaches, and outcome information was obtained from their hospital records.

Inpatient Alcohol and Drug Abusers

A sample of 832 male and 340 female substance abusers was obtained from an inpatient substance abuse treatment program (McKenna & Butcher, 1987). Patients were administered the MMPI-2 during their orientation to the program, usually several days after being admitted to the facility. In addition to the Restandardization Project forms, patients completed a substance-abuse history form.

Criteria for Excluding Subjects from the Sample

After deleting incomplete records, the following exclusion criteria were applied:

1. Item omissions of greater than 40.
2. F Scale raw scores of greater than 25.
3. A raw score of greater than 25 on the F_B scale, an infrequency scale comparable to the F Scale developed to assess random responding to the items that appeared later in the AX booklet.

Derivation of Uniform T-Scores

Several problems with the existing linear T scores for the MMPI scales led the Restandardization Committee to consider several solutions. Dissimilar distributions, and the consequent lack of percentile equivalence for equal T-scores, have long been a source of difficulty in interpreting MMPI T scores on both the clinical and supplementary scales. One possibility, used by other researchers in recent MMPI projects (e.g., Colligan, Osborne, Swenson, & Offord, 1983), was to derive normalized T scores. However, that procedure requires making a number of assumptions the restandardization Committee was not prepared to accept. Normalization procedures are based on the assumption that the sampled distribution is somehow distorted and needs to be corrected. It is assumed that, had sampling been adequate, the resultant distribution would have been normal. As detailed in the *MMPI-2 Manual*, the normative sample of 2600 individuals represented quite adequately the population of the United States, thus there was no basis for assuming that nonnormal distributions resulted from sampling error. Furthermore, there is no empirical evidence that the various forms of psychopathology assessed by the MMPI are normally distributed.

In addition to relying on questionable assumptions, normalized T-scores would alter significantly the character of the MMPI profile. Hsu and Betman (1986) demonstrated that use of the normalized T scores developed by Colligan and colleagues (1983) can lead to differences as high as 20 points between linear and normalized T scores. Furthermore, Green (1985) and Hsu and Betman (1986) have shown that MMPI code-types are altered considerably when T scores are normalized. Differences between linear and normalized T scores are directly proportional to score elevation, resulting in greater changes at higher score levels. In other words, normalized T-scores are most likely to exert their altering effects at the most clinically significant levels. Furthermore, since all extant correlates for MMPI profiles are based on linear T scores, the use of normalized T-scores would cause serious difficulties in profile interpretation.

Having concluded that normalized T scores would be inappropriate for MMPI-2, the Restandardization Committee sought an alternative way to ensure scale comparability. Auke Tellegen (1988) developed uniform T scores for eight of the basic clinical scales, excluding scales 5 and 0. As we describe in Chapter 3, uniform T scores were also developed for the MMPI-2 Content Scales.

Computationally, first linear T scores were derived using the formula $T = 50 + [10 (X - M)]/SD$, where X is the raw score, and M and SD are the mean and standard deviation of the raw scores on the particular scale for each normative group. Next, a set of normative "composite T-score" values, associated with a series of percentile values, was derived as follows: for each percentile the associated linear T-score value was derived from each of the 16 distributions, and these 16 values were averaged. The resulting series of average or composite T-score values (corresponding to the series of percentiles) was then used as the uniform standard in deriving regression formulas and look-up tables for individual scales (separately for each sex). The look-up tables transform the raw scores of each scale into corresponding composite T-score estimates. These estimates constitute the uniform T scores for that scale. As was intended, the resulting uniform T-score distributions are very similar from scale to scale, with approximately equal numbers of scores at each level of T-score elevation.

Using the same set of composite T-score values (the one just described) throughout, uniform T scores were derived from the K-corrected and non-

K-corrected raw scores of the basic clinical scales (except for scales 5 and 0, which were excluded because of their distinctive methods of derivation and distribution) and for the raw scores of the new Content Scales as well.

The MMPI-2 Booklet

The normative and clinical data collected on the AX booklet provided the basis for including items in the MMPI-2 booklet (Appendix A). The MMPI Restandardization Committee reduced the item pool to 567 according to several criteria. First, it was decided that most of the items on the existing clinical and validity scales were "protected" from deletion except in rare cases where the original item was thought to be so problematic (objectionable or obsolete) that it had to be deleted. Second, a number of supplementary scales, such as MAC, were considered to be valuable assessment measures and the items on the scale were retained if the content was not objectionable. Finally, items making up the MMPI-2 Content Scales described in this book were retained because of the initial strong empirical support for their efficacy.

Several criteria were employed in excluding items. Those that had been demonstrated to be objectionable or offensive — items referring to religion, bowel and bladder function, or sexual preference (See Butcher & Tellegen, 1966) — were eliminated. Items thought to be outmoded, such as the "drop the handkerchief" item, were also eliminated.

Chapter 3
Development of the MMPI-2 Content Scales

The MMPI-2 Content Scales were developed using multi-stage, multi-method procedures that combined rational and statistical methods. These procedures most closely approximated the deductive approach, to use Burisch's (1984) terms (Chapter 1). Figure 1 provides a summary of the development stages and the multiple steps taken within each stage. The first stage involved a rational identification of the content areas and classification of items into each area. The second stage was designed to enhance the convergent validity of the rationally constructed scales by using statistical procedures to identify items not appropriately assigned to the content areas or scales. Items were deleted from and added to the scales accordingly. The third and fourth stages were designed to enhance the discriminant validity of the Content Scales using further rational review and statistical verification procedures. The fourth stage also included the development of uniform T scores for the Content Scales. The fifth stage simply provided rationally derived scale descriptions based on item content.

FIGURE 1. Developmental Stages of MMPI-2 Content Scales

Rational Identification of Content Areas
— Definition of Content Dimensions
— Independent Rater Selection of Items
— Group Consensus Selection of Items

Statistical Verification of Item-Scale Membership
— Identification and Deletion of Items Not Correlated with Scales
— Identification and Addition of Items Correlated with Scales but Not Previously Selected

Final Rational Review
— Inspection and Revision of the Changed Content Dimensions
— Deletion of Statistically Related but Content Inappropriate Items
— Elimination of Most Item Overlap

Final Statistical Refinement
— Elimination of Items More Highly Correlated with Other Scales
— Derivation of Uniform T Scores for Content Scales

Rational Descriptions for Scales
— Items Inspected and Descriptions Written for Each Scale

Stage One: Rational Identification of Content Areas

Step 1: Definition of Content Dimensions

The first step in the development of the Content Scales consisted of defining clinically relevant content areas in the MMPI Form AX experimental booklet. Twenty-two possible content categories were identified by Butcher on the basis of the existing literature on content dimensions within the original MMPI (Dahlstrom, Welsh, & Dahlstrom, 1975), a factor-analytic study of the original MMPI item pool (Johnson, Butcher, Null, and Johnson, 1984), and a review of the additional item content written for Form AX. These content categories were considered to have promise in representing the item domains contained in the revised MMPI. The original item domains were:

Self-Alienation

Aggressive Loss of Control

Rigid Thinking

Traditional Sex Role Discontent

Anti-Social Ideas and Practices

Social Avoidance

Negative Family Relationships: Past

Negative Family Relationships: Current

Type A Behavior

Perceived Poor Health

Low Tolerance for Pain

Suspicion-Mistrust

Depressed Mood

Self-Indulgent Life-Style

Anxiety

Fears and Phobias

Sexual Concerns

Authority Conflict

Well-Being

Religious Fundamentalism

Negative Work Attitudes

Low Treatment Amenability

Butcher provided definitions for each of the domains to be used by the raters in the second step of this stage.

Step 2: Independent Rater Selection of Items

The full 704-item pool of Form AX was reviewed by three of the authors (JNB, JRG, and CLW) who independently assigned items into the above 22 content domains. Judges were allowed to add other potential categories that they thought would be useful during this step. If deemed appropriate, based on category definitions, they could assign items to more than one content domain.

Following the initial item review, the three separate lists of item groupings were consolidated into provisional content scales if at least two of the three raters placed the items in the same content domain. Next, the raters were asked to review independently the provisional scales, indicate if they agreed with the inclusion of items on the scales, and indicate the scoring direction for the items. Raters (JG and CW) suggested new content domains as well, but there were not enough items in the pool to develop additional scales for these domains.

Step 3: Group Consensus Selection of Items

Once the individual item-rating process was complete, the three raters, in a group meeting, reviewed all items and evaluated whether the item content was appropriate for the content scale it was placed in during the previous reviews. At this meeting, the raters discussed any disagreements about scale-item membership until there was full agreement by all three raters. One scale, Low Tolerance for Pain, was dropped from further consideration since the raters were unable to identify an acceptable number of items to assess this domain. Table 6 lists the remaining 21 scales and the number of items assigned to each scale.

Stage Two: Statistical Verification of Item-Scale Membership

Stage Two was designed to enhance the convergent validity of the content scales through the use of statistical procedures. It consisted of two steps, the first aimed at identifying rationally selected items that detracted from the internal consistency of the scales, the second intended to identify non-selected items that correlated substantially with the "purified" scales. These items would then be candidates for inclusion on those scales. Decision-making during Stage Two was guided by a conservative approach founded on the tenet that the rational scales constructed during Stage One should serve as the core domains to be tapped by the Content Scales. Nevertheless, substantial modifications were made on several scales, and four scales were dropped.

TABLE 6. Scale Names and Number of Items Following Stages One and Two: Rational Construction and Empirical Refinement

Scale	# of Items Stage One	# of Items Deleted Stage Two	# of Items Added Stage Two
Self-Alienation	21	2	29
Aggressive Loss of Control	18	2	5
Rigid Thinking	20	3	17
Traditional Sex Role Discontent	39	scale dropped	
Anti-Social Ideas and Practices	27	3	1
Social Avoidance	31	4	0
Negative Family Relationships: Past	14	scale dropped	
Negative Family Relationships: Current	27	2	7
Type A Behavior	24	4	2
Perceived Poor Health	49	2	3
Suspicion-Mistrust	24	0	6
Depressed Mood	33	0	31
Self-Indulgent Life-Style	15	scale dropped	
Anxiety	20	0	21
Fears and Phobias	25	1	0
Sexual Concerns	13	scale dropped	
Authority Conflict	24	2	3
Well-Being	25	2	20
Religious Fundamentalism	15	2	0
Negative Work Attitudes	25	4	34
Low Treatment Amenability	24	4	24
Cynicism	20[a]	0	2

[a]Added during Stage 2, indicates number of items before statistical analysis.

Step 1: Identification and Deletion of Items Not Correlated With Scales

The goal of this step in scale construction was to identify any rationally selected items that detracted from the uniformity of the scales, that is, items whose low correlations with the total scale score (minus that item) meant that their inclusion would reduce the scale's internal consistency. For this procedure item analyses were conducted using the college sample and the inpatient psychiatric sample described in Chapter 2. Analyses were conducted separately for each of the 21 scales. For every scale each item's correlation with the total scale score (minus that item) was computed, as well as the (Cronbach) coefficient alpha when that item was deleted.

The decision to use both the college (i.e., normal) and clinical samples was guided by the conservative approach we adopted for this stage as outlined above. Thus, for an item to be deleted, its inadequate empirical contribution to its scale had to be demonstrated in both samples and for both genders. In other words, it had to meet our criterion for deletion in all four samples (inpatient males and females and college males and females). The criterion was that the item's Pearson Product-Moment correlation with the corrected total scale score be substantially lower than the correlations for the majority of the items on that scale and that its deletion would increase the scale's alpha by two points (e.g., .78 rises to .80) or more.

The scale-by-scale analyses revealed that four scales (Traditional Sex Role Discontent, Negative Family Relationships: Past, Self-Indulgent Life-Style, and Sexual Concerns) had unacceptably low internal consistencies. These scales were dropped from further consideration. The number of items deleted from the remaining 17 scales is provided in the second column of Table 6. This number ranged from zero (Suspicion-Mistrust, Depressed Mood, and Anxiety scales) to four items (Social Avoidance, Type A Behavior, Negative Work Attitudes, and Low Treatment Amenability scales).

Examination of the item content covered by the four deleted scales disclosed that a content category revealed by a previous item factor analysis (Johnson et al., 1984) was now missing from the content scales. This was the factor termed Cynicism. We thus decided to add this 20-item factor as an additional Content Scale and subject it to the same analyses as the rest of the scales. Our item-scale analysis revealed that all 20 items correlated adequately with the corrected scale score, and that the scale possessed ample internal consistency. This scale is also included in Table 6.

Step 2: Identification and Addition of Items Correlated with Scales but Not Previously Selected

This step was designed to identify items that were not rationally assigned to the scales, that might nevertheless contribute to the assessment of the content areas defined by the now purified scales. For these analyses we split the inpatient samples into the Minnesota and Ohio subsamples, each of which served as a cross-validating sample for the other. Here, too, we adopted a conservative approach since we were not interested in substantially altering the content domains tapped by the rationally derived scales.

For each of the 18 scales, Pearson Product-Moment correlations between the entire 704-item pool (minus the scale items) and that scale were computed. Items whose correlation with a scale was .50 or higher in one sample (male or female) and whose cross-validated correlation was .45 (allowing for some shrinkage) or higher in the cross-validating sample (same gender) were added to that scale.

Table 6 also presents the number of items added to each scale following this procedure. These numbers varied considerably. Thus, three scales (i.e., Social Avoidance, Fears and Phobias, and Religious Fundamentalism) received no additional items, while other scales (e.g., Negative Work Attitudes, Depressed Mood, and Self-Alienation) received about 30 new items. The next two stages were designed to ensure that only those items that were genuinely related to their core content areas would be retained.

Stage Three: Final Rational Review

Inspection of the item domains added to the Content Scales during the previous stage revealed that not all of the newly added items were related conceptually to their content areas. In some cases inclusion of these items on the scales could be justified by broadening or refining the definition of a particular content area. Thus, for example, many of the items added to the Self-Alienation Scale were not clear markers of that construct, but most of the items could be defined as indicating low self-esteem. Thus, Stage Three consisted of two steps: first, the content domain of each of the 18 expanded scales was inspected to determine whether the definition (and consequently the scale name) should be modified. Second, the entire set of items for each content scale was inspected to rationally determine whether each item fit its content area, with particular attention paid to overlapping items (appearing on more than one scale) in an attempt to hold their number to a minimum.

Step 1: Inspection and Revision of Changed Content Domains

This step was designed to identify content areas that had been broadened and to adjust their definitions appropriately before deleting nonfitting items. In the process of evaluating and comparing the domains, we discovered that two were essentially overlapping domains. Thus, the Well-Being Scale to a great extent overlapped the Depressed Mood Scale, and the Authority Conflict Scale overlapped the Anti-Social Ideas and Practices and the Cynicism scales. Since neither of these two scales appeared to represent a unique area, both were dropped from further consideration. One more scale, Religious Fundamentalism, was also dropped at this stage following the Restandardization Committee's decision to delete religious items from MMPI-2 because of their controversial nature. A small number of additional objectionable items were also deleted at this stage for the same reason. These came primarily from the Perceived Poor Health Scale.

The remaining 15 scales were then evaluated to determine whether scale name or definition changes were in order. Table 7 lists the revised scale names and the number of items on each scale at this point. Three scales, Anxiety, Cynicism, and Type A Behavior, retained the names and definitions they had in previous stages. Four scales received new names: Fears (previously Fears and Phobias), Depression (Depressed Mood), Health Concerns (Perceived Poor Health), and Anti-Social Attitudes (Anti-Social Ideas and Practices).

Both name and definition were revised for the remaining eight scales. Self-Alienation was renamed Low Self-Esteem and its definition revised accordingly. Rigid Thinking was expanded to include additional forms of obsessive behavior and renamed Obsessiveness. Suspicion-Mistrust was expanded to include additional forms of bizarre thinking and behavior, and renamed Bizarre Mentation. Aggressive Loss of Control was expanded to include additional forms of anger-expressive behavior and renamed Anger. Social Avoidance was expanded to include additional indicators of social discomfort and renamed accordingly. Negative Family Relationships: Current was expanded to include past family problems from the previously deleted Negative Family Relationships: Past Scale. This scale was renamed Family Problems. Negative Work Attitudes was expanded to include additional sources of work interference and renamed accordingly. And, finally, Low Treatment Amenability was expanded to include additional negative treatment indicators and renamed accordingly.

TABLE 7. Scale Names and Number of Items Following Stage Three: Rational Modification

Scale	# of Items Step One	# of Items Deleted Step Two
Anxiety	41	15
Fears	24	0
Obsessiveness	34	17
Depression	62	20
Health Concerns	50	10
Bizarre Mentation	30	4
Anger	21	4
Cynicism	22	0
Antisocial Attitudes	25	1
Type A Behavior	22	2
Low Self-Esteem	48	19
Social Discomfort	27	1
Family Problems	32	6
Work Interference	55	18
Negative Treatment Indicators	44	13

Step 2: Deletion of Statistically Related but Content Inappropriate Items

This step had two main goals: First to delete items whose content did not fit their scale's definition, and second to reduce unnecessary item overlap. Both of these goals were designed to enhance the scales' discriminant validity. We were aware that some of the items added to the scales in stage two might not be directly related to their content areas, but, rather, to the general factor of psychopathology so prominent in many of the MMPI items and scales. Items that correlated with a scale but were not directly related to its content would tend to reduce its discriminant validity, while their deletion would enhance it.

The issue of item overlap (items belonging to more than one scale) is controversial and some might argue for eliminating all item overlap for the sake of discriminant validity. We decided to conform to this principle when deletion would not hamper a scale's construct validity. Thus, to the extent that two constructs overlap (e.g., Cynicism and Anti-Social Attitudes), we would expect and accept a certain degree of item overlap between scales designed to measure them. Deleting such items from one scale would result in obtaining only a fragmentary representation of that scale's construct. All overlapping items were inspected and where it was deemed that deletion of an item from one scale would not hamper the assessment of its construct that item was eliminated.

Table 7 presents the number of items deleted from each scale during step two of this stage. This number varied from zero on the Fears and Cynicism scales to as many as 20 items on the expanded Depression scale.

Stage Four: Final Statistical Refinement

Step 1: Elimination of Items More Highly Correlated with Other Scales

This step of scale construction was designed to ensure statistically that the goals set down for Stage Three (and pursued rationally) were met. For the purpose of this step, all clinical subsamples were combined into one mixed-gender sample. Our goal here was to enhance discriminant validity for both genders and therefore the advantages of having a larger (albeit mixed) sample were deemed to outweigh the (unlikely) potential of gender confounds.

Pearson Product-Moment correlations were computed between all Content Scale items and the entire set of scales (minus the item if it belonged to the scale). Each scale's items were then analyzed separately to determine whether an item correlated higher or to the same degree with other content scales. In the few cases where an item from one scale correlated significantly higher with another scale, that item was either deleted or transferred to the second scale if justified by its content. In cases where an item from one scale showed the same correlation with its scale and another, a similar decision was made unless the item's content clearly indicated that it should remain on the original scale. Finally, where similar or higher correlations resulted from item overlap an approach similar to the one used in Stage Three was taken. That is, the item was deleted from one or both scales unless it was clear that item overlap reflected construct overlap.

Table 8 displays the results of these analyses and the final number of items on each of the 15 content scales. The number of items deleted during this step ranged from zero on Cynicism to nine on Depression. Items were added (i.e., transferred) to Obsessiveness (2), Cynicism (1), Type A Behavior (1), and Low Self-Esteem (1).

Having completed the preceding stages, we were interested in finding out how much the initial list of items had changed. Table 9 presents these numbers. The Health Concerns Scale lost the greatest number of items; how-

TABLE 8. Item Deletions and Additions during Stage Four: Final Empirical Refinements

Scale	# of Items Deleted	# of Items Added	# of Items Final
Anxiety	3	0	23
Fears	1	0	23
Obsessiveness	3	2	16
Depression	9	0	33
Health Concerns	4	0	36
Bizarre Mentation	2	0	24
Anger	1	0	16
Cynicism	0	1	23
Antisocial Attitudes	2	0	22
Type A Behavior	2	1	19
Low Self-Esteem	6	1	24
Social Discomfort	2	0	24
Family Problems	1	0	25
Work Interference	4	0	33
Negative Treatment Indicators	5	0	26

TABLE 9. Changes in Scale Composition from Initial to Final Stages

Scale	# of Items Common to Initial and and Final List	# of Items Deleted from Initial List	# of New Items added in Final List
Anxiety	14	6	9
Fears	23	2	0
Obsessiveness	11	9	5
Depression	27	6	6
Health Concerns	35	14	1
Bizarre Mentation	21	3	3
Anger	15	3	1
Cynicism	20	0	3
Antisocial Attitudes	22	5	0
Type A Behavior	18	6	1
Low Self-Esteem	16	5	8
Social Discomfort	24	7	0
Family Problems	24	3	1
Work Interference	19	6	14
Negative Treatment Indicators	15	9	11

ever, many of these were deleted "administratively" after the Restandardization Committee decided to eliminate "bowel and bladder function" items. At the other extreme, no items were deleted from the Cynicism scale, which is not surprising given that this was the only scale whose initial list was derived from an inductive (factor) analysis. The greatest number of additions was made to scales whose initial definition was expanded following Stage Two (e.g., Work Interference (14) and Negative Treatment Indicators (11)). No items were added to the initial lists developed for the Fears, Anti-Social Attitudes, and Social Discomfort scales.

Item Overlap between the MMPI-2 Content Scales. As noted earlier, some of the constructs underlying the MMPI-2 Content Scales are conceptually related — for example, depression (DEP) and the tendency to view oneself in negative terms (LSE). We were aware that some items might, rationally and statistically, "belong" to more than one scale. The scale construction procedures employed, particularly Step 1 of Stage 4, tended to reduce item overlap considerably. However, a few items, because of their relevance to several constructs appear on more than one Content Scale. Table 10 shows the item overlap in the MMPI-2 Content Scales. Item overlap was kept to a minimum, with the most overlap occurring in two of the general problem scales: WRK and TRT.

TABLE 10. Number of Overlapping Items on the MMPI-2 Content Scales

	ANX	FRS	OBS	DEP	HEA	BIZ	ANG	CYN	ASP	TPA	LSE	SOD	FAM	WRK	TRT
ANX	—	—	2	—	—	—	—	—	—	—	—	—	—	5	—
FRS		—	—	—	—	—	—	—	—	—	—	—	—	—	—
OBS			—	—	—	—	—	—	2	—	—	4	5
DEP				—	—	1	—	—	—	—	—	1	6
HEA					—	—	—	—	—	—	—	—	—
BIZ						—	—	—	—	—	1	—	—
ANG							—	—	—	3	—	—	—	1	1
CYN								—	—	1	—	—	—	1	1
ASP									—	1	—	—	—	—	—
TPA										—	—	—	—	2	—
LSE											—	—	—	1	2
SOD												—	—	—	—
FAM													—	1	—
WRK														—	2
TRT															—

Step 2: Derivation of Uniform T Scores for the Content Scales

To ensure a maximal degree of comparability between T scores for the newly developed Content Scales and the standard MMPI clinical scales, uniform T scores for the Content Scales were derived in the same manner as the uniform T scores for the clinical scales (see Chapter 2). This made it possible to express eight of the clinical scales and the 15 Content Scales on a common metric. In turn, comparability both within and between the two sets of scales was ensured. This had not been the case with the Wiggins Content Scales, where differential distributions limited the ability to make comparisons among the Content Scales and between the Wiggins and clinical scales. Such differential patterns were particularly disturbing when scales measuring similar areas were compared (e.g., the clinical D and Wiggins DEP scales). Tables for converting Content Scale raw scores into uniform T scores are provided in Appendix J.

Stage Five: Rational Descriptors for Scales

A final rational procedure involved writing descriptions of each of the content scales based on item content (Table 11). This resulted in one last name change for one of the Content Scales. Antisocial Attitudes was renamed Antisocial Practices, given the behavioral emphasis in many of the items and to distinguish it further from Cynicism, primarily an attitude scale.

Information concerning the items comprising the Content Scales is provided in Appendixes H and I.

TABLE 11. Description of MMPI-2 Content Scales

ANX (ANXIETY) 23 items. High scorers on ANX report general symptoms of anxiety including tension, somatic problems (i.e., heart pounding and shortness of breath), sleep difficulties, worries, and poor concentration. They fear losing their minds, find life a strain, and have difficulty making decisions. They appear to be aware of these symptoms and problems, and admit to having them.

FRS (FEARS) 23 items. A high score on FRS indicates an individual with many specific fears. These include the sight of blood; high places; money; animals such as snakes, mice, or spiders; leaving home; fire; storms and natural disasters; water; the dark; being indoors; and dirt.

OBS (OBSESSIVENESS) 16 items. High scorers on OBS have tremendous difficulty making decisions and are likely to ruminate excessively about issues and problems, causing others to become impatient. Having to make changes distresses them, and they may report some compulsive behaviors like counting or saving unimportant things. They are excessive worriers who frequently become overwhelmed by their own thoughts.

DEP (DEPRESSION) 33 items. High scores on this scale characterize individuals with significant depressive thoughts. They report feeling blue, uncertain about their future, and uninterested in their lives. They are likely to brood, be unhappy, cry easily, and feel hopeless and empty. They may report thoughts of suicide or wishes that they were dead. They may believe that they are condemned or have committed unpardonable sins. Other people may not be viewed as sources of support.

HEA (HEALTH CONCERNS) 36 items. Individuals with high scores on HEA report many physical symptoms across several body systems. Included are gastro-intestinal symptoms (e.g., constipation, nausea and vomiting, stomach trouble), neurological problems (e.g., convulsions, dizzy and fainting spells, paralysis), sensory problems (e.g., poor hearing or eyesight), cardiovascular symptoms (e.g., heart or chest pains), skin problems, pain (e.g., headaches, neck aches), respiratory trouble (e.g., coughs, hay fever or asthma). These individuals worry about their health and feel sicker than the average person.

BIZ (BIZARRE MENTATION) 24 items. Psychotic thought processes characterize individuals high on the BIZ scale. They may report auditory, visual, or olfactory hallucinations and may recognize that their thoughts are strange and peculiar. Paranoid ideation (e.g., the belief that they are being plotted against or that someone is trying to poison them) may be reported as well. These individuals may feel that they have a special mission or special powers.

ANG (ANGER) 16 items. High scores on the ANG scale suggest anger-control problems. These individuals report being irritable, grouchy, impatient, hotheaded, annoyed, and stubborn. They sometimes feel like swearing or smashing things. They may lose self-control and report having been physically abusive toward people and objects.

CYN (CYNICISM) 23 items. Misanthropic beliefs characterize high scorers on CYN. They expect hidden, negative motives behind the acts of others — for example, believing that most people are honest simply because they fear being caught. Other people are to be distrusted, because people use each other and are friendly only for selfish reasons. They are likely to hold negative attitudes about those close to them, including fellow workers, family, and friends.

ASP (ANTISOCIAL PRACTICES) 22 items. In addition to having misanthropic attitudes similar to those of high scorers on the CYN scale, high scorers on the ASP scale report problem behaviors during their school years and antisocial practices such as being in trouble with the law, stealing or shoplifting. They report sometimes enjoying the antics of criminals and if not explicitly endorsing unlawful conduct, they believe it is all right to get around the law.

TPA (TYPE A) 19 items. High scorers on TPA are hard-driving, fast-moving, and work-oriented individuals, who frequently become impatient, irritable, and annoyed. They do not like to wait or be interrupted. There is never enough time in a day for them to complete their tasks. They are direct and may be overbearing in their relationships with others.

LSE (LOW SELF-ESTEEM) 24 items. High scores on LSE characterize individuals with low opinions of themselves. They do not believe that they are liked by others or that they are important. They hold many negative attitudes about themselves, including thinking they are unattractive, awkward and clumsy, useless, and a burden to others. They certainly lack self-confidence, and find it hard to accept compliments from others. They may be overwhelmed by all the faults they see in themselves.

SOD (SOCIAL DISCOMFORT) 24 items. SOD high scorers are very uneasy around others, preferring to be by themselves. When in social situations, they are likely to sit alone, rather than joining in the group. They see themselves as shy and dislike parties and other group events.

FAM (FAMILY PROBLEMS) 25 items. Considerable family discord is reported by high scorers on FAM. Their families are described as lacking in love, quarrelsome, and unpleasant. They even may report hating members of their families. Their childhood may be portrayed as abusive, and their marriages as unhappy and lacking in affection.

WRK (WORK INTERFERENCE) 33 items. A high score on WRK is indicative of behaviors or attitudes likely to contribute to poor work performance. Some of the problems relate to low self-confidence, concentration difficulties, obsessiveness, tension and pressure, and decision-making problems. Others suggest lack of family support for the career choice, personal questioning of career choice, and negative attitudes toward co-workers.

TRT (NEGATIVE TREATMENT INDICATORS) 26 items. High scores on TRT indicate individuals with negative attitudes toward doctors and mental-health treatment. High scorers do not believe that anyone can understand or help them. They have issues or problems that they are not comfortable discussing with anyone. They may not want to change anything in their lives, nor do they feel that change is possible. They prefer giving up to facing a crisis or difficulty.

Chapter 4

Psychometric Characteristics of the MMPI-2 Content Scales

A major test of a psychometric scale's utility is its reliability. In this chapter we provide reliability data and other statistics describing the psychometric properties of the Content Scales in four of the samples discussed in Chapter 2: the MMPI-2 normative sample, an inpatient sample of alcoholics (McKenna & Butcher, 1987), a sample of military personnel (Butcher et al., 1988), and the inpatient psychiatric sample (Graham & Butcher, 1988) that was used in the development of the scales.

Reliability

Table 12 provides two indexes of the reliability of the Content Scales in the MMPI-2 normative sample (Butcher et al., 1989). The first two columns of the table contain a measure of the test-retest reliability of the Content Scales in a subsample of the MMPI-2 normative sample who agreed to take form AX a second time. Examination of these two columns shows that the test-retest reliability of the Content Scales is well within the acceptable range for both males and females drawn from a normative sample of the United States population. In comparison with the range of one- to two-week test-retest reliabilities of the clinical scales in normal samples, as summarized by Graham (1987), all the coefficients reported here fall at the highest end of the range of reliabilities.

Columns 3 and 4 of Table 12 contain a measure of the internal consistency of the Content Scales in the MMPI-2 normative sample. As described in Chapter 3, the Content Scales were designed to possess high internal consistencies. Examination of their consistency in independent samples provides a crucial test of this aspect of the test design. Table 13 provides the internal consistencies of the scales in three other samples — the psychiatric sample that was used in the development of the scales, a clinical sample of alcoholics who were tested at an inpatient setting that provides treatment for chemical dependency, and a "normal" sample of military women and men.

Examination of Tables 12 and 13 shows that the Content Scales possess ample internal consistency and that their alphas, for the most part, did not regress substantially from those found in the psychiatric sample in which the alphas were maximized. This indicates that the degree of content homogeneity achieved in developing the scales is maintained both in other clinical samples and in samples of nonclinical subjects. The one notable exception is the BIZ scale, which appears to regress more than the others. It is likely that this is due to the highly restricted variance of responses to its items in non-inpatient psychiatric samples. Nevertheless, its internal consistency is still well within an acceptable range in the other three samples,

**TABLE 12. Reliability of the MMPI-2 Content Scales
in the Normative Sample**

Scale	Test-Retest[a]		Internal Consistency[b,c]	
	Males n = 82	Females n = 111	Males n = 1,138	Females n = 1,462
ANX	.90	.87	.82	.83
FRS	.81	.86	.72	.75
OBS	.83	.85	.74	.77
DEP	.87	.88	.85	.86
HEA	.81	.85	.76	.80
BIZ	.78	.81	.73	.74
ANG	.85	.82	.76	.73
CYN	.80	.89	.86	.85
ASP	.81	.87	.78	.75
TPA	.82	.79	.72	.68
LSE	.84	.86	.79	.83
SOD	.91	.90	.83	.84
FAM	.84	.83	.73	.77
WRK	.90	.91	.82	.84
TRT	.79	.88	.78	.80

[a]Average retest interval was nine days.
[b]Cronbach's (1951) coefficient alpha.
[c]Subjects who responded "Cannot Say" to an item on a scale were deleted from that scale. The minimum number of subjects was 1,090 males and 1,384 females.

and its test-retest reliability (Table 12) is also adequate for psychometric assessment.

An interesting comparison can be made between the test-retest reliabilities and internal consistencies of the Content Scales and those of the MMPI-2 clinical scales reported in the test manual (1989), which are based on the same sample reported here in the first two columns of Table 12. The test-retest coefficients for the clinical scales range from .58 for Pa in females to .92 for Si in males. On average, they are somewhat lower than those reported here for the MMPI-2 Content Scales.

A similar comparison can be made between the internal consistencies of the MMPI-2 clinical scales and the Content Scales. Here, of course, the Content Scales have a distinct advantage in that they were developed specifically to possess a high degree of internal consistency, which played no role in the development of the clinical scales. As expected, the internal consistencies reported here are considerably higher than those reported in the MMPI-2 manual (1989) for the clinical scales.

Another comparison of interest can be made between the new Content Scales and the Wiggins Content Scales for the original MMPI. Such a comparison can be made, since, as described in Chapter 2, the experimental form of the MMPI booklet contained all of the Wiggins items. Table 14 con-

TABLE 13. Internal Consistencies of the MMPI-2 Content Scales in Psychiatric, Alcoholic, and Military Samples

	Sample					
	Psychiatric		Alcoholic		Military	
	Males	Females	Males	Females	Males	Females
Scales	(n = 232)	(n = 191)	(n = 832)	(n = 380)	(n = 1,156)	(n = 167)
ANX	.90	.90	.87	.87	.84	.82
FRS	.84	.78	.71	.73	.75	.78
OBS	.83	.84	.78	.81	.78	.78
DEP	.94	.93	.90	.90	.87	.87
HEA	.88	.88	.84	.85	.83	.85
BIZ	.90	.90	.77	.79	.81	.84
ANG	.79	.84	.81	.78	.78	.78
CYN	.89	.87	.85	.86	.85	.84
ASP	.80	.80	.76	.78	.78	.72
TPA	.80	.76	.75	.74	.74	.75
LSE	.87	.89	.85	.87	.83	.86
SOD	.88	.84	.87	.89	.81	.82
FAM	.86	.84	.80	.82	.78	.77
WRK	.91	.90	.89	.88	.87	.87
TRT	.88	.88	.83	.83	.82	.78

Note: Subjects who responded "Cannot Say" to an item on a scale were deleted from that scale. The minimum number of subjects was 211 males and 166 females for the psychiatric sample, 793 males and 341 females for the alcoholic sample, and 1,121 males and 150 females for the military sample.

TABLE 14. Reliability of the Wiggins Content Scales in the Normative Sample

	Test-Retest[a]		Internal Consistency[b]	
Scale	Males (n = 82)	Females (n = 111)	Males (n = 1,138)	Females (n = 1,462)
HEA	.78	.80	.71	.73
DEP	.92	.87	.81	.83
ORG	.80	.78	.74	.78
FAM	.81	.77	.65	.69
AUT	.75	.85	.77	.75
FEM	.81	.83	.58	.48
REL	.94	.95	.87	.87
HOS	.81	.87	.77	.75
MOR	.87	.91	.82	.85
PHO	.83	.86	.72	.74
PSY	.84	.81	.78	.77
HYP	.77	.76	.71	.69
SOC	.91	.91	.83	.84

Note: Subjects who responded "Cannot Say" to an item on a scale were deleted from that scale. The minimum number of subjects was 1,090 males and 1,384 females.
[a]Average retest interval was nine days.
[b]Cronbach's (1951) coefficient alpha.

tains the test-retest coefficients and internal consistencies of the Wiggins scales in the MMPI-2 normative sample.

With respect to test-retest reliability, a comparison of Tables 12 and 14 shows that the two sets of scales are generally comparable. There is no clear pattern of one set of scales having greater test-retest reliability, and all the coefficients for scales measuring similar constructs are roughly equivalent.

TABLE 15. Internal Consistencies for the Wiggins Content Scales in Psychiatric, Alcoholic, and Military Samples

	Sample					
	Psychiatric		Alcoholic		Military	
	Males	Females	Males	Females	Males	Females
Scales	n = 232	n = 191	N = 832	n = 380	n = 1,156	n = 167
HEA	.78	.79	.80	.79	.73	.76
DEP	.92	.91	.88	.88	.87	.84
ORG	.89	.86	.82	.84	.84	.86
FAM	.77	.74	.71	.76	.69	.71
AUT	.79	.79	.73	.77	.77	.71
FEM	.61	.53	.60	.51	.52	.58
REL	.79	.75	.82	.79	.78	.74
HOS	.84	.83	.79	.81	.81	.81
MOR	.88	.88	.88	.88	.86	.85
PHO	.82	.78	.72	.74	.74	.79
PSY	.92	.92	.82	.81	.85	.87
HYP	.77	.82	.71	.71	.72	.66
SOC	.87	.85	.88	.89	.80	.80

Note: Subjects who responded "Cannot Say" to an item on a scale were deleted from that scale. The minimum number of subjects was 211 males and 166 females for the psychiatric sample, 793 males and 341 females for the alcoholic sample, and 1,121 males and 150 females for the military sample.

Table 14 also contains measures of the internal consistencies of the Wiggins scales in the normative sample. Table 15 provides these measures for the psychiatric, alcoholic, and military samples. A comparison of the Content Scales and the Wiggins scales shows that, on average, the Content Scales possess a higher degree of internal consistency. Similarly named scales such as FAM, HEA, and DEP are good examples of this phenomenon. Thus, insofar as reliability is concerned, it appears that the new Content Scales offer a viable replacement for the Wiggins scales without detriment to test-retest reliability and in some cases, improving on the internal consistencies of the Wiggins scales.

Descriptive Statistics

Following are three types of descriptive statistics for the MMPI-2 Content Scales: the uniform T-score transformation (Tellegen, 1988) for deriving standard scores for the Content Scales; the means and standard deviations of Content Scale scores for the four samples included in this chapter; and item-scale correlations for the psychiatric sample.

The Uniform Distribution

As described in Chapter 2, the purpose of deriving uniform T scores was to transform the distribution of each individual scale to that of a composite of the clinical-scale distributions. Tables 16 and 17 provide data that can be used to assess the effect and success of this effort.

TABLE 16. Effects of Uniform T-Score Transformation on Skewness and Kurtosis in the Normative Sample

	Skewness				Kurtosis			
	Males		Females		Males		Females	
Scale	Lin	Uni	Lin	Uni	Lin	Uni	Lin	Uni
ANX	.86	.73	.73	.71	.38	.55	0	.39
FRS	.99	.78	.47	.68	1.15	1.01	−.06	.52
OBS	.67	.74	.47	.78	.07	.44	−.54	.51
DEP	1.60	.71	1.33	.70	3.10	.71	1.74	.48
HEA	1.41	.68	1.23	.72	2.75	.60	1.88	.69
BIZ	1.45	.94	1.71	.77	2.24	.96	3.47	.57
ANG	.53	.75	.44	.76	−.30	.52	−.30	.50
CYN	.23	.80	.46	.77	−.75	.44	−.43	.47
ASP	.29	.74	.52	.71	−.62	.55	−.14	.47
TPA	.13	.77	.22	.80	−.65	.35	−.38	.74
LSE	1.19	.79	.90	.70	1.43	.97	.21	.52
SOD	.58	.77	.72	.76	−.25	.50	.05	.55
FAM	.85	.67	.81	.73	.50	.45	.41	.46
WRK	1.08	.75	.80	.75	1.24	.61	.14	.64
TRT	1.11	.79	1.01	.73	1.30	.81	.65	.48
Mean	.86	.76	.79	.74	.77	.63	.45	.53
SD	.46	.06	.40	.03	1.25	.21	1.10	.09
Range	1.47	.27	1.49	.12	3.85	.66	4.01	.35

Table 16 presents the skewness and kurtosis of the Content Scales scored both as linear and uniform T scores. Linear T scores were derived by the following transformation:

$$\text{Linear T score} = \frac{(\text{Raw Score-Normative Mean}) \times 10}{\text{Normative SD}} + 50$$

The derivation of uniform T scores is described in Chapter 2, and the tables for converting Content Scale raw scores to uniform T scores are provided in Appendix J.

Examination of Table 16 demonstrates very clearly that the uniform transformation is successful in making the Content Scale distributions much closer in terms of skewness and kurtosis than are the linear T-score distributions. As would be expected, the means of the linear and uniform skewness and kurtosis are quite similar, since the objective was to create a uniform distribution representative of the composite of the linear distributions. They are not identical because the composite was based on the clinical scales rather than the Content Scales. The overall effect of the uniform transformation is represented by the standard deviations and ranges of the linear and uniform skewness and kurtosis. We would expect the means of the linear and uniform skewness and kurtosis to be comparable, since it is precisely the goal of the uniform transformation to represent an "average" distribution. The extent of the differences in skewness and kurtosis among the linear distributions is represented by their ranges and standard deviations, and the success of the uniform transformation in creating similar distributions among the scales may be evaluated by examining the degree to which these ranges and standard deviations shrink in the uniform distributions.

In Table 16 we see quite clearly that the uniform transformation is successful in creating uniform distributions. For example, the standard deviation of the skewness of the Content Scales drops from .46 to .06, while the range drops from 1.47 to .27 when comparing the linear and uniform scales in males. As discussed in Chapter 2, this enables direct comparisons between T scores on different content and clinical scales.

Table 17 provides a different perspective on the same phenomenon, presenting the *actual* percentile of linear and uniform T scores of 70 and 80 for each of the scales. If the scales were all normally distributed, we would expect all linear T scores of 70 to correspond to the percentile equivalent of two standard deviations above the mean — 97.7 — and all linear T scores of 80 to correspond to the percentile equivalent of three standard deviations above the mean — 99.9. A comparison of the linear and uniform percentiles at T scores 70 and 80 again demonstrates the success of the uniform transformation in creating more similar distributions, thus making the same T score more equally interpretable across scales.

As was the case in Table 16, the means for the linear and uniform percentiles are quite close, and the effect of the uniform transformation is seen in the standard deviations and ranges. As for the means, they, of course, do not correspond precisely to the two figures quoted above as the percentile equivalents of T scores 70 and 80 because the uniform distribution is not a normal distribution. The reasons for preferring this distribution over a normal one (i.e., normalized T scores) are discussed in Chapter 2.

TABLE 17. Linear versus Uniform T-Score Percentiles at T Scores 70 and 80

| | T Score 70 | | | | T Score 80 | | | |
| | Males | | Females | | Males | | Females | |
Scale	Lin	Uni	Lin	Uni	Lin	Uni	Lin	Uni
ANX	96.3	96.3	96.4	96.4	99.4	99.4	99.9	99.6
FRS	96.6	97.1	97.1	96.8	99.2	99.3	99.8	99.5
OBS	96.5	96.5	97.1	96.5	99.8	99.8	99.9	99.8
DEP	95.1	96.7	95.6	96.3	98.4	99.3	98.7	99.4
HEA	96.0	96.9	95.8	96.6	98.5	99.2	98.8	99.1
BIZ	95.2	96.9	95.9	96.9	99.2	99.6	98.2	99.6
ANG	97.5	97.0	97.2	96.6	99.9	99.5	100.0	99.7
CYN	98.1	95.7	97.5	96.1	100.0	99.7	100.0	99.8
ASP	98.2	96.3	96.9	96.3	99.9	99.7	99.9	99.6
TPA	98.5	96.7	98.2	96.7	100.0	99.8	99.9	99.5
LSE	95.5	96.0	96.0	96.6	99.2	99.5	99.7	99.5
SOD	95.9	95.2	95.8	95.8	99.9	99.6	99.8	99.6
FAM	96.2	96.9	95.7	96.1	99.4	99.4	99.7	99.6
WRK	96.0	96.4	96.4	96.4	99.2	99.5	99.7	99.5
TRT	95.7	96.4	95.8	96.2	99.3	99.4	99.4	99.5
Mean	96.5	96.5	96.5	96.4	99.4	99.5	99.5	99.5
SD	1.1	0.52	0.79	0.29	0.51	0.18	0.55	0.17
Range	3.4	1.9	2.6	1.1	1.6	0.6	1.8	0.7

Sample Means and Standard Deviations

The means and standard deviations of the raw scores and uniform T scores of the four samples discussed in this chapter may be used as points of reference for comparing both individual and group scores on the content scales.

As seen in Table 18 the uniform T transformation was successful not only in enhancing the comparability of the Content Scales, but also in deriving means and standard deviations of the expected magnitude of 50 and 10, respectively, in the MMPI-2 normative sample.

Table 19 provides means and standard deviations on the Content Scales for the psychiatric sample that was used in the development of the scales. Though this fact may bias these descriptive indexes somewhat, it is clear that on average in a psychiatric sample most of the Content Scales reach levels that are clinically interpretable.

In Table 20 we see that this is not the case in a sample of alcoholics hospitalized for treatment. This finding is not surprising, since we would not expect alcoholics receiving treatment for a *specific* problem to show elevations across the board as did the omnibus sample of inpatient psychiatric patients.

Finally, in Table 21 we see that subjects in the military sample obtain scores that, for the most part, are almost identical to those obtained by the normative sample. This finding led Butcher et al. (in press) to conclude that

TABLE 18. Raw and Uniform T-Score Means and Standard Deviations for the Normative Sample

	Raw Scores				T Scores			
	Males (n = 1,138)		Females (n = 1,462)		Males (n = 1,138)		Females (n = 1,462)	
Scale	M	SD	M	SD	M	SD	M	SD
ANX	5.5	4.2	6.5	4.5	50.0	9.8	49.9	10.0
FRS	3.8	3.0	6.6	3.6	50.0	10.0	50.0	9.9
OBS	4.9	3.1	5.5	3.3	49.8	9.8	50.0	9.8
DEP	4.8	4.6	5.9	5.0	50.2	10.0	49.9	10.0
HEA	5.3	3.9	6.2	4.5	50.0	10.0	50.0	9.9
BIZ	2.3	2.5	2.2	2.5	50.0	9.7	50.3	9.7
ANG	5.6	3.3	5.7	3.1	50.0	9.9	49.9	9.8
CYN	9.5	5.4	8.7	5.2	50.0	10.0	50.0	9.8
ASP	7.9	4.2	6.2	3.7	50.0	9.9	49.9	9.9
TPA	8.1	3.7	7.4	3.3	49.9	9.9	49.8	9.9
LSE	4.3	3.7	5.2	4.2	50.0	10.0	50.0	9.9
SOD	7.6	4.8	7.5	4.8	49.9	10.0	50.0	9.9
FAM	5.3	3.5	6.1	3.8	50.1	9.9	49.9	9.8
WRK	7.3	5.0	8.5	5.4	50.0	9.9	50.0	9.9
TRT	4.7	3.7	5.0	4.0	50.0	10.0	50.0	9.9

TABLE 19. Raw and Uniform T-Score Means and Standard Deviations for the Psychiatric Sample

	Raw Scores				T Scores			
	Males (n = 232)		Females (n = 191)		Males (n = 232)		Females (n = 191)	
Scale	M	SD	M	SD	M	SD	M	SD
ANX	11.9	6.1	13.0	6.1	65.1	14.5	64.5	14.0
FRS	6.3	4.6	9.7	4.5	58.1	15.3	59.0	13.2
OBS	7.9	4.2	9.2	4.1	59.6	13.8	61.9	13.5
DEP	15.6	9.0	16.2	8.6	70.3	16.0	68.4	14.8
HEA	10.5	6.9	12.0	7.5	61.7	15.1	61.8	14.9
BIZ	6.9	5.6	7.6	5.7	66.4	19.9	67.7	17.8
ANG	7.9	3.8	8.0	4.0	56.9	12.2	57.9	13.9
CYN	12.6	6.1	12.7	5.8	56.6	12.8	57.9	12.1
ASP	11.2	4.6	9.6	4.6	58.6	12.7	59.4	13.0
TPA	9.3	4.4	9.6	4.0	53.7	12.8	57.2	13.6
LSE	9.9	5.8	10.9	6.1	64.5	14.8	63.7	14.7
SOD	11.3	5.9	11.0	5.1	57.9	13.1	57.1	10.8
FAM	10.7	5.7	11.7	5.3	65.0	15.8	64.3	13.8
WRK	15.3	7.9	16.6	7.8	65.1	14.8	65.3	15.0
TRT	10.7	6.4	11.5	6.2	65.3	16.2	65.9	15.2

TABLE 20. Raw and Uniform T-Score Means and Standard Deviations for the Alcoholic Sample

| | Raw Scores | | | | T Scores | | | |
| | Males (n = 832) | | Females (n = 380) | | Males (n = 832) | | Females (n = 380) | |
Scale	M	SD	M	SD	M	SD	M	SD
ANX	10.4	5.5	11.6	5.6	61.6	12.9	61.3	12.7
FRS	4.4	3.1	7.2	3.7	51.9	10.2	51.8	10.3
OBS	6.9	3.5	7.6	3.7	56.2	11.6	56.4	11.7
DEP	10.6	6.6	12.4	6.9	61.8	12.0	62.1	12.0
HEA	7.8	5.6	9.3	6.1	55.9	12.9	56.5	12.5
BIZ	3.6	3.1	3.6	3.3	54.8	11.5	55.5	11.3
ANG	8.0	3.8	7.4	3.5	57.4	12.2	55.8	12.0
CYN	10.5	5.3	9.1	5.4	51.8	10.1	50.8	10.2
ASP	9.5	4.2	7.1	4.1	53.7	10.5	52.6	11.4
TPA	9.5	3.9	8.5	3.7	53.9	11.4	53.4	12.0
LSE	6.4	4.7	8.5	5.3	55.5	12.3	57.5	12.5
SOD	8.6	5.5	8.4	5.7	52.1	11.7	51.9	11.9
FAM	7.8	4.4	8.6	4.8	56.9	12.3	56.4	12.3
WRK	11.4	6.9	13.3	7.0	57.8	13.1	58.7	13.2
TRT	6.6	4.5	7.3	4.7	55.1	11.7	55.6	11.5

TABLE 21. Raw and Uniform T-Score Means and Standard Deviations for the Military Sample

| | Raw Scores | | | | T Scores | | | |
| | Males (n = 1,156) | | Females (n = 167) | | Males (n = 1,156) | | Females (n = 167) | |
Scale	M	SD	M	SD	M	SD	M	SD
ANX	6.0	4.5	5.5	3.8	51.0	10.6	47.6	8.2
FRS	3.7	2.8	5.0	3.3	49.5	9.4	45.8	9.1
OBS	4.6	3.3	4.6	3.1	48.6	10.9	47.4	9.0
DEP	5.3	4.8	5.2	4.5	51.3	10.3	48.6	9.3
HEA	5.3	4.2	4.9	4.0	50.0	10.5	47.1	9.4
BIZ	3.1	3.1	3.1	3.2	53.1	11.4	53.7	11.7
ANG	6.2	3.5	5.7	3.5	51.9	10.8	50.3	11.2
CYN	11.7	5.4	11.9	5.1	54.3	10.9	56.0	10.4
ASP	9.6	4.4	8.0	3.6	54.2	11.2	54.8	9.7
TPA	8.2	3.8	7.5	3.7	50.2	10.3	50.5	11.3
LSE	3.8	3.7	3.6	3.6	48.5	10.4	46.3	8.9
SOD	6.7	4.6	5.2	4.0	48.0	9.5	45.2	8.4
FAM	5.9	3.8	5.7	3.5	51.8	10.6	48.8	9.2
WRK	6.9	5.5	7.0	5.0	54.4	6.8	47.0	9.4
TRT	5.0	3.9	4.3	3.4	50.7	10.4	48.4	8.7

separate MMPI norms are not needed for use with military subjects as previous researchers had suggested.

Item-Scale Correlations

For each Content Scale item the correlation was derived by deleting its contribution from the total raw score and then computing the point-biserial correlation between the item and the corrected scale score. Item-scale correlations are provided for the MMPI-2 normative sample and for the combined psychiatric sample employed in the development of the scales in Tables 22 and 23. Examination of these figures reveals some degree of attenuation in the correlations obtained in the normative sample when compared to those found in the psychiatric sample. This is to be expected both because of the effects of restricted variance on some items and scales in the normative sample in comparison with the psychiatric one and because of the statistical phenomenon of regression, since items were selected for inclusion on a particular scale based on their correlations with the scale in subsets of the psychiatric sample. Overall, the item-scale correlations are quite adequate in both samples.

TABLE 22. Item-Scale Correlations in the Normative Sample

Scale	Item #	Males	Females	Scale	Item #	Males	Females
ANX	15	.29	.26	FRS	186	.07	.11
	30	.13	.20	(cont.)	317	.17	.14
	31	.34	.32		322	.12	.17
	39	.24	.32		329	.08	.13
	140	.30	.37		334	.11	.07
	170	.28	.30		385	.34	.37
	196	.53	.50		392	.41	.41
	208	.24	.31		395	.28	.35
	223	.30	.34		397	.40	.42
	273	.46	.47		401	.32	.34
	290	.42	.38		435	.28	.38
	299	.41	.36		438	.38	.35
	301	.47	.49		441	.28	.28
	305	.38	.39		447	.29	.29
	339	.52	.52		453	.34	.32
	405	.34	.35		458	.35	.34
	408	.40	.45		462	.31	.39
	415	.49	.53		468	.15	.30
	463	.29	.34		471	.26	.32
	469	.45	.51		555	.12	.23
	496	.35	.34				
	509	.34	.33	OBS	55	.19	.26
	556	.48	.47		87	.38	.41
					135	.40	.51
FRS	115	.20	.22		196	.40	.41
	154	.30	.27		309	.32	.31
	163	.43	.42		313	.19	.18

Scale	Item #	Males	Females	Scale	Item #	Males	Females
OBS	327	.31	.26	HEA	53	.31	.43
(cont.)	328	.39	.43	(cont.)	57	.34	.35
	394	.40	.46		59	.31	.38
	442	.40	.35		91	.29	.34
	482	.41	.54		97	.24	.31
	491	.30	.46		101	.24	.32
	497	.36	.35		111	.32	.43
	509	.40	.45		117	.22	.21
	547	.22	.26		118	.28	.22
	553	.21	.17		141	.34	.40
					142	.17	.14
DEP	3	.23	.32		149	.21	.31
	9	.42	.37		159	.16	.21
	38	.35	.39		164	.28	.42
	52	.39	.37		175	.34	.31
	56	.47	.49		176	.30	.33
	65	.48	.53		179	.32	.36
	71	.33	.39		181	.17	.17
	75	.26	.27		194	.18	.16
	82	.42	.42		204	.19	.14
	92	.32	.23		224	.46	.50
	95	.45	.50		247	.27	.26
	130	.45	.49		249	.19	.17
	146	.17	.28		255	.23	.19
	215	.44	.50		295	.26	.27
	234	.21	.14		404	.24	.23
	246	.16	.07				
	277	.47	.48	BIZ	24	.19	.29
	303	.30	.32		32	.37	.32
	306	.35	.27		60	.15	.19
	331	.36	.31		96	.32	.23
	377	.51	.50		138	.25	.15
	388	.43	.48		162	.05	.00
	399	.36	.29		198	.26	.26
	400	.42	.53		228	.21	.23
	411	.47	.53		259	.38	.38
	454	.28	.31		298	.33	.38
	506	.31	.29		311	.33	.36
	512	.23	.23		316	.42	.45
	516	.41	.36		319	.28	.34
	520	.30	.28		333	.31	.33
	539	.36	.41		336	.15	.19
	546	.25	.20		355	.16	.19
	554	.45	.51		361	.29	.20
					427	.32	.23
HEA	11	.16	.24		466	.26	.33
	18	.18	.23		490	.25	.34
	20	.21	.22		508	.37	.36
	28	.26	.37		543	.29	.37
	33	.33	.35		551	.36	.44
	36	.17	.13				
	40	.20	.38	ANG	29	.23	.19
	44	.18	.32		37	.42	.36
	45	.36	.34		116	.34	.36
	47	.39	.35		134	.37	.32

Scale	Item #	Males	Females	Scale	Item #	Males	Females
ANG	302	.41	.38	ASP	374	.48	.47
(cont.)	389	.47	.39	(cont.)	412	.32	.23
	410	.23	.21		418	.36	.38
	414	.35	.28		419	.26	.24
	430	.42	.42				
	461	.31	.26	TPA	27	.32	.23
	486	.36	.35		136	.33	.35
	513	.47	.44		151	.25	.26
	540	.27	.18		212	.19	.16
	542	.46	.45		302	.45	.39
	548	.38	.27		358	.33	.27
	564	.29	.31		414	.34	.29
					419	.36	.31
CYN	50	.37	.39		420	.33	.31
	58	.47	.45		423	.41	.31
	76	.44	.44		430	.35	.29
	81	.49	.50		437	.17	.12
	104	.47	.40		507	.47	.40
	110	.50	.47		510	.14	.14
	124	.47	.44		523	.29	.24
	225	.38	.42		531	.13	.09
	241	.41	.37		535	.37	.34
	254	.44	.44		541	.12	.12
	283	.33	.32		545	.19	.22
	284	.37	.40				
	286	.46	.46	LSE	61	.21	.27
	315	.34	.28		70	.35	.39
	346	.35	.36		73	.46	.52
	352	.40	.38		78	.13	.14
	358	.48	.42		109	.23	.24
	374	.57	.57		130	.43	.52
	399	.33	.34		235	.28	.22
	403	.51	.50		326	.44	.47
	445	.48	.46		369	.34	.41
	470	.37	.34		376	.33	.33
	538	.40	.39		380	.34	.29
					411	.47	.49
ASP	26	.17	.18		421	.41	.49
	35	.30	.26		450	.17	.24
	66	.15	.15		457	.35	.44
	81	.46	.45		475	.43	.44
	84	.32	.21		476	.23	.28
	104	.38	.36		483	.30	.29
	105	.30	.22		485	.52	.59
	110	.45	.42		503	.38	.39
	123	.42	.37		504	.24	.33
	227	.31	.33		519	.35	.48
	240	.21	.16		526	.26	.23
	248	.33	.27		562	.30	.38
	250	.25	.24				
	254	.34	.38	SOD	46	.32	.34
	266	.22	.17		49	.53	.55
	269	.38	.36		86	.31	.27
	283	.34	.21		158	.35	.35
	284	.42	.44		167	.50	.53

Scale	Item #	Males	Females	Scale	Item #	Males	Females
SOD	185	.37	.45	WRK	108	.04	.04
(cont.)	262	.21	.35	(cont.)	135	.39	.50
	265	.46	.45		233	.41	.46
	275	.28	.29		243	.34	.40
	280	.46	.45		299	.43	.40
	281	.29	.26		302	.29	.31
	321	.27	.41		318	.20	.28
	337	.55	.59		339	.47	.48
	340	.29	.27		364	.44	.51
	349	.24	.26		368	.40	.40
	353	.49	.47		394	.45	.49
	359	.41	.40		409	.37	.35
	360	.40	.49		428	.28	.23
	363	.24	.24		445	.27	.24
	367	.44	.43		464	.39	.39
	370	.57	.53		491	.39	.49
	479	.32	.32		505	.38	.40
	480	.38	.32		509	.44	.44
	515	.27	.24		517	.22	.14
					521	.20	.19
FAM	21	.32	.38		525	.33	.38
	54	.24	.14		545	.31	.30
	83	.25	.36		554	.42	.47
	125	.26	.34		559	.32	.21
	145	.28	.39		561	.29	.36
	190	.25	.31		566	.29	.24
	195	.31	.40				
	205	.39	.37	TRT	22	.31	.34
	217	.19	.14		92	.26	.16
	256	.35	.37		274	.37	.41
	292	.29	.31		306	.33	.27
	300	.14	.26		364	.39	.47
	323	.22	.20		368	.39	.40
	378	.31	.27		373	.23	.23
	379	.22	.28		375	.33	.33
	382	.35	.43		376	.39	.37
	383	.32	.32		377	.41	.37
	413	.28	.28		391	.38	.42
	449	.29	.25		399	.38	.39
	455	.29	.36		482	.37	.45
	478	.04	.10		488	.20	.16
	543	.33	.37		491	.35	.46
	550	.33	.31		493	.12	.10
	563	.24	.29		494	.26	.31
	567	.20	.25		495	.23	.22
					497	.39	.38
WRK	10	.12	.15		499	.25	.17
	15	.16	.17		500	.39	.38
	17	.29	.27		501	.14	.15
	31	.37	.38		504	.24	.32
	54	.21	.11		528	.20	.25
	73	.39	.50		539	.37	.41
	98	.23	.29		554	.40	.45

Note: Correlations are point bi-serial. Each item was removed from the total score before the correlation was computed.

TABLE 23. Item-Scale Correlations in the Psychiatric Sample

Scale	Item #	Males	Females	Scale	Item #	Males	Females
ANX	15	.48	.33	OBS	327	.40	.40
	30	.37	.40	(cont.)	328	.50	.54
	31	.56	.56		394	.58	.48
	39	.51	.54		442	.43	.32
	140	.56	.58		482	.56	.52
	170	.50	.56		491	.53	.52
	196	.60	.63		497	.58	.60
	208	.39	.33		509	.33	.38
	223	.50	.42		547	.44	.45
	273	.64	.59		553	.42	.40
	290	.32	.34				
	299	.52	.49	DEP	3	.51	.55
	301	.60	.61		9	.58	.57
	305	.36	.30		38	.45	.44
	339	.51	.61		52	.56	.46
	405	.39	.46		56	.59	.49
	408	.54	.51		65	.66	.59
	415	.54	.54		71	.28	.18
	463	.58	.55		75	.54	.62
	469	.64	.65		82	.53	.55
	496	.46	.59		92	.66	.57
	509	.38	.45		95	.66	.51
	556	.36	.44		130	.49	.55
					146	.28	.22
FRS	115	.37	.21		215	.53	.43
	154	.30	.31		234	.42	.38
	163	.24	.30		246	.42	.59
	186	.33	.19		277	.45	.38
	317	.41	.39		303	.63	.55
	322	.52	.26		306	.55	.49
	329	.41	.38		331	.63	.61
	334	.30	.28		377	.56	.44
	385	.38	.19		388	.53	.52
	392	.53	.36		399	.45	.43
	395	.56	.52		400	.54	.59
	397	.57	.49		411	.56	.69
	401	.32	.27		454	.60	.63
	435	.54	.69		506	.59	.57
	438	.29	.26		512	.39	.31
	441	.44	.44		516	.68	.66
	447	.30	.31		520	.61	.63
	453	.33	.22		539	.56	.56
	458	.33	.15		546	.53	.46
	462	.40	.16		554	.64	.64
	468	.42	.40				
	471	.46	.41	HEA	11	.43	.49
	555	.49	.41		18	.40	.32
					20	.33	.45
OBS	55	.27	.44		28	.41	.43
	87	.45	.41		33	.35	.23
	135	.45	.44		36	.22	.32
	196	.51	.50		40	.53	.50
	309	.41	.49		44	.47	.52
	313	.26	.27		45	.37	.34

Scale	Item #	Males	Females	Scale	Item #	Males	Females
HEA	47	.42	.44	ANG	134	.41	.45
(cont.)	53	.53	.46	(cont.)	302	.52	.47
	57	.46	.37		389	.40	.51
	59	.44	.44		410	.23	.27
	91	.50	.42		414	.38	.34
	97	.43	.41		430	.47	.52
	101	.54	.41		461	.23	.43
	111	.39	.48		486	.57	.64
	117	.29	.29		513	.37	.52
	118	.14	.42		540	.34	.27
	141	.37	.39		542	.55	.52
	142	.27	.28		548	.39	.34
	149	.41	.29		564	.26	.37
	159	.45	.19				
	164	.44	.49	CYN	50	.51	.44
	175	.31	.27		58	.42	.48
	176	.47	.43		76	.54	.60
	179	.35	.51		81	.53	.53
	181	.41	.47		104	.43	.38
	194	.22	.33		110	.59	.50
	204	.24	.40		124	.54	.43
	224	.53	.52		225	.49	.49
	247	.42	.35		241	.44	.38
	249	.22	.29		254	.43	.40
	255	.34	.37		283	.65	.62
	295	.37	.40		284	.34	.35
	404	.27	.38		286	.38	.43
					315	.51	.53
BIZ	24	.57	.52		346	.30	.38
	32	.49	.53		352	.41	.45
	60	.41	.46		358	.47	.59
	96	.41	.43		374	.46	.35
	138	.57	.53		399	.54	.42
	162	.47	.46		403	.50	.45
	198	.49	.56		445	.59	.44
	228	.49	.53		470	.38	.30
	259	.43	.55		538	.49	.44
	298	.49	.62				
	311	.57	.51	ASP	26	.36	.21
	316	.56	.57		35	.28	.43
	319	.43	.49		66	.26	.19
	333	.59	.47		81	.39	.28
	336	.53	.53		84	.48	.38
	355	.49	.52		104	.37	.29
	361	.49	.65		105	.40	.32
	427	.51	.32		110	.49	.38
	466	.46	.50		123	.38	.43
	490	.49	.49		227	.21	.36
	508	.42	.44		240	.33	.25
	543	.50	.50		248	.33	.30
	551	.60	.51		250	.33	.38
					254	.31	.40
ANG	29	.24	.48		266	.31	.39
	37	.52	.62		269	.39	.40
	116	.36	.40		283	.52	.45

Scale	Item #	Males	Females	Scale	Item #	Males	Females
ASP	284	.25	.37	SOD	167	.44	.42
(cont.)	374	.42	.46	(cont.)	185	.36	.26
	412	.35	.34		262	.38	.10
	418	.32	.37		265	.46	.52
	419	.33	.29		275	.29	.35
					280	.54	.54
TPA	27	.40	.42		281	.44	.34
	136	.39	.41		321	.45	.37
	151	.39	.20		337	.51	.44
	212	.31	.35		340	.41	.34
	302	.54	.35		349	.54	.49
	358	.36	.41		353	.55	.37
	414	.39	.40		359	.37	.37
	419	.41	.32		360	.49	.39
	420	.41	.44		363	.46	.55
	423	.41	.37		367	.48	.41
	430	.44	.38		370	.56	.56
	437	.32	.29		479	.33	.30
	507	.49	.36		480	.52	.36
	510	.22	.21		515	.29	.21
	523	.39	.15				
	531	.25	.29	FAM	21	.39	.32
	535	.42	.40		54	.40	.36
	541	.19	.19		83	.43	.37
	545	.41	.34		125	.46	.35
					145	.52	.38
LSE	61	.35	.33		190	.48	.44
	70	.24	.40		195	.56	.54
	73	.40	.50		205	.50	.50
	78	.53	.54		217	.25	.20
	109	.40	.44		256	.24	.33
	130	.40	.50		292	.46	.48
	235	.42	.26		300	.47	.39
	326	.42	.53		323	.36	.30
	369	.39	.41		378	.42	.42
	376	.51	.47		379	.53	.48
	380	.51	.59		382	.39	.40
	411	.48	.55		383	.27	.29
	421	.44	.51		413	.42	.32
	450	.39	.58		449	.33	.34
	457	.39	.51		455	.38	.39
	475	.60	.57		478	.39	.22
	476	.39	.35		543	.50	.40
	483	.49	.43		550	.41	.41
	485	.64	.58		563	.39	.39
	503	.48	.47		567	.35	.38
	504	.42	.56				
	519	.44	.43	WRK	10	.23	.35
	526	.46	.46		15	.50	.33
	562	.42	.40		17	.42	.48
					31	.57	.62
SOD	46	.42	.33		54	.35	.19
	49	.59	.52		73	.28	.19
	86	.42	.35		98	.55	.50
	158	.38	.48		108	.42	.30

Scale	Item #	Males	Females	Scale	Item #	Males	Females
WRK	135	.46	.45	TRT	22	.53	.59
(cont.)	233	.39	.37		92	.53	.49
	243	.56	.61		274	.51	.42
	299	.55	.47		306	.42	.41
	302	.57	.57		364	.46	.54
	318	.53	.43		368	.39	.58
	339	.61	.38		373	.41	.51
	364	.44	.57		375	.45	.38
	368	.38	.51		376	.48	.50
	394	.36	.24		377	.55	.42
	409	.62	.65		391	.57	.59
	428	.27	.28		399	.51	.51
	445	.55	.53		482	.57	.47
	464	.57	.57		488	.32	.27
	491	.58	.57		491	.29	.43
	505	.54	.57		493	.57	.60
	509	.46	.42		494	.25	.12
	517	.23	.28		495	.55	.57
	521	.56	.52		497	.62	.59
	525	.57	.64		499	.40	.28
	545	.39	.35		500	.21	.21
	554	.60	.58		501	.57	.50
	559	.31	.29		504	.49	.37
	561	.31	.47		528	.28	.37
	566	.31	.23		539	.18	.14
					554	.49	.43

Note: Correlations are point bi-serial. Each item was removed from the total score before the correlation was computed.

Intercorrelation among the MMPI-2 Content Scales

The intercorrelations among the MMPI-2 Content Scales for the MMPI-2 normative sample are reported in Table 24. The intercorrelations for the full MMPI-2 Content Scales range from .11 to .77 for males and from .11 to .79 for females. Since several of the Content Scales contain overlapping items (see Table 10 in Chapter 3) the scale intercorrelations were also computed with the overlapping items removed from the scales. The intercorrelations of the scales with the overlapping items removed are footnoted in Table 24. The range of correlations for the MMPI-2 Content Scales, with overlapping items removed, remains approximately the same — between .11 and .76 for males and .11 and .75 for females. As expected, the correlation between pairs of scales does change when overlapping items are removed (see note to Table 24).

TABLE 24. MMPI-2 Content Scale Intercorrelations

	ANX	FRS	OBS	DEP	HEA	BIZ	ANG	CYN	ASP	TPA	LSE	SOD	FAM	WRK	TRT
ANX	—	.34	.66^a	.72	.48	.43	.51	.44	.38	47	.57	.28	.57	.76^h	.64
FRS	.35		.39	.32	.35	.25	.20	.33	.23	.30	.34	.17	.27	.39	.40
OBS	.72^a	.40		.60	.36	.45	.48	.51	41	.53	.65^f	.29	.51	.76^i	.67^p
DEP	.75	.32	.67		.43	.43	.46	.49^b	41	.39	.69	.34	.58	.75^j	.76^q
HEA	.54	.32	.43	.48		.38	.32	.30	.25	.27	. 37	.20	.31	.43	.40
BIZ	.41	.32	.45	.45	.39		.41	.51	.45	.35	.34	.06	.45^g	.41	.37
ANG	.58	.30	.56	.56	.38	.40		.49	.51	.69^c	.36	.14	.49	.49^k	.46^r
CYN	.46	.41	.52	.51^b	.39	.53	.47		.76	.60^d	.43	.19	.52	.53^l	.54^s
ASP	.37	.25	.41	.41	.29	.45	.46	.74		.54^e	.35	.11	.47	.42	.45
TPA	.49	.34	.51	.43	.32	.39	.66^c	.54^d	.46^e		.36	.18	.47	.50^m	.47
LSE	.62	.33	.70^f	.72	.37	.35	.43	.45	34	.39		.41	.45	.74^n	.72^t
SOD	.31	.18	.30	.39	.20	.11	.19	.21	.13	. 20	.44		.24	.40	.42
FAM	.58	.26	.50	.61	.40	.47^g	.56	.50	41	.45	.47	.26		.57^o	.54
WRK	.79^h	.36	.79^i	.79^j	.45	41	.57^k	.53^l	.42	.52^m	.76^n	.43	.55^o		.77^u
TRT	.65	.40	.72^p	.78^q	.41	.42	. 49^r	.58^s	.47	.47	.77^t	.43	.53	.79^u	—

Note: Males are presented in the upper right, females in the lower left. N = 1,138 males, 1,462 females. The following footnotes indicate the intercorrelations of these scales when item overlap is eliminated: male intercorrelations/female inter-correlations (number of overlapping items).

[a].44/.52 (2)   [g].40/.41 (1)   [l].45/.44 (1)   [q].55/.56 (6)
[b].45/.46 (1)   [h].56/.62 (5)   [m].31/.29 (2)   [r].40/.37 (1)
[c].50/.44 (3)   [i].45/.48 (4)   [n].61/.62 (1)   [s].49/.51 (1)
[d].49/.45 (1)   [j].64/.68 (1)   [o].48/.47 (1)   [t].49/.53 (2)
[e].34/.25 (1)   [k].37/.45 (1)   [p].40/.43 (5)   [u].51/.53 (2)
[f].45/.47 (2)

Summary

The test-retest reliability of the Content Scales in a subsample of the MMPI-2 normative sample was, on average, somewhat greater than that of the MMPI-2 clinical scales. In comparison to the original MMPI Wiggins Content Scales, the MMPI-2 Content Scales were generally similar in test-retest reliability.

The Content Scales greatly outperformed the MMPI-2 clinical scales on internal consistency. To a lesser degree, the internal consistencies of the Content Scales were also higher than those of the original MMPI Wiggins Content Scales in all four of the samples for which data were reported.

Analyses of the effect of employing the uniform T-score transformation demonstrated that the uniform transformation was quite successful in making the T score distributions of the Content Scales more similar (in terms of their skewness and kurtosis) than distributions of *linear* T scores for these scales would have been. Also, applying the uniform distribution makes equal uniform T scores much more equivalent (in terms of percentiles) than are linear T scores.

The means and standard deviations of both raw scores and uniform T scores for the normative, psychiatric, alcoholic, and military samples show that the uniform transformation was successful in producing means of 50 and standard deviations of 10 for the normative sample on the MMPI-2 Content Scales; the psychiatric sample obtained clinically interpretable mean scores on most of the Content Scales; the alcoholic sample obtained meaningful elevations only on specific scales related to characterological aspects of alcoholism; and the military sample obtained scores that were quite similar to those of the normative sample.

Finally, corrected item-scale point-biserial correlations for each item on each of the MMPI-2 Content Scales in the normative and psychiatric samples revealed an expected degree of attenuation in the normative sample (owing to restricted variance as compared with the psychiatric sample and regression), though in general the correlations were quite adequate in both samples.

Our initial examination of the psychometric characteristics of the MMPI-2 Content Scales reveals that these are reliable, homogeneous, uniformly distributed, and adequately differentiating scales.

Chapter 5

Validation of the MMPI-2 Content Scales

Before new personality scales can be used effectively in clinical prediction their relationship to existing personality measures and their ability to accurately assess external (behavioral) variables must be delineated. Evidence for the internal and external validity of the MMPI-2 Content Scales is the subject of this chapter. Internal validity refers to the correlations of the Content Scales with other MMPI scales; external validity refers to correlations with extra-test data.

Correlation with Other MMPI Measures

Much can be learned about a scale by examining its interrelationships with other personality and clinical measures. Users of the Content Scales are likely to be most familiar with other MMPI scales they have used in the past. Examining correlations of the Content Scales with these previously established MMPI scales will help mark the "territory" and boundaries of the MMPI-2 Content Scales. Since a number of correlations with large samples were computed, only correlations of the highest magnitude, usually greater than .70, will be reported for the Content Scales and the original validity and clinical scales, the Wiggins Content Scales, and supplementary scales A, R, and Es. (See Tables 25–28).

Behavioral Correlate Data for External Validation of the Scales

Information on the external validity of the MMPI-2 Content Scales was obtained from personality ratings of subjects in the adult normative sample by their spouses. As part of the MMPI restandardization, a number of subjects at each testing site were asked to bring their spouse to the testing session; over 800 couples participated. After completing the MMPI materials, they were asked to complete the Dyadic Adjustment Scale (Spanier and Filsinger, 1983) and a Couple's Rating Form on their spouse. These personality ratings (see the form reproduced in Appendix G) cover a broad range of both positive and negative behaviors on which the spouse would likely have information. After deleting incomplete records, invalid MMPIs, and nonheterosexual couples, the analyses were performed on 822 couples, 92 percent of whom were married. The median length of time that the spouses had known each other was 13.5 years. Ninety-one percent indicated that they had a very close or extremely close relationship with their partners. The subjects in the couples sample did not differ markedly from the total restan-

TABLE 25. Intercorrelations between the Content Scales and the MMPI Validity and Clinical Scales for Normative Sample Males (N = 1,138)

	L	F	K	Hs	D	Hy	Pd	Mf	Pa	Pt	Sc	Ma	Si
ANX	-.27	.47	-.61	.50	.45	.04	.50	.20	.33	.80	.69	.31	.43
FRS	-.07	.24	-.29	.34	.22	.02	.16	.01	.09	.37	.35	.06	.28
OBS	-.30	.40	-.63	.40	.26	-.16	.29	.12	.18	.77	.64	.31	.44
DEP	-.17	.57	-.56	.48	.52	.02	.58	.16	.38	.80	.75	.27	.48
HEA	-.06	.47	-.29	.89	.45	.39	.35	.10	.25	.50	.55	.18	.29
BIZ	-.14	.51	-.44	.38	.03	-.09	.36	.08	.33	.51	.62	.48	.11
ANG	-.38	.34	-.66	.33	.01	-.21	.36	-.02	.15	.55	.53	.42	.19
CYN	-.17	.39	-.71	.33	.07	-.43	.26	-.17	-.16	.51	.53	.42	.32
ASP	-.34	.42	-.60	.26	.01	-.36	.37	-.15	-.12	.45	.50	.51	.18
TPA	-.37	.29	-.68	.29	.05	-.30	.22	-.05	.04	.53	.48	.38	.25
LSE	-.19	.48	-.52	.42	.42	-.11	.27	.07	.18	.72	.61	.11	.59
SOD	-.07	.31	-.31	.24	.39	-.19	.04	.11	.09	.40	.36	-.20	.85
FAM	-.27	.53	-.55	.32	.21	-.11	.57	.18	.21	.59	.66	.43	.31
WRK	-.26	.53	-.63	.49	.44	-.09	.41	.14	.21	.81	.73	.23	.59
TRT	-.19	.54	-.57	.46	.40	-.12	.40	.02	.19	.72	.68	.20	.56

Note: Correlations < – .09 and > .09 are significant at p < .001.

TABLE 26. Intercorrelations between the Content Scales and the MMPI Validity and Clinical Scales for Normative Sample Females (N = 1,462)

	L	F	K	Hs	D	Hy	Pd	Mf	Pa	Pt	Sc	Ma	Si
ANX	-.24	.47	-.67	.58	.60	.17	.51	.10	.39	.83	.71	.34	.48
FRS	.02	.16	-.41	.34	.20	-.01	.13	.00	.06	.39	.33	.11	.32
OBS	-.26	.39	-.69	.45	.40	-.06	.36	.08	.25	.79	.65	.36	.47
DEP	-.19	.58	-.63	.54	.63	.12	.61	.01	.44	.83	.77	.31	.55
HEA	-.07	.42	-.43	.91	.45	.48	.33	.00	.25	.55	.59	.29	.31
BIZ	-.07	.49	-.46	.36	.11	-.03	.39	-.14	.31	.51	.65	.50	.15
ANG	-.34	.38	-.69	.39	.20	-.06	.44	.00	.25	.62	.60	.44	.27
CYN	-.08	.41	-.70	.41	.17	-.24	.32	-.24	-.06	.51	.54	.46	.35
ASP	-.30	.41	-.57	.30	.09	-.25	.37	-.28	-.09	.44	.51	.51	.23
TPA	-.29	.31	-.65	.32	.15	-.16	.23	-.05	.13	.53	.49	.36	.28
LSE	-.16	.44	-.60	.44	.53	-.04	.31	.01	.23	.74	.61	.14	.65
SOD	-.04	.28	-.38	.24	.43	-.17	.06	.07	.19	.43	.35	-.17	.84
FAM	-.21	.56	-.57	.40	.32	.04	.61	.04	.33	.60	.72	.45	.33
WRK	-.23	.50	-.69	.52	.58	.02	.44	.04	.29	.82	.72	.27	.63
TRT	-.15	.50	-.63	.45	.50	-.05	.42	-.04	.26	.72	.69	.24	.61

Note: Correlations < – .08 and > .08 are significant at p < .001.

dardization sample in terms of major demographic characteristics of age, race, and educational level.

The 110 items on the Rater Information Form were submitted to a factor analysis to summarize and reduce the variables and provide factor scores for the resulting dimensions. The principal components analysis followed by a varimax rotation was performed on the rating data using the SAS factor analysis program (SAS/STAT, 1985). The factor scales were constructed by selecting the items based upon the absolute value of the factor loadings.

TABLE 27. Intercorrelations between the MMPI-2 Content Scales and A, R, ES, Wiggins Content Scales for Normative Sample Males (N = 1,138)

	A	R	ES	HEA	DEP	ORG	FAM	AUT	FEM	REL	HOS	MOR	PHO	PSY	HYP	SOC
ANX	.80	-.16	-.44	.52	.80	.46	.51	.37	.01	-.04	.51	.74	.44	.53	.43	.30
FRS	.39	-.02	-.37	.34	.38	.37	.21	.23	.06	.12	.26	.39	.91	.28	.20	.18
OBS	.80	-.23	-.46	.37	.69	.43	.41	.41	.03	.03	.54	.72	.46	.51	.44	.33
DEP	.82	-.10	-.45	.45	.89	.47	.49	.39	.04	-.03	.48	.79	.39	.54	.34	.36
HEA	.42	.04	-.45	.79	.47	.82	.30	.23	.03	.03	.31	.37	.43	.39	.20	.18
BIZ	.49	-.29	-.40	.34	.46	.41	.37	.44	.09	.14	.47	.42	.29	.84	.48	.06
ANG	.52	-.43	-.25	.30	.51	.32	.43	.48	-.15	-.04	.79	.44	.24	.47	.56	.11
CYN	.55	-.35	-.34	.29	.52	.33	.39	.84	-.06	.10	.62	.52	.35	.58	.49	.18
ASP	.45	-.36	-.20	.27	.43	.27	.39	.88	-.10	-.05	.61	.42	.27	.49	.48	.10
TPA	.53	-.42	-.21	.28	.47	.28	.37	.55	-.09	-.05	.80	.45	.32	.45	.58	.13
LSE	.74	-.06	-.42	.39	.70	.46	.33	.34	.02	.00	.41	.79	.40	.39	.27	.46
SOD	.39	.32	-.21	.21	.36	.23	.18	.10	-.05	-.13	.16	.39	.29	.17	-.07	.92
FAM	.60	-.26	-.29	.33	.59	.33	.82	.45	.05	-.07	.56	.56	.34	.51	.41	.23
WRK	.85	-.12	-.47	.46	.79	.49	.47	.40	.01	.00	.53	.82	.46	.51	.39	.44
TRT	.76	-.10	-.44	.43	.75	.45	.40	.44	-.04	-.01	.50	.75	.45	.47	.33	.45

Note: Correlations < -.09 and > .09 are significant at p < .001.

TABLE 28. Intercorrelations between the MMPI-2 Content Scales and A, R, ES, Wiggins Content Scales for Normative Sample Females (N = 1,462)

	A	R	ES	HEA	DEP	ORG	FAM	AUT	FEM	REL	HOS	MOR	PHO	PSY	HYP	SOC
ANX	.84	-.14	-.58	.56	.83	.55	.53	.38	.01	-.05	.55	.77	.47	.55	.42	.31
FRS	.41	.01	-.49	.30	.39	.35	.19	.33	.19	.21	.33	.39	.92	.36	.26	.20
OBS	.83	-.21	-.59	.43	.75	.48	.44	.44	.07	.02	.58	.79	.49	.56	.45	.32
DEP	.86	-.08	-.57	.50	.91	.52	.53	.41	-.02	-.03	.56	.80	.43	.59	.33	.38
HEA	.51	-.01	-.60	.81	.51	.84	.34	.31	.01	.07	.37	.41	.37	.45	.31	.18
BIZ	.51	-.23	-.47	.35	.48	.44	.33	.46	.02	.13	.51	.42	.35	.82	.47	.09
ANG	.62	-.39	-.38	.37	.61	.38	.50	.46	-.05	-.04	.80	.56	.36	.50	.52	.15
CYN	.57	-.24	-.50	.35	.54	.42	.41	.86	.02	.15	.62	.52	.41	.64	.47	.19
ASP	.46	-.29	-.29	.27	.44	.31	.35	.87	-.06	-.05	.60	.42	.27	.51	.42	.11
TPA	.56	-.36	-.34	.29	.50	.33	.38	.49	-.02	-.04	.78	.50	.37	.49	.53	.16
LSE	.78	.01	-.55	.38	.73	.48	.38	.35	.03	.02	.45	.83	.41	.44	.27	.50
SOD	.42	.29	-.29	.21	.39	.22	.19	.11	-.11	-.04	.20	.43	.33	.22	-.07	.92
FAM	.62	-.24	-.40	.38	.62	.42	.86	.42	-.05	-.04	.59	.54	.34	.57	.39	.22
WRK	.88	-.08	-.58	.48	.82	.52	.47	.43	.00	.00	.58	.85	.46	.55	.38	.46
TRT	.79	-.04	-.58	.40	.76	.50	.42	.48	.02	.00	.54	.78	.48	.54	.32	.45

Note: Correlations < -.08 and > .08 are significant at p < .001.

Items were included on a factor if the absolute value was greater than .30 for both males and females or if the item had the highest value for one gender and all the loadings for the other gender were less than .30.

Six factors were extracted from the rating data:

Factor 1. General Maladjustment

The first factor emerging from the couples' rating data was marked by personality items related to General Maladjustment, such as having a tendency toward shyness, sadness, moodiness, nervousness, and feelings of impending doom. The items loading on this factor reflected psychological symptoms such as health concerns, sexual conflicts, sleep problems, worrying, crying easily, negative self-views, and suspicion.

Factor 2. Hostile-Overbearing

The second factor was a negative dimension marked by aggressive behavior such as the tendency to be argumentative, stubborn, irritable, and angry. In addition, resentful attitudes, stubborn behavior, hostile behavior, and swearing and cursing were found to load on this factor.

Factor 3. Outgoing-Helpful

This positive behavioral dimension was the third factor to emerge. Items loading on this factor include such personality characteristics as behavior that is friendly, cheerful, thoughtful of others, generous, cooperative, affectionate, pleasant, and relaxed. In addition, positive activities such as volunteering for projects, willingness to try new things, constructive behavior, showing feelings easily, and enjoying parties loaded on this factor.

Factor 4. Histrionic-Verbosity/ Hyperactive Behavior

This fourth factor is a mildly negative dimension. Items loading on this factor include oppositional, distractible, and flirtatious traits and behaviors such as excessive talking, bragging, giving advice too freely, driving too fast and recklessly, and starting projects without completing them.

Factor 5. Perfectionistic-Responsibility

A fifth factor extracted from the couple's rating data was a generally positive one. Items loading on this factor reflect personality characteristics such as ambition, dependability, good judgment, and responsibility. In addition, behaviors such as being creative in problem-solving, trying too hard, being sought by others for advice, and preferring to do things right also loaded on this factor.

Factor 6. Antisocial Behavior

The final factor is an interesting one, given that the subject population was solicited randomly from the community and not from mental-health or correctional institutions. This factor reflects negative behaviors such as being arrested or in trouble with the law, threatening to harm people, getting into fights, drinking alcohol to excess, getting angry and breaking things, and taking drugs not prescribed by a doctor.

Adequacy of the Rating Data

The effectiveness of the couples' rating data as external correlates for the Content Scales may be limited for several reasons. First, the individuals rated were "normals," that is, they were obtained through random sampling in several comunities in the United States. These individuals, for the most part, were not psychologically troubled and exhibited no extreme behaviors or psychological problems. Consequently, the range of the ratings is somewhat restricted in terms of psychopathological expression. Similarly, the normative sample's variance on the Content Scales is also somewhat restricted. This is particularly true for some of the more pathologically oriented scales such as Bizarre Mentation. The restricted variances in the two sets of scores had an attenuating effect on the correlations between the Content Scales and the behavioral data. We would expect that correlations of a higher magnitude would be obtained in more pathological samples, and studies are currently under way to test this hypothesis. Despite the attenuation of *magnitude*, the correlational *patterns* provide highly useful information concerning external correlates of the Content Scales.

Second, items in the rating form were believed to be: (1) relevant for "normal" couples; (2) ratable by couples (i.e., it was assumed that most married individuals would know if their spouse was characterized by the behavior); and (3) informative about various aspects of personality and interpersonal behavior.

Very extreme behaviors and symptoms with a low base rate in the normal population were not included. Extremely intimate and potentially offensive items also were not included. Nevertheless, we believe that the data serve as an important source of empirical descriptors for validating the new Content Scales. Comparisons between the correlates obtained for MMPI-2

Content Scales and the MMPI-2 clinical scales indicate that the Content Scales performed at least as well as and in many cases much better than the clinical scales when predicting relevant behaviors from the couples' ratings. (See the external correlate data for the MMPI-2 clinical and validity scales in the MMPI-2 *Manual* (1989).)

Validity of the Content Scales: Clinical Data

Data obtained on psychiatric patients and pain patients, described in Chapter 2, will be used for some scales to evaluate the range and operation of the scales in clinical populations.

ANX (Anxiety)

MMPI-2 Correlates

This scale measures the negative affectivity dimension marked by the first factor of the MMPI-2. For the MMPI-2 normative sample the ANX scale is most highly correlated with the Welsh Anxiety Scale (.80 for males and .84 for females), the Pt scale (.80 for males and .83 for females), the Wiggins DEP (.80 for males and .83 for females) and MOR (.74 for males and .77 for females) scales. The intercorrelations are high enough that these scales could be considered alternate measures of the anxiety dimension contained in MMPI-2.

Behavioral Correlates

These correlates resemble the correlates of other anxiety-focused measures within the MMPI such as the Welsh Anxiety Scale. Therefore, it is not surprising that in the normative couple sample both men and women who scored high on the ANX scale are viewed by their spouses as being characterized by general maladjustment (F1) and are viewed as not being outgoing and helpful as reflected in the negative association with Factor 3 (Outgoing-Helpful); in addition, the women were viewed as hostile and overbearing (F2).

Elevations in males on the ANX Scale, as seen in Table 29, are correlated with having many fears, worrying a great deal, worrying about the future, being nervous and jittery, being tense, lacking self-confidence, and being moody. Although behavioral correlates for females are a bit broader, they tend to center around similar anxieties. In addition, women who score high on the ANX scale are viewed as being hostile, irritable, argumentative, and uncooperative.

TABLE 29. Behavioral Correlates for the ANX Scale Derived from Spouse's Ratings

Item	r
Males	
Has many fears	.27
Seems convinced that something dreadful is about to happen	.27
Worries and frets over little things	.27
Worries about the future	.26
Complains of headaches, stomach trouble, or other ailments	.24
Is moody	.22
Is very upset by small but unexpected events	.21
Feels people do not care about him	.21
Gets very sad or blue and is slow to come out of it	.21
Gets nervous and jittery	.19
Is envious or jealous of others	.19
Is irritable and grouchy over even minor things	.19
Lacks an interest in things	.18
Whines and demands special attention	.18
Puts own self down	.18
Gives up too easily	.18
Lacks energy	.18
Has a very hard time making any decisions	.18
Is cheerful	−.21
Is self–confident	−.23
Is pleasant and relaxed	−.25
Factors	
F1 General Maladjustment	.36
F3 Outgoing–Helpful	−.23
Females	
Gets very sad or blue and is slow to come out of it	.31
Has many fears	.28
Has bad dreams	.28
Worries and frets over little things	.28
Puts own self down	.28
Worries about the future	.28
Gets nervous and jittery	.27
Is moody	.27
Complains of headaches, stomach trouble, or other ailments	.26
Blames self for things that go wrong	.25
Is restless	.24
Lacks control over emotions	.24
Has troubles sleeping at night	.23
Breaks down and cries easily	.23
Seems convinced that something dreadful is about to happen	.23
Worries about health a great deal	.23
Lacks energy	.22
Appears worn out	.21
Acts bored and restless	.21
Thinks others are talking about her	.21
Argues about minor things	.20
Gives up too easily	.20
Is very concerned about death	.20

TABLE 29. Behavioral Correlates for the ANX Scale Derived from Spouse's Ratings (continued)

Item	r
Females (cont.)	
Feels people do not care about her	.19
Is irritable and grouchy over even minor things	.19
Is very upset by small but unexpected things	.19
Gets annoyed easily	.19
Has a very hard time making any decisions	.18
Is envious or jealous of others	.18
Is overly sensitive to any rejection	.18
Nags a lot	.18
Has a good sense of humor	−.18
Gets along well with others	−.18
Is cooperative	−.18
Is cheerful	−.23
Is pleasant and relaxed	−.23
Is self-confident	−.26
Factors	
F1 General Maladjustment	.41
F2 Hostile/Overbearing	.18
F3 Outgoing/Helpful	−.22

FRS (Fears)

MMPI-2 Correlates

Unlike the ANX Scale, which focuses on generalized anxiety, this scale assesses more specific fears. Consequently, it is less highly correlated with general anxiety measures such as the Welsh A scale and the Pt scale and more highly correlated with the Wiggins PHO scale (.91 for males and .92 for females) in the MMPI-2 normative sample.

Behavioral Correlates

The number of behavioral correlates for this scale in the normative couples sample is lower than for the other scales, perhaps because this scale addresses very specific and somewhat extreme behaviors, fears that are not common in normals. No significant behavioral correlates for FRS were found for males, which may be related to cultural expectations that men do not express fear. Females who are high scorers on the FRS Scale tended to be viewed as generally maladjusted (F1) and were rated by their spouses as fearful, nervous, and concerned about death.

TABLE 30. Behavioral Correlates for the FRS Scale Derived from Spouse's Ratings

Item	r
Males	
None	
Females	
Gets nervous and jittery	.24
Is very concerned about death	.22
Has many fears	.20
Is passive and obedient to superiors	.19
Factors	
F1 General Maladjustment	.20

OBS (Obsessiveness)

MMPI-2 Correlates

Obsessiveness has several pathological covariates among other MMPI-2 scales. In the MMPI-2 normative sample, the OBS scale is most significantly correlated with other scales measuring anxiousness and cognitive problems such as the Pt scale (.77 for males and .79 for females), and the Welsh Anxiety Scale (.80 for males and .83 for females). Among the Wiggins Content Scales the OBS scale appears to be most significantly correlated with MOR (.72 for males and .79 for females) and DEP (.69 for males and .75 for females).

Behavioral Correlates

In normal populations OBS appears to be related to general fearfulness and maladjusted behavior, as well as to problems in cognitive processing. For both males and females the spouse-rating correlates showed that worry and fretting over small details were a significant feature of their spouses' behavior.

High OBS males and females were rated by their spouses as high on Factor 1 (General Maladjustment). For males, Factor 3 (Outgoing-Helpful) was negatively associated with high scores on OBS.

The couples' item-correlation data show that high OBS males are viewed as lacking in self-confidence, lacking an interest in things, and having difficulty making decisions. In addition, an examination of the correlates listed in Table 31 reveals that, for males, fearfulness, somatic distress, and tension were important components of their behavior as viewed by their wives. High OBS scale scores are associated with fearfulness, worry, and helplessness in women as viewed by their husbands. Wives are seen as being unrealistic about their ability, self-critical, having low self-confidence, and being self-blaming. They tend to be viewed by their husbands as emotional and having difficulty making decisions.

TABLE 31. Behavioral Correlates for the OBS Scale Derived from Spouse's Ratings

Item	r
Males	
Worries and frets over little things	.22
Has many fears	.19
Complains of headaches, stomach troubles, or other ailments	.19
Has a very hard time making important decisions	.19
Gives up too easily	.19
Lacks an interest in things	.18
Thinks others are talking about him	.18
Is self-confident	−.18
Is pleasant and relaxed	−.19
Factors	
F1 General Maladjustment	.27
F3 Outgoing-Helpful	−.18
Females	
Has many fears	.25
Gets nervous and jittery	.25
Puts own self down	.25
Worries and frets over little things	.23
Has a very hard time making important decisions	.22
Lacks control over emotions	.21
Is unrealistic about own abilities	.21
Gets very sad or blue and is slow to come out of it	.20
Worries about the future	.20
Blames self for things that go wrong	.19
Gives up too easily	.19
Has bad dreams	.19
Acts bored and restless	.18
Is very concerned about death	.18
Acts helpless	.18
Shows sound judgment	−.18
Is creative in solving problems and meeting challenges	−.20
Is self-confident	−.26
Factors	
F1 General Maladjustment	.32
F3 Outgoing–Helpful	−.18

DEP (Depression)

MMPI-2 Correlates

This scale contains content related to tension, low mood, and morale problems, and in the MMPI-2 normative sample it is related significantly to Welsh's A scale (.82 for males and .86 for females). The most significant correlates among the Wiggins scales are DEP (.89 for males and .91 for females) and MOR (.79 for males and .80 for females). Among the MMPI-2 clinical scales the DEP scale is most highly correlated with the Pt scale (.80 for males and .83 for females), the Sc scale (.75 for males and .77 for females), and the D scale (.52 for males .63 for females).

Behavioral Correlates

Gender differences emerged on the spouse's ratings on the DEP scale, with high-scoring females being viewed as having more extensive and more severe problems than the males. In general low mood, negative self-views, and maladaptive functioning characterize both males and females who have elevated scores on DEP. As shown in Table 32, men with high DEP scores are viewed by their spouses as lacking an interest in things, lacking energy, being overly sensitive to rejection, being indecisive, and being ineffective in meeting daily challenges. High DEP males feel that others do not care about them, and they tend to put themselves down as well. They are seen by their spouses as tense, passive, and worried about present health problems and concerned about the future.

Females who score high on the DEP scale appear to be viewed by their husbands as quite maladjusted. Husbands rate these women as generally depressed, moody, nervous, lacking in control, irritable and angry, lacking in self-confidence, emotional, and demanding. They are also viewed as unpleasant, resentful, and not very constructive or helpful.

TABLE 32. Behavioral Correlates for the DEP Scale Derived from Spouse's Ratings

Item	r
Males	
Has many fears	.24
Lacks an interest in things	.24
Gets very sad or blue and is slow to come out of it	.22
Is moody	.22
Gives up too easily	.21
Is unrealistic about own abilities	.21
Worries and frets over little things	.21
Lacks energy	.21
Puts own self down	.20

TABLE 32. Behavioral Correlates for the DEP Scale Derived from Spouse's Ratings (continued)

Item	r
Males (cont.)	
Seems convinced that something dreadful is about to happen	.20
Appears worn out	.20
Has a very hard time making any decisions	.20
Feels people do not care about him	.19
Is overly sensitive to any rejection	.19
Is irritable and grouchy over even minor things	.18
Worries about the future	.18
Complains of headaches, stomach trouble, or other ailments	.18
Shows sound judgment	−.18
Is pleasant and relaxed	−.20
Is creative in solving problems and meeting challenges	−.20
Is cheerful	−.21
Is self-confident	−.24
Factors	
F1 General Maladjustment	.34
F2 Hostile Overbearing	.18
F3 Outgoing-Helpful	−.23
Females	
Gets very sad or blue and is slow to come out of it	.33
Has many fears	.28
Is moody	.26
Breaks down and cries easily	.26
Has bad dreams	.25
Acts bored or restless	.25
Gives up too easily	.25
Gets nervous and jittery	.25
Feels people do not care about her	.24
Worries and frets over little things	.24
Puts own self down	.24
Lacks an interest in things	.23
Complains of headaches, stomach trouble, or other ailments	.23
Seems convinced that something dreadful is about to happen	.23
Is overly sensitive to any rejection	.23
Is very concerned about death	.23
Lacks control over emotions	.22
Acts helpless	.22
Is unrealistic about own abilities	.22
Lacks energy	.21
Thinks others are talking about her	.21
Avoids contact with people for no reason	.21
Whines and demands special attention	.21
Is irritable and grouchy over even minor things	.21
Gets annoyed easily	.21
Has a very hard time making any decisions	.21
Blames self for things that go wrong	.21
Worries about the future	.20
Appears worn out	.20
Worries about health a great deal	.19

Is resentful	.19
Is envious or jealous of others	.19
Is restless	.19
Is suspicious of others	.19
Is very upset by small but unexpected events	.18
Gets very angry and yells	.18
Has trouble sleeping at night	.18
Acts to keep people at a distance	.18
Is creative in solving problems and meeting challenges	−.19
Shows sound judgment	−.19
Is constructive and helpful	−.19
Gets along well with others	−.20
Is cooperative	−.21
Has good sense of humor	−.21
Is pleasant and relaxed	−.22
Is cheerful	−.27
Is self-confident	−.29

Factors	
F1 General Maladjustment	.40
F2 Hostile-Overbearing	.19
F6 Antisocial Behaviors	.19
F4 Histrionic-Verbosity	.19
F5 Perfectionistic-Responsibility	−.20
F3 Outgoing-Helpful	−.28

HEA (Health Concerns)

MMPI-2 Correlates

The most significant correlates for the HEA scale in the MMPI-2 normative sample are those scales focusing on expression of somatic complaints such as the MMPI-2 Hs scale (.89 for males and .91 for females) and the Wiggins HEA (.79 for males and .81 for females) and ORG (.82 for males and .84 for females) scales.

Behavioral Correlates

HEA shows a number of behavioral correlates similar for males and females. High scorers on HEA are viewed as having problems of adjustment. They are seen as worried over their health, as complaining a great deal about their physical symptoms, and as appearing "worn out" and lacking in energy. They are viewed as worried and nervous and are seen as having sleep problems. (See Table 33.)

Validity of HEA: Chronic Pain Patients versus Normative Subjects

Individuals who experience and seek treatment for chronic pain score significantly higher on the HEA scale than individuals in the normative sample.

TABLE 33. Behavioral Correlates for the HEA Scale Derived from Spouse's Ratings

Item	r
Males	
Worries about health a great deal	.31
Complains of headaches, stomach trouble, or other ailments	.30
Lacks energy	.23
Appears worn out	.21
Seems convinced that something dreadful is about to happen	.21
Has bad dreams	.19
Has many fears	.19
Gets nervous and jittery	.19
Has trouble sleeping at night	.18
Factors	
F1 General Maladjustment	.29
Females	
Worries about health a great deal	.31
Complains of headaches, stomach trouble, or other ailments	.31
Has trouble sleeping at night	.24
Has bad dreams	.22
Gets nervous and jittery	.19
Appears worn out	.19
Has many fears	.19
Worries and frets over little things	.19
Is restless	.18
Factors	
F1 General Maladjustment	.24

In an extensive study of chronic pain and the MMPI-2 (Keller & Butcher, 1990), the distribution of chronic pain cases on the HEA scale was compared with individuals in the MMPI-2 normative sample. For both males and females the chronic pain patients are generally distributed in the upper ranges of uniform T scores while the normative subjects are approximately normally distributed around a mean score of 50 (see Figures 2 and 3).

An inspection of these T-score distributions reveals that employing a cutoff score of about $T = 65$ on the HEA scale classifies most of the chronic pain subjects as having health problems and includes a relatively small number of subjects from the normative samples who are likely to have health problems. These data show that chronic pain patients, in general, endorse higher numbers of health concerns (as measured by HEA) than subjects in the MMPI-2 normative sample. Moreover, the data presented here support the view that practical test interpretation of the MMPI-2 Content

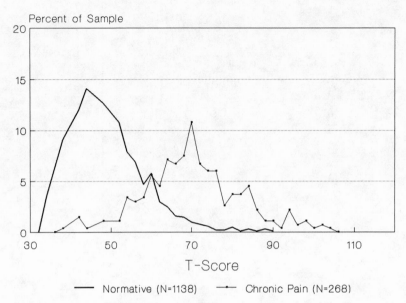

Figure 2: Uniform T-Score Distributions for HEA: Normative Sample vs. Pain Patients (Men).

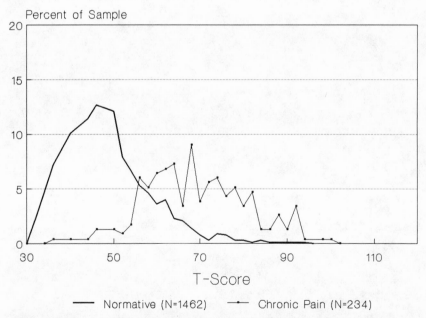

Figure 3: Uniform T-Score Distributions for HEA: Normative Sample vs. Pain Patients (Women)

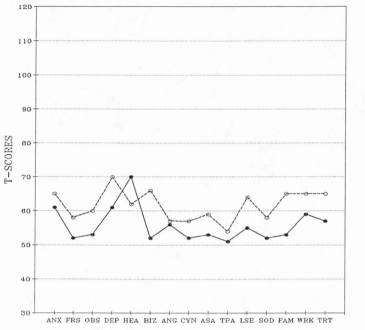

Figure 4: Content Scale Mean Profile, Pain vs. Psych Sample (Men).

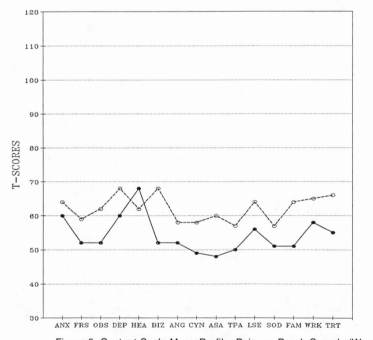

Figure 5: Content Scale Mean Profile, Pain vs. Psych Sample (Women).

Scales should begin at a T = 65 level of scale elevation (see the discussion in Butcher, et al., 1989).

It is also interesting and informative to compare the responses of chronic pain patients with other clinical groups. Clear discriminant validity is present when chronic pain patients are compared with inpatient psychiatric patients (Graham & Butcher, 1988) on the MMPI-2 Content Scales. The differential response of pain patients to HEA item content is marked. The psychiatric patients, on the other hand, endorse content addressing severe mental-health symptoms that produce elevations on the BIZ and DEP scales. (See Figures 4 and 5.)

BIZ (Bizarre Mentation)

MMPI-2 Correlates

In the MMPI-2 normative sample this scale is most significantly associated with scales measuring severe psychological problems and confusion such as the Sc scale (.62 for males and .65 for females), the Pt scale (.51 for males and .51 for females), and the F scale (.51 for males and .49 for females). In addition, the Wiggins PSY scale was highly corelated with BIZ (.84 for males and .82 for females.)

Behavioral Correlates

For reasons described earlier, the couples' rating form contained limited bizarre content. Consequently, there were no reported significant correlates for males and only a few for females, including general maladjustment, fears and nightmares, suspicion and mistrust, and poor judgment.

ANG (Anger)

MMPI-2 Correlates

This scale is most clearly and consistently correlated in the MMPI-2 normative sample with scales defined by the expression of anger or hostility such as the Wiggins HOS scale (.79 for males and .80 for females). Of the MMPI-2 clinical scales ANG is most highly associated with the Pt (.55 for males and .62 for females), Sc (.53 for males and .60 for females), and K (-.72 for males and -.70 for females.)

TABLE 34. Behavioral Correlates for the BIZ Scale Derived from Spouse's Ratings

Item	r
Males	
None	
Females	
Has bad dreams	.20
Is suspicious of others	.19
Has many fears	.18
Shows sound judgment	−.18
Factors	
F1 General Maladjustment	.20

Behavioral Correlates

In general, these correlates for males and females in the couples' rating data contain many similar elements — moodiness, anger expression, and loss of self-control. However, because there were some differences in the expression of anger, each gender will be described separately.

Men scoring high on ANG are viewed by their spouses in highly negative terms, as reflected in the factor scores of the couples' rating data. By far the highest correlation is on F2 (Hostile-Overbearing); the high correlation on F1 (General Maladjustment) suggests that males with high scores are also viewed as having significant interpersonal adjustment problems. ANG for males was positively correlated with F4 (Histrionic-Verbosity/Hyperactivity) as well and negatively correlated with F3 (Outgoing-Helpful). Most of the individual behavioral items attributed to the males who score high on ANG are negative and center around having temper tantrums, getting very angry, getting annoyed easily, swearing and cursing, smashing things in anger, getting upset by small events, and being generally hostile. The descriptions include having angry thoughts as well as engaging in overtly aggressive physical acts. These individuals are viewed as unpleasant, stubborn, and suspicious.

Although most of the behavioral correlates for females and males are identical, a few differences were found. Females who score high on ANG were also rated as being high on the Antisocial Factor (F6). In addition, females were thought to get sad or blue and be slow to come out of it.

TABLE 35. Behavioral Correlates for the ANG Scale Derived from Spouse's Ratings

Item	r
Males	
Has temper tantrums	.36
Gets very angry and yells	.32
Gets annoyed easily	.30
Is irritable and grouchy over even minor things	.28
Swears and curses	.27
Gets angry and actually breaks things	.25
Acts very bossy	.25
Argues about minor things	.24
Talks back to others	.24
Is very upset by small but unexpected events	.23
Acts hostile and unfriendly	.22
Resents being told what to do	.21
Lacks control over emotions	.20
Acts stubborn	.20
Nags a lot	.20
Is moody	.20
Whines and demands special attention	.20
Gets nervous and jittery	.19
Is suspicious of others	.19
Complains of headaches, stomach troubles, or other ailments	.19
Tells people off about their faults and mistakes	.19
Seems convinced that something dreadful is about to happen	.19
Is overly sensitive to any rejection	.18
Upsets routine of others for no good reason	.18
Is resentful	.18
Is cooperative	−.18
Gets along well with others	−.19
Goes to religious services and functions	−.20
Is pleasant and relaxed	−.25
Factors	
F2 Hostile-Overbearing	.37
F6 Antisocial Behavior	.26
F1 General Maladjustment	.24
F4 Histrionic-Verbosity	.19
F3 Outgoing-Helpful	−.19
Females	
Is irritable and grouchy over even minor things	.28
Gets annoyed easily	.27
Is moody	.27
Gets very angry and yells	.26
Is restless	.25
Has many fears	.25
Lacks control over emotions	.25
Has temper tantrums	.24
Argues about minor things	.24
Gets very sad or blue and is slow to come out of it	.23
Nags a lot	.23
Acts stubborn	.22

TABLE 35. Behavioral Correlates for the ANG Scale Derived from Spouse's Ratings (continued)

Item	r
Females (cont.)	
Has bad dreams	.22
Gets angry and actually breaks things	.22
Worries about the future	.21
Acts hostile and unfriendly	.21
Acts bored and restless	.20
Gets nervous and jittery	.20
Whines and demands special attention	.20
Tells people off about their faults and mistakes	.20
Is very upset by small but unexpected events	.19
Breaks down and cries easily	.18
Worries and frets over little things	.18
Is thoughtful of others	−.19
Is cheerful	−.21
Is pleasant and relaxed	−.21
Is cooperative	−.22
Factors	
F2 Hostile-Overbearing	.31
F1 General Maladjustment	.29
F4 Histrionic-Verbosity	.22
F6 Antisocial Behavior	.21
F3 Outgoing-Helpful	−.20

CYN (Cynicism)

MMPI-2 Correlates

In the MMPI-2 normative sample this scale is defined, in part, by its association with scales measuring externalization of negative attitudes such as the Wiggins AUT (.84 for males and .86 for females) and HOS scales (.62 for males and .62 for females) and its negative relation to the K scale (-.71 for males and -.70 for females).

Behavioral Correlates

The items on the Couples' Behavior Rating Form did not allow for as clear a definition of this scale as of other Content Scales; however, some useful correlates did emerge in the analyses. The behavioral correlates appear to be somewhat different for males and females.

Males high on CYN are viewed by their wives as having psychological problems centering around hostility since they were high on Hostile-Overbearing (F2) and General Maladjustment (F1) and negatively associated with Outgoing-Helpful (F3). The males were reported to have more temper tantrums and to be whiny and demanding. They also were described as showing a lack of interest in things.

The females who scored high on CYN were viewed by their husbands as having psychological problems; they were high on General Maladjustment (F1) and Histrionic-Verbosity (F4). In addition, they were seen as not being very friendly and sociable. There was a negative correlation with Outgoing-Helpful (F3). Women were viewed as suspicious and nervous, and were thought to have little interest in things going on around them. They were also rated as not having sound judgment.

TABLE 36. Behavioral Correlates for the CYN Scale Derived from Spouse's Ratings

Item	r
Males	
Has temper tantrums	.19
Lacks an interest in things	.18
Whines and demands special attention	.18
Tells lies for no apparent reason	.18
Nags a lot	.18
Factors	
F2 Hostile-Overbearing	.19
F1 General Maladjustment	.19
F3 Outgoing-Helpful	−.19
Females	
Is suspicious of others	.22
Lacks an interest in things	.20
Gets nervous and jittery	.19
Is very concerned about death	.18
Shows sound judgment	−.19
Factors	
F1 General Maladjustment	.22
F4 Histrionic-Verbosity	.19
F3 Outgoing-Helpful	−.19

ASP (Antisocial Practices)

MMPI-2 Correlates

In the MMPI-2 normative sample this scale is most closely associated with the Wiggins Authority Problems scale AUT (.88 for males and .87 for females.) To a lesser degree, it is also correlated with the Wiggins Hostility scale (HOS) (.61 for males and .60 for females). The highest correlates with the MMPI-2 clinical scales are Ma (.51 for males and .51 for females), Sc

(.50 for males and .51 for females), and K (-.60 for males and -.57 for females). It is interesting that the intercorrelation of ASP and Pd was only .37 for males and .37 for females, probably because Pd is a somewhat heterogeneous scale that reflects more than antisocial attitudes and practices.

Behavioral Correlates

The behavioral ratings of couples were not expected to provide much discriminating information on clinical problem areas since the subjects were "normals" drawn at random from the community and the items on the rating scale were limited in their clinical focus. However, information provided by spouses was quite consistent and relevant for individuals who scored high on ASP. In fact, one of the factors that emerged from the factor analysis of the behavioral ratings was called Antisocial Behaviors (F6). Both males and females from the community sample who scored high on ASP were described by their spouses as displaying antisocial behaviors. There were some differences in the way high scorers were viewed by their spouses. Males were rated high on General Maladjustment (F1). Females were viewed as being more Histrionic-Verbose (F4), less Outgoing-Helpful (F3), and less Perfectionistic-Responsible (F5). The behavioral ratings at the item level were similarly informative. High ASP males were described as: taking drugs, having been arrested, swearing and cursing, demanding, having temper tantrums, and not going to religious services. High ASP females were viewed as less blatantly aggressive but still having problems such as lack of interests, telling lies, threatening people who disagree with them, not being very constructive or helpful, not being very thoughtful, and not showing very sound judgment.

TABLE 37. Behavioral Correlates for the ASP Scale Derived from Spouse's Ratings

Item	r
Males	
Takes drugs other than those prescribed by a doctor	.22
Has been arrested or in trouble with the law	.21
Swears and curses	.20
Whines and demands special attention	.20
Has temper tantrums	.20
Drinks alcohol to excess (gets sick or passes out)	.18
Is pleasant and relaxed	−.18
Goes to religious services and functions	−.23
Factors	
F6 Antisocial Behaviors	.26
F2 Hostile–Overbearing	.22
F3 Outgoing–Helpful	−.18

Females

Lacks an interest in things	.21
Threatens to harm people who disagree with her	.19
Tells lies for no apparent reason	.18
Is constructive and helpful	−.19
Is thoughtful of others	−.20
Goes to religious services and functions	−.20
Shows sound judgment	−.20

Factors	
F4 Histrionic-Verbosity	.22
F6 Antisocial Behaviors	.20
F3 Outgoing-Helpful	−.19
F5 Perfectionistic-Responsibility	-.22

TPA (Type A Behavior)

MMPI Correlates

The TPA scale was most highly correlated with Wiggins HOS (.80 for males and .78 for females), AUT (.55 for males and .49 for females), and HYP (.58 for males and .53 for females). Among the MMPI clinical scales TPA was negatively correlated with K (-.68 for males and -.65 for females) and positively correlated with Pt (.53 for males and .53 for females.)

Behavioral Correlates

The behavioral correlates of males scoring high on the Type A scale are similar to many of those appearing in the literature on the Type A behavior pattern (Rosenman, Brand, Jenkins, Friedman, and Straus, 1975), negative behaviors relating to anger expression and competitiveness as central themes in spouse ratings. The high-scoring Type A individual was also viewed as being less outgoing or helpful.

Specific behaviors described by spouses of high TPA males include having temper tantrums, acting bossy, arguing over minor things, becoming upset by unexpected events, and being irritable, critical, angry, and tense. It should be noted that only the negative aggressive-hostile component of the Type A pattern emerged in the couple rating data for high Type A males and not the schedule-driven component often found in this behavior pattern. No items were included in the rating scale to address that aspect of the Type A personality.

It is interesting that the Type A pattern does not appear as prominently or in the same form for females as it does for males. Gender differences in responding to the items on TPA were evident in the relatively lower alpha coefficients obtained for females (see the alpha coefficients reported in Chapter 4). These data suggest that the TPA scale is not as homogeneous a measure of the construct with women. The relatively few behavioral correlates for women in the couples' rating data suggest that the scale may not be as useful a diagnostic measure for females as for males. Instead, the TPA scale appears to be measuring general maladjustment in females, with these women being viewed as restless, nervous, and jittery. They are also viewed as being suspicious of others.

TABLE 38. Behavioral Correlates for the TPA Scale Derived from Spouse's Ratings

Item	r
Males	
Has temper tantrums	.23
Acts very bossy	.22
Is very upset by small but unexpected events	.22
Argues about minor things	.21
Is irritable and grouchy over even minor things	.21
Acts hostile and unfriendly	.21
Gets annoyed easily	.20
Talks back to others	.20
Is suspicious of others	.19
Is critical of other people	.19
Gets very angry and yells	.18
Gets nervous and jittery	.18
Nags a lot	.18
Is pleasant and relaxed	−.22
Factors	
F2 Hostile-Overbearing	.28
F3 Outgoing-Helpful	−.21
Females	
Is restless	.20
Gets nervous and jittery	.20
Is suspicious of others	.18
Is pleasant and relaxed	−.18
Factors	
F1 General Maladjustment	.19
F3 Outgoing-Helpful	−.18

LSE (Low Self-Esteem)

MMPI-2 Correlates

This scale appears to have markers in the scales that measure negative affect, low morale, and low mood in the MMPI-2 normative sample. The highest correlations among the clinical scales were with Pt (.72 for males and

.74 for females), Sc (.61 for males and .61 for females), and Si (.59 for males and .65 for females). LSE is highly correlated with the Welsh A scale (.74 for males and .78 for females), Wiggins MOR (.79 for males and .83 for females) and DEP (.70 for males and .73 for females).

Behavioral Correlates

LSE has highly similar correlates for males and females. Both are viewed by their spouses as having psychological adjustment problems, but females tended to show somewhat more negative correlates including an indication of social maladjustment. High scorers from both sexes are viewed by their spouses as tending to put themselves down, giving up too easily, being overly sensitive to rejection, and low in self-confidence. Moreover, they tend to worry a great deal, have many fears, and have difficulty making decisions. The high-scoring LSE individual is viewed as having a difficult time meeting challenges, solving problems, and making decisions.

TABLE 39. Behavioral Correlates for the LSE Scale Derived from Spouse's Ratings

Item	r
Males	
Puts own self down	.27
Lacks an interest in things	.22
Is unrealistic about own abilities	.22
Worries and frets over little things	.19
Gives up too easily	.18
Feels people do not care about him	.18
Has many fears	.18
Is overly sensitive to any rejection	.18
Is creative in solving problems and meeting challenges	−.19
Is self-confident	−.25
Factors	
F1 General Maladjustment	.26
Females	
Puts own self down	.27
Gives up too easily	.24
Is unrealistic about own abilities	.24
Blames self for things that go wrong	.23
Has a very hard time making decisions	.21
Lacks an interest in things	.20
Has many fears	.20
Avoids contact with people for no reason	.20
Worries and frets over little things	.19
Gets very sad or blue and slow to come out of it	.19
Gets nervous and jittery	.18

TABLE 39. Behavioral Correlates for the LSE Scale Derived from Spouse's Ratings (continued)

Item	r
Females (cont.)	
Acts helpless	.18
Shows sound judgment	−.18
Is creative in solving problems and meeting challenges	−.20
Is self-confident	−.32
Factors	
F1 General Maladjustment	.29
F3 Outgoing-Helpful	−.20

SOD (Social Discomfort)

MMPI-2 Correlates

In the MMPI-2 normative sample this scale is correlated with Si (.85 for males and .84 for females) and is highly similar to Wiggins SOC (.92 for males and .92 for females).

Behavioral Correlates

SOD appears to have similar behavioral correlates for males and females. Men and women scoring high on SOD were viewed by their spouses as not very outgoing and helpful. In addition, high-scoring women were viewed by their husbands as generally maladjusted. Behavioral ratings of husbands and wives show generally the same pattern. Individuals with high SOD scores are seen as very shy, avoidant, quiet, unfriendly, and as not enjoying parties and having friends over. (See Table 40.)

TABLE 40. Behavioral Correlates for the SOD Scale Derived from Spouse's Ratings

Item	r
Males	
Acts very shy	.30
Avoids contact with people for no reason	.28
Acts to keep people at a distance	.24
Lacks energy	.19
Volunteers for projects	−.18
Talks too much	−.19
Is willing to try new things	−.19
Laughs and jokes with people	−.22

Is friendly	–.22
Enjoys parties, entertainments, or having friends over	–.29

Factors

F3 Outgoing-Helpful	–.25

Females	
Acts very shy	.31
Avoids contact with people for no reason	.31
Acts to keep people at a distance	.30
Puts own self down	.18
Laughs and jokes with people	–.21
Is self-confident	–.24
Enjoys parties, entertainments, or having friends over	–.31

Factors

F1 General Maladjustment	.20
F3 Outgoing-Helpful	–.26

FAM (Family Problems)

MMPI-2 Correlates

Not surpisingly, in the MMPI-2 normative sample FAM appears to be most highly associated with Wiggins FAM (.86 for males and .82 for females). However, correlations with other scales, such as Wiggins HOS (.59 for males and .56 for females) and Welsh A (.62 for males and .60 for females), also help define the network of interrelations for this scale. FAM is most highly correlated with clinical scales Sc (.66 for males and .72 for females) and Pd (.57 for males and .61 for females).

Behavioral Correlates

FAM is the content scale with the broadest range of correlates in the normative couples data. Both males and females with high scores on this scale appear to be viewed by their spouses as having many negative personality characteristics and problems (see Table 41). This finding may result from a "negative halo effect," suggesting that individuals who see themselves as having family problems (i.e., they score high on FAM) are viewed by their spouse as indiscriminately troubled. Significant correlates are found for FAM with most of the factor groupings for males and all of the factors for females. Thus, males scoring high on FAM appear to be viewed by their spouses as generally maladjusted, hostile, overactive, unhelpful, and antisocial. High-scoring FAM females are viewed as being generally maladjusted, hostile, overactive, antisocial, not very helpful, and not reliable or responsible.

Individual ratings for both males and females cover a broad range of negative behaviors from items relating to intrapsychic problems, such as fearfulness and tension, to those showing externalization of anger, such as irritability, moodiness, and aggression.

TABLE 41. Behavioral Correlates for the FAM Scale Derived from Spouse's Ratings

Item	r
Males	
Is moody	.24
Has many fears	.23
Is irritable and grouchy over even minor things	.23
Is very upset by small but unexpected events	.23
Is suspicious of others	.22
Has temper tantrums	.22
Whines and demands special attention	.22
Is resentful	.22
Appears worn out	.21
Argues about minor things	.21
Gets very angry and yells	.21
Acts very bossy	.20
Lacks an interest in things	.19
Gets annoyed easily	.19
Worries and frets about little things	.19
Thinks others are talking about him	.19
Talks back to others	.19
Nags a lot	.19
Acts to keep people at a distance	.19
Seems convinced that something dreadful is about to happen	.19
Feels people do not care about him	.18
Gets very sad or blue and is slow to come out of it	.18
Lacks control over emotions	.18
Is overly sensitive to any rejection	.18
Craves attention	.18
Swears and curses	.18
Is critical of other people	.18
Acts hostile and unfriendly	.18
Is constructive and helpful	−.18
Shows sound judgment	−.19
Is cooperative	−.19
Gets along well with others	−.21
Is pleasant and relaxed	−.22
Is cheerful	−.25
Factors	
F1 General Maladjustment	.29
F2 Hostile-Overbearing	.29
F4 Histrionic-Verbosity	.23
F6 Antisocial Behaviors	.19
F3 Outgoing-Helpful	−.24

Females

Has many fears	.30
Feels people do not care about her	.28
Gets very sad or blue and is slow to come out of it	.28
Gets annoyed easily	.27
Lacks control over emotions	.27
Is moody	.26
Gets very angry and yells	.26
Has bad dreams	.25
Is resentful	.25
Gets nervous and jittery	.24
Acts bored and restless	.24
Is irritable and grouchy over even minor things	.24
Is restless	.24
Argues about minor things	.23
Nags a lot	.23
Worries and frets about little things	.22
Breaks down and cries easily	.22
Gives up too easily	.22
Has temper tantrums	.22
Is suspicious of others	.21
Is very upset by small but unexpected things	.21
Lacks an interest in things	.20
Complains of headaches, stomach trouble, or other ailments	.20
Is overly sensitive to any rejection	.20
Acts hostile and unfriendly	.20
Acts helpless	.20
Seems convinced that something dreadful is about to happen	.20
Appears worn out	.19
Worries about the future	.19
Thinks others are talking about her	.19
Does just the opposite of what is asked	.19
Is envious or jealous of others	.19
Has problems or conflicts over sex	.19
Lacks energy	.18
Gets angry and actually breaks things	.18
Acts stubborn	.18
Has a very hard time making any decisions	.18
Whines and demands special attention	.18
Has good sense of humor	−.18
Is constructive and helpful	−.18
Gets along well with others	−.20
Shows sound judgment	−.20
Is self-confident	−.21
Is friendly	−.21
Is thoughtful of others	−.24
Is cheerful	−.24
Is pleasant and relaxed	−.27
Is cooperative	−.28

Factors

F1 General Maladjustment	.38
F2 Hostile-Overbearing	.29
F4 Histrionic-Verbosity	.24
F6 Antisocial Behaviors	.21
F5 Perfectionistic-Responsibility	−.19
F3 Outgoing-Helpful	−.29

WRK (Work Interference)

MMPI-2 Correlates

A number of scale relationships in the MMPI-2 normative sample help define the characteristics assessed by this scale. The WRK correlates highly with several measures, such as Welsh A (.88 for males and .85 for females), Wiggins DEP (.82 for males and .79 for females), and MOR (.85 for males and .82 for females.) A number of clinical scales show high intercorrelations with WRK: Pt (.81 for males and .82 for females), Sc (.73 for males and .72 for females), and Si (.59 for males and .63 for females).

Behavioral Correlates: A Study of Group Mean Differences

The ability to function in a work environment varies between groups. To illustrate with an extreme case, individuals who are actively pursuing a professional career are likely to possess different and probably more adaptive personal work-related attitudes than people who have dropped out of society or are not functioning productively in life. Moreover, groups with different occupational aspirations and work histories are likely to differ in work attitudes. To the extent that the WRK scale measures negative characteristics centering around work, we would expect such groups to differ on this scale. To test this hypothesis, scores on the WRK Scale obtained from four samples were compared. The groups, composed entirely of males, were: airline pilot applicants (N = 274), active-duty military personnel (N = 1,478), hospitalized alcoholics (N = 832), and psychiatric inpatients (N = 232).

The results of the study are shown in Table 42. Clearly, the significant mean differences were in the expected direction. The active-duty military personnel who volunteered to participate in this study were, as a group, not experiencing occupational problems. Their performance on WRK was at the mean level of the normative sample on this scale. By contrast, hospitalized alcoholics and psychiatric inpatients scored over 1 and 2 standard deviations above the mean, respectively. Individuals in inpatient alcohol treatment typically have considerable employment-related problems and many are unemployed at the time of evaluation. Similarly, the inpatient psychiatric patients had considerable work-adjustment problems and many had never held active jobs. It is interesting that the airline-pilot applicant group scored about two standard deviations below the mean on this scale, reflecting the presentation of highly successful work skills and positive attitudes toward work at the time of testing. These findings provide strong support for the hypothesis tested.

TABLE 42. Mean Scores on WRK for Four Groups of Males

Sample	N	M	S.D.	SE	95% Confidence Interval
Pilots	274	.79	1.43	.09	.62-.96
Military	1,478	7.49	5.77	.15	7.19-7.78
Alcoholics	832	11.39	6.86	.24	10.92-11.85
Psychiatric	232	15.26	7.93	.52	14.24-16.29

Note: The mean score of the male MMPI-2 normative sample on WRK is 7.30 and the S.D. is 4.98.
Analysis of Variance: $F(3,2812) = 320.1, p < .00001$
Multiple Range Test:
    Tukey's honestly significant difference post-hoc comparison: All groups differ significantly at the corrected .05 level.

Behavior Ratings

The most salient behaviors reported by wives of husbands with high scores on WRK appear in Table 43. High scores on WRK were associated with elevations on Factor F1 (General Maladjustment), suggesting that the high WRK husband is viewed as having psychological adjustment problems and as not very friendly or cooperative and distant from others. Specific behaviors characterizing high-scoring males are: appears not to be very ambitious and lacks energy; gives up too easily on tasks; lacks interest in life; has low problem-solving ability; cannot make decisions easily; is unrealistic about himself, lacks confidence, and feels rejected easily. As a result, high WRK males tend to put themselves down a lot, are fearful, tense, unpleasant, and not relaxed. They are also viewed as having too many physical complaints.

The behavioral correlates for women are similar, but there tend to be more significant behaviors reported for high-scoring wives than for husbands. The most salient of these behaviors can be seen in Table 43. High scores on WRK were associated with behaviors loading on Factor F1 (General Maladjustment), suggesting that the high WRK wife is viewed as having psychological adjustment problems. Moreover, high WRK scores were negatively associated with ratings on the F3 or Outgoing-Helpful factor. These women are viewed by their husbands as not very friendly or cooperative, and as distant from others. Wives who are high on WRK also tend to receive significantly lower ratings on Factor 5 (Perfectionistic-Responsibility), suggesting that they are viewed as not very ambitious, undependable, not very responsible, and uncreative at problem-solving.

Specific behaviors characteristic of high-scoring females are: appears not to be very ambitious and lacks energy; gives up too easily on tasks; is depressed and lacks interest in life; has low problem-solving ability; cannot make decisions easily; and lacks sound judgment. They are further described as being unrealistic about themselves, lacking confidence, and feeling rejected easily. As a result they tend to put themselves down a lot. High-scoring females are viewed as fearful, tense, and unpleasant; they are thought to worry about the future and tend to be moody and emotional, and to avoid other people.

TABLE 43. Behavioral Correlates for the WRK Scale Derived from Spouse's Ratings

Item	r
Males	
Gives up too easily	.24
Lacks an interest in things	.21
Has many fears	.20
Worries and frets over little things	.20
Has a very hard time making decisions	.20
Complains of headaches, stomach trouble, or other ailments	.20
Is unrealistic about own abilities	.19
Is overly sensitive to any rejection	.19
Seems convinced that something dreadful is about to happen	.19
Lacks energy	.19
Puts own self down	.18
Appears worn out	.18
Is cheerful	−.19
Is pleasant and relaxed	−.19
Is ambitious	−.19
Is creative in solving problems and meeting challenges	−.24
Is self-confident	−.25
Factors	
F1 General Maladjustment	.29
F3 Outgoing-Helpful	−.21
F5 Perfectionistic-Responsibility	−.20
Females	
Has many fears	.26
Puts own self down	.26
Gets very sad or blue and is slow to come out of it	.25
Gives up too easily	.24
Gets nervous and jittery	.24
Has a very hard time making any decisions	.23
Worries and frets over little things	.22
Avoids contact with people for no reason	.22
Has bad dreams	.22
Lacks energy	.21
Acts bored and restless	.21
Acts helpless	.21
Blames self for things that go wrong	.20
Is unrealistic about own abilities	.20
Lacks an interest in things	.20
Lacks control over emotions	.20
Worries about the future	.19

Appears worn out	.18
Is moody	.18
Thinks others are talking about her	.18
Is very concerned about death	.18
Shows sound judgment	−.18
Is constructive and helpful	−.18
Is creative in solving problems and meeting challenges	−.19
Is pleasant and relaxed	−.20
Is cheerful	−.20
Is self-confident	−.29

Factors

F1 General Maladjustment	.34
F5 Perfectionistic-Responsibility	−.18
F3 Outgoing-Helpful	−.24

TRT (Negative Treatment Indicators)

MMPI-2 Correlates

In the MMPI-2 normative sample TRT is most highly correlated with Welsh A (.79 for males and .76 for females), Wiggins DEP (.76 for males and .75 for females) and MOR (.78 for males and .75 for females.) The clinical scales having the most significant association with TRT were Pt (.72 for males and .72 for females) and Sc (.68 for males and .69 for females).

Behavioral Correlates

The couples' rating data provide information on how high scorers on TRT, most of whom are not in psychological treatment, are viewed by someone who knows them well. Males who score high on TRT are viewed by their spouses as likely to have psychological problems; that is, these scores tend to be associated with high scores on General Maladjustment (F1). In addition, the high-scoring male is viewed as not very outgoing or helpful (F3). Behaviors attributed to males who score high on TRT include: lacking an interest in things, lacking energy, giving up too easily, and being fearful of the future. Moreover, these men are viewed as not self-confident, tense, and not very creative in meeting challenges and solving problems, and not showing sound judgment.

Females who score high on TRT are also viewed by their spouses as likely to have psychological problems, their scores tending to be associated with high scores on General Maladjustment (F1). In addition, the high-scoring female is viewed as not very outgoing or helpful (F3) and low on Perfectionistic-Responsibility (F5). More behaviors are attributed to females who score high on TRT than to males. They include: avoidance, nervousness, lacking an interest in things, lacking energy, giving up too easily, and being fearful of the future and death. Moreover, high-scoring females are viewed as not self-confident, tense, not very creative in meeting challenges and solving problems, and not showing sound judgment.

TABLE 44. Behavioral Correlates for the TRT Scale Derived from Spouse's Ratings

Item	r
Males	
Lacks an interest in things	.26
Gives up too easily	.22
Lacks energy	.21
Seems convinced that something dreadful is about to happen	.20
Is overly sensitive to any rejection	.19
Worries and frets over little things	.18
Acts hostile and unfriendly	.18
Is constructive and helpful	−.18
Is cheerful	−.20
Is creative in solving problems and meeting challenges	−.20
Is pleasant and relaxed	−.20
Is self-confident	−.21
Factors	
F1 General Maladjustment	.26
F3 Outgoing-Helpful	−.25
Females	
Lacks an interest in things	.23
Avoids contact with people for no reason	.22
Gives up too easily	.22
Gets nervous and jittery	.22
Acts bored and restless	.21
Gets very sad or blue and is slow to come out of it	.21
Has many fears	.21
Is unrealistic about own abilities	.20
Has a very hard time making any decisions	.20
Puts own self down	.20
Worries and frets over little things	.19
Is very concerned about death	.19
Acts helpless	.19
Seems convinced that something dreadful is about to happen	.19
Is overly sensitive to any rejection	.18
Acts to keep people at a distance	.18
Is cheerful	−.19
Is creative in solving problems and meeting challenges	−.19
Shows sound judgment	−.20
Is self-confident	−.23

Factors

F1 General Maladjustment	.30
F5 Perfectionistic-Responsibility	−.19
F3 Outgoing-Helpful	−.24

Summary

The correlates identified in this chapter are highly informative concerning the validity of the MMPI-2 Content Scales. They offer an encouraging first look. Further studies will be necessary to obtain a clearer and more detailed picture of their usefulness in clinical assessment.

Chapter 6

**Interpretation of the
MMPI-2 Content
Scales**

The success of any measure of personality is determined, in large part, by how well it describes and depicts behavior in individual cases in assessment settings. In this chapter we will present a number of cases from a variety of settings to illustrate how the MMPI-2 Content Scales differentially reflect problems and issues individuals report through their responses to the MMPI-2 items.

A General Interpretive Strategy for the MMPI-2 Content Scales

Validity Considerations

Individuals being seen in mental-health settings typically are highly motivated to describe their problems and behaviors in the clinical evaluation, and usually produce honest, believable self-reports (Landis & Katz, 1934). However, in some contexts or in some clinical applications, patients may be motivated to provide a distorted view of their current adjustment either by trying to make an overly favorable impression (e.g., as in personnel screening or in domestic court settings) or by presenting the view that they are more psychologically or physically disordered than they actually are (e.g., as in work compensation and disability determination contexts or in determining competency to stand trial.)

Since content measures may be particularly vulnerable to response distortion (Lachar & Alexander, 1978), it is important for the clinician to ensure that the individual has responded consistently and appropriately to the test items. There are several traditional measures in the original MMPI that provide valuable information about the client's test-taking attitudes. The Cannot Say Score, the total number of omitted items, provides the clinician with an appraisal of how cooperative the individual was in disclosing personal information. Large numbers of item omissions (e.g., more than 10) indicate that the individual has not cooperated fully with the evaluation. The L and K scales are two measures for assessing a subject's tendency to claim excessive virtue or to present an overly favorable view of themselves. The F score provides a good indication of random responding or exaggeration of psychological problems. Attention to the individual's performance on these measures will provide information about the believability of his or her responses to the items.

There are several new validity measures on the MMPI-2 that will provide additional information to the clinician in assessing the credibility of a client's self-report. F_B, or Back F Scale, like the original MMPI F scale, provides information about the individual's tendency to exaggerate symptoms or to answer in a random manner. Like many of the items on the Content Scales, most of the items on the F_B scale appear later in the MMPI-2 booklet after the original F items. Thus, it is particularly important to note the client's scores on the F_B Scale before interpreting the Content Scale scores.

Attention to these validity indexes should provide the clinician with sufficient information to determine the credibility of the individual's self-disclosure and determine how much confidence can be placed in interpreting the MMPI-2 Content Scales. If the MMPI-2 validity scales are within acceptable limits, the interpreter can proceed with an evaluation of the MMPI-2 Content Scales. The interpretive approach suggested in this chapter both *supplements* information from the clinical scales and provides novel hypotheses about the patients' behavior and problems.

The MMPI-2 Content Scales as Supplemental Information

The original MMPI clinical scales, derived according to the external or empirical test-construction strategy, are heterogeneous in content and only interpretable through reference to the established personality correlates for the scales. It is, at times, difficult to understand precisely what the empirical scales measure, since we do not know which of the many possible reference criteria or behavioral correlates to apply to the client. For example, we may know from the patient's profile only that the individual's score on the Pd scale is notably elevated. We do not know precisely which of the many possible scale correlates apply to the client. We know that high elevations on the Pd scale are often associated with such aberrant behaviors as impulsivity, irresponsibility, poor judgment, unconventionality, family problems, and so forth across a number of different research populations.

The use of content scales can be of considerable value in sharpening or refining the meaning of clinical-scale elevations. For example, a clinical-scale elevation on the Pd scale (e.g., T > 65) could indicate one of several possible interpretations:

— The individual could be manifesting extreme antisocial behavior.

— The individual could be an immature, irresponsible person who tends to act impulsively and exercise poor judgment at times. The person, a care-free, fun-loving sort, shows no antisocial personality features.

— The individual could be an unconventional nonconforming person who resists traditional mores (e.g., like many of the hippies of the '60s) yet be a highly goal-oriented and socially concerned person. The person does not engage in antisocial or criminal behavior.

— The high scorer on Pd could be an individual who is experiencing some family turmoil or who is angry at his/her spouse or parents. Clinicians have been aware for some time that there is a "situational" aspect to the Pd scale that should be addressed.

Through a consideration of the MMPI-2 Content Scales, the clinician is able to clarify the client's Pd scale elevation. By evaluating the relative elevation on the ASP scale, for example, the clinician can learn if the Pd elevation actually reflects the presence of antisocial attitudes or practices. Similarly, if the FAM scale is the most salient Content Scale elevation, and ASP is relatively low, then the Pd elevation may be largely the result of family conflict. If both ASP and FAM are elevated, then both issues are likely to be salient in this particular case.

The MMPI-2 Content Scales as an Additional Source of Information

The Content Scales do not acquire their interpretive value *only* as supplementary guides for interpreting the clinical scales. Rather, as the validation data in Chapter 5 show, the Content Scales stand alone both in terms of their theoretical meaning and their predictive power. The external validation data presented in Chapter 5 from the couple's study show the content scales to have validity coefficients paralleling those of the more established clinical scales.

Some MMPI-2 Content Scales provide views of the client's symptoms of current personality functioning that are not available in the clinical scales. Two examples of more focused information on clients are the Obsessiveness and Anger scales. Although both sets of behavior were, to some extent, assessed in the original MMPI, they were not incorporated as specific measures of these constructs. For example, obsessive-compulsive behaviors are reflected on scales Pt, D, and A; and anger symptoms were included on F, Pd, Pa, and Sc. However, the items were embedded in the context of many differently focused item contents and thus were not separately evaluated from those other, possibly unrelated, behaviors.

As measures of theoretically defined, homogeneous constructs, the Content Scales provide reliable, valid indexes the clinician can employ in personality description. High scores on the ANG scale reflect a pattern of behavior associated with loss of control; high scores on the OBS scale reflect cognitive-processing problems such as indecision, unproductive rumination, and so forth.

Some of the MMPI-2 Content Scales consist largely of item content that was added during the restandardization to assess important personality constructs that were not part of the original instrument — readiness for psychological treatment (TRT) or Type A Behavior (TPA). An initial demonstration of the validity of these new scales was provided in Chapter 5. In addition to empirical validity, the Content Scales also possess face validity. They can readily be interpreted by applying the defined scale meanings to appropriate scale elevations.

The Content Scale Interpretive Strategy

The scales have been arranged on the profile sheet to facilitate a clear organization of interpretive hypotheses. It is useful to view the content scales as assessing four general clinical areas: (1) symptoms of distress; (2) externalizing-aggressive tendencies; (3) negative self-views; and (4) general problem areas: social, familial, work, and treatment. Each of these symptom groups will be described further.

1. Internal Symptomatic Behaviors.

The first group of symptoms includes the first six scales on the profile: Anxiety, Fears, Obsessiveness, Depression, Health Concerns, and Bizarre Mentation. The scales included in this group reflect internal or cognitive behaviors that are symptomatic of psychological disorder—for example, anxious or depressive thoughts. These behaviors are found to accompany many types of adjustment problems ranging from anxiety-based disorders to affective, schizophrenic, and organic disorders. The symptomatic behavior reflected by high elevations on these scales is taken at face value to indicate that the client is showing relatively more concerns than most others:

Anxiety. A high score reflects excessive worry, tension, vague feelings of insecurity, anxiousness, accelerated heart rate, shortness of breath, sleep difficulties, poor concentration, indecisiveness, and fear of losing one's mind.

Fears. A high score on this scale indicates that the client has endorsed a large number of specific fears such as the sight of blood, high places, money, animals, leaving home, fire, storms, or natural disasters.

Obsessiveness. An elevated score suggests indecisiveness, worry, pathological rumination, and irrational thoughts. Having to make changes distresses high scorers, and they may report some compulsive behaviors like counting or saving unimportant items.

Depression. High scores indicate that the individual experiences low mood, depressive thoughts, worry about the future, feelings of hopelessness, uncertainty about the future. They are likely to brood a great deal and be unhappy about their lives. They cry easily, and feel hopeless and empty. They may report thoughts of suicide or may wish they were dead. They may believe that they are condemned or have committed unpardonable sins. Other people may be viewed as uninterested in them.

Health Concerns. High-scoring individuals report being in poor health. They worry about their physical well being and focus excessively upon minor physical problems. They are having difficulty functioning because of their perceived physical ills or pain.

Bizarre Mentation. The high-scoring individual acknowledges unusual beliefs, including hallucinations or delusions. The client shows distorted, autistic thinking.

2. External Aggressive Tendencies

The next four Content Scales reflect externalizing behavior. They assess aspects of how the individual responds to others — either in terms of attitudinal dispositions, such as cynical beliefs, or through overt behaviors such as having engaged in physical fights or verbal abuse.

Anger. This scale assesses loss of control under frustration or stress. The individual reports being grouchy, irritable, and annoyed over minor things. Physical or verbal abuse and loss of temper are manifestations. This scale suggests a history of loss of control including possibly aggressive and violent behavior.

Cynicism. High scores on this scale suggest that the individual holds negative views about the motives of others and views other people as untrustworthy. The client reports feeling the need to be "on guard" about other people's intentions toward him/her.

Antisocial Practices. High-scoring individuals report having a history of problem behaviors or antisocial acts. They appear to condone negative or antisocial acts.

Type A Behavior. An elevated score on this scale suggests intense, fast-moving, task-oriented activity. Individuals with elevated scores on this scale are described as overbearing, aggressive, overly direct. They appear to be so oriented toward tasks or work that they distress others with their aggressiveness.

3. Negative Self-Views

Psychological maladjustment is often characterized by negative self-views. Feelings of low self-esteem and worthlessness are central processes in many psychological adjustment problems. Our approach to assessing negative self-views involved incorporating items dealing with low self-efficacy and self-criticism in one homogeneous scale that was separate from other forms of psychopathology such as depression or anxiety. The LSE scale appears to perform well, based on the validation data reported in Chapter 5, measuring the tendency for some individuals to "put themselves down" and to consider themselves unworthy of anyone's interest or attention.

Low Self-Esteem. High elevations on this scale reflect negative self-views. These individuals have low opinions of themselves; they believe they are unattractive, awkward and clumsy, useless, and a burden to others. They do not think they are liked by others and they do not feel they are important. They are usually overwhelmed by all the faults they see in themselves.

4. General Problem Areas: Social, Familial, Work, and Treatment

Many of the MMPI clinical scales are trait-based measures that provide information about specific personality traits. Similarly, several of the MMPI-2 Content Scales, especially those dealing with symptomatic behavior, focus on specific trait or situational problems. Scales such as OBS or FRS are quite narrow in terms of the problems addressed. The last four measures on the Content Scale profile sheet are somewhat different from the previously described scales. The Social Discomfort, Family Problems, Work Interference, and Negative Treatment Indicators are general scales that address clinically relevant behavioral patterns.

Two content scales aimed at assessing general problem areas were included in the original MMPI, the Wiggins FAM and SOC scales. These general problem scales, FAM and SOD in the MMPI-2, were constructed using a number of social or family-oriented behaviors and served as indicators of broad problems clients have in those contexts.

Family Problems. Family relationships are addressed by the content of this scale. High scorers report considerable family discord. Their families are described as lacking in love, quarrelsome, and unpleasant. They may even report hating members of their families. Their childhood is likely to be portrayed as abusive, and their marriages seen as unhappy and lacking in affection.

Social Discomfort. This scale provides an indication of the way in which the individual relates to others. High scorers are very uneasy around other people, preferring to be by themselves. They are likely to sit alone when in a social situation. They are shy, somewhat reclusive, and dislike parties and other group events.

Two additional general-problem scales, WRK and TRT, were incorporated in the MMPI-2. Based mostly on new item content, they address issues somewhat different from most trait- or symptom-oriented MMPI scales. These scales incorporate broader problem behaviors that influence the adaptive efforts the individual makes toward work and toward the treatment process itself. They can aid the clinician in assessing the individual's potential to cooperate in rehabilitation and readjustment efforts.

Work Interference. This scale assesses the individual's attitudes toward productive work. A high score on WRK is indicative of behaviors or attitudes likely to result in poor work performance. Some of the problems relate to low self-confidence, concentration difficulties, obsessiveness, tension and pressure, and decision-making problems. Others suggest lack of family support for the career choice, personal questioning of career choice, and negative attitudes toward co-workers.

Negative Treatment Indicators. Attitudes measured by this scale include a reluctance to change and an inability to discuss problems or to self-disclose personal information to others. High scorers on TRT have negative attitudes toward doctors in general and toward mental-health treatment specifically. High scorers do not believe that anyone can understand or help them. They have issues or problems that they are not comfortable discussing with others. They may not want to change anything in their lives, nor do they feel that change is possible. They prefer giving up rather than facing a crisis or difficulty.

Use of the MMPI-2 Content Scales with Clients: Case Illustrations

The cases selected for discussion in this chapter were drawn at random from the clinical settings described in Chapter 2: inpatient psychiatric (Graham & Butcher, 1988); chronic pain program (Keller & Butcher, 1988); airline personnel selection program (Butcher, 1987); and a study of marital couples in therapy (Hjemboe & Butcher, 1989). An outpatient treatment case of one of the authors is also included. They illustrate how the MMPI-2 Content Scales should be included in the interpretation of an individual's profile. The first case to be presented illustrates the usefulness of the MMPI-2 Content Scales in understanding patients who are experiencing severe personality disorganization and confusion. The patient's scores on the MMPI-2 clinical scales are relatively similiar to many individuals in inpatient treatment facilities and reflect a psychotic process. Her Content Scale elevations provide additional information about what characterizes her thinking and some clues about her attitudes toward rehabilitation.

CASE 1

Setting: State Psychiatric Hospital

Patient Characteristics:

Age: 31   Occupation: None   Gender: Female

Marital Status: Single   Ethnicity: Black

Referral Problems

Ms. D. is a single, black female who was committed recently by the court to a state hospital after becoming verbally abusive and threatening to kill staff at the previous community psychiatric facility at which she was residing. Her symptoms included delusional thinking, an irrational, and at times disabling, fear of rats and other animals, paranoid ideation, refusal to eat, and physically aggressive behavior toward others. She frequently exhibited hostile, belligerent behavior, and, at times, displayed inappropriate sexual behavior. She manifested frequent outbursts of verbal and physical violence which left her vulnerable to physical abuse and retaliation by others. Her aggressive outbursts appeared to be cyclic and were not amenable to treatment by psychotropic medication.

History and Family Characteristics

Ms. D was the youngest of three children. Her father's parental rights were terminated when she was an infant. Her history suggested a strong possibility of physical and sexual abuse, both in her original family and in a foster family. She was placed in a number of foster homes beginning at age six. Emotional difficulties were first noted at age ten, and she was first hospitalized in early adolescence.

Ms. D. had one child, although her parental rights to this child ended following several incidents in which she was abusive toward the child. She was not married to the child's father although she did live with him for several years. This relationship was terminated when Ms. D. could no longer tolerate this man's physical abuse of her. She has had no contact with her two sisters or any other family members for many years.

Previous psychological testing indicated that Ms. D's intellectual functioning was at the borderline mentally retarded level. Her highest educational level was the ninth grade in high school. She was never able to hold a steady job and supported herself mainly through prostitution. Her most recent diagnosis was Schizo-affective disorder and alcohol, marijuana, and amphetamine abuse.

Treatment History

Ms. D. was hospitalized numerous times for treatment of her mental illness and chemical dependency. All previous provisional discharges were unsuc-

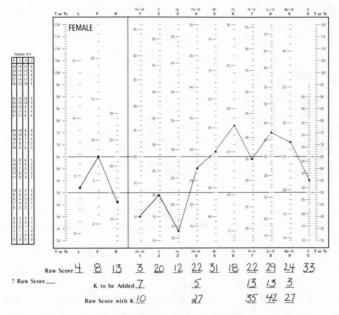

Raw Score 4 8 13 3 20 12 22 31 18 22 29 24 33

? Raw Score___   K to be Added 7   5   13 13 3

Raw Score with K 10   27   35 42 27

Case 1 (Ms. D.) Occupation: None; Age: 31; Marital status: single.

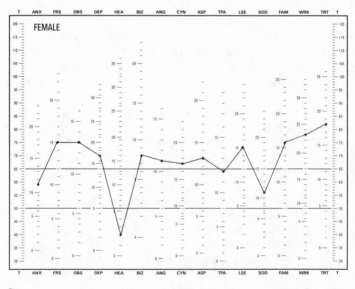

Raw Score 11 15 13 17 2 8 11 17 13 12 15 11 16 23 18

Case 1 (Ms. D.) Occupation: None; Age: 31; Marital status: single.

cessful. She had great difficulty adapting to an independent living situation. Behavioral management of her aggressive acting out continued to be problematic throughout her current hospitalization.

Interpretation of MMPI-2 Validity and Clinical Scales

Ms. D produced a valid MMPI, responding to the items in an open and frank manner, and admitting numerous psychological difficulties. Her F scale, though somewhat elevated, was at a level frequently found at inpatient psychiatric settings. There is some indication that Ms. D likely showed little insight into her own motives and behavior and was probably ineffective in dealing with the problems of everyday life.

Ms. D.'s clinical-scale profile resembles those frequently found among psychiatric inpatients. Her extreme scores, particularly on Sc and Pa suggest that she manifests frankly psychotic behavior, has disturbed thinking, has delusions of persecution and/or grandeur, and is angry and resentful of others. There is also an indication that Ms. D. shows poor judgment, has difficulty at times separating reality from fantasy, is emotionally labile, has difficulty controlling her impulses, and is unable to form meaningful relationships.

Interpretation of MMPI-2 Content Scales

Ms. D.'s scores on the MMPI-2 Content Scales provide additional information about her current functioning. In general, her high scores on BIZ and CYN are consistent with the high elevations on the Pa and Sc scales. However, the MMPI-2 Content Scales also reveal her intense fearfulness and self-doubt. The content of her responses indicates that she experiences a large number of specific and distinct fears; in addition, she endorses content reflective of severe obsessional thinking—she has difficulty making decisions and likely ruminates excessively about her difficulties and problems. Ms D. has a very low opinion of herself, believing that she cannot be liked by others. Ms. D reported that she has experienced considerable family discord and views her present family situation as unpleasant and her family relationships as unrewarding. Ms. D is likely to experience great difficulties in work; she reports having a very poor work history and possesses many characteristics that would make functioning in a work environment very problematic. Ms. D also reports a number of attitudes and beliefs that suggest a very low likelihood that she will benefit from psychotherapeutic intervention.

Case Two, is also from a state mental hospital and illustrates the utility of the MMPI-2 Content Scales at providing information about the specific problems or personality factors underlying the individual's psychopathology, information quite distinct from that provided by the MMPI-2 clinical and supplementary scales.

CASE 2

Setting: State Psychiatric Hospital

Patient Characteristics

Age: 53   Occupation: None   Gender: Male

Marital Status: Divorced   Ethnicity: White

Reason for Referral

Mr. K was recently committed to a state hospital by court order, having been found to be mentally ill and chemically dependent. He currently displays physically aggressive behavior, hypersexuality, sleeplessness, emotional lability, irritability, agitation, and grandiose delusions.

History and Family Characteristics

Mr. K was born and raised in a rural community in the Midwest. He graduated from high school in the middle of his class and was an active participant in high-school athletics. His father was a store manager and his mother a homemaker. Both parents had psychiatric disorders that required hospitalization at one time or another.

Following his graduation from high school, Mr. K attended college for two quarters, but was then forced to discontinue his studies owing to a lack of funds. He subsequently joined the armed forces from which he received an honorable discharge after four years. He married at the age of 23 while still in the service. Upon his discharge he obtained further education while working part-time and later assumed a teaching position. Shortly thereafter he violently assaulted three of his four children, apparently in response to persecutory delusions, causing them serious harm. Mr. K was found not guilty by reason of insanity and committed to a psychiatric hospital for a period of two years.

Since his initial commitment, Mr K has had numerous psychiatric hospitalizations. He is usually successfully stabilized on medications and has also been noted to benefit from group psychotherapy. In addition to his psychotic disorder he has been treated, with some success, for chemical dependency. He has made three known suicide attempts. Mr. K's primary diagnosis is Schizophrenia, Paranoid Type, Chronic, and he has a secondary diagnosis of Alcohol Abuse, in remission.

Interpretation of MMPI-2 Validity and Clinical Scales

Mr. K produced a valid profile reporting a wide range of psychological symptoms and difficulties. His F score, though highly elevated, is not uncommon in psychiatric inpatients with psychotic disorders.

Persons with profiles such as the one produced by Mr. K may harbor intense feelings of inferiority, insecurity, and guilt. Withdrawal from everyday activities and emotional apathy are common, and suicidal ideation may be present. They

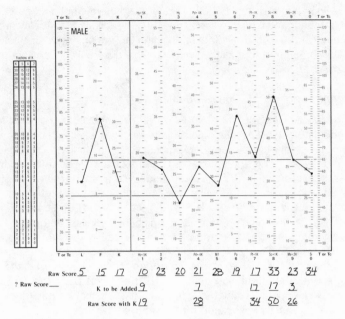

Raw Score 5 15 17 10 23 20 21 28 19 17 33 23 34
? Raw Score ___
K to be Added 9   7   17 17 3
Raw Score with K 19   28   34 50 26

Case 2 (Mr. K) Occupation: Teacher; Education: 16; Age: 53; Marital Status: Divorced.

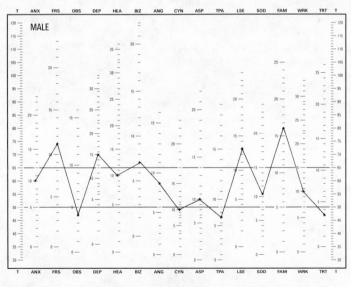

Raw Score 10 11 4 15 10 7 9 10 10 7 13 11 16 10 3

Case 2 (Mr. K) Occupation: Teacher; Education: 16; Age: 53; Marital Status: Divorced.

are suspicious and distrustful of others and avoid deep emotional ties. Delusions of grandeur and hallucinations coupled with feelings of unreality are frequently reported by individuals with Mr. K's profile. Among psychiatric patients this profile is frequently found in individuals with a diagnosis of Schizophrenia, Paranoid Type.

Interpretation of MMPI-2 Content Scales

Mr. K's MMPI-2 Content Scale scores provide considerable additional information about his current psychological functioning and thinking. He reports experiencing a variety of specific fears, including such things as blood, high places, money, animals, and storms and natural disasters, as reflected in his extremely high score on the FRS scale. In addition, he reports many symptoms of a depressed mood such as feeling blue, uncertain about the future, and occasional thoughts about suicide. Mr. K's high score on the LSE scale suggests that he has a very low opinion of himself, which may involve the belief that he is unworthy of others' care and attention and a negative self-image. His most extreme Content Scale score was on FAM, suggesting that he feels greatly alienated from his family. He reported considerable family discord in the past and/or present. It is interesting that his TRT score was quite low for an individual in an inpatient psychiatric facility, suggesting that he has many personality characteristics associated with good treatment response.

Treatment History

Mr. K has been in and out of state psychiatric hospitals for the past 31 years. He is generally well liked by both patients and staff, and is an active participant in group acitivities. The only relative with whom he is maintaining contact is his brother. His condition has stabilized and he is viewed as a "good patient." However, as a result of his history of maladjustment outside the hospital, there is no plan for his discharge any time soon.

The MMPI is widely used in medical settings for assessing the possible role of psychological factors in somatic disease. In recent years, the MMPI has gained broad acceptance as the personality instrument of choice for evaluating individuals experiencing chronic pain or who are participating in a pain treatment program. The MMPI-2 Content Scales provided useful information about a patient in a pain treatment program including her attitudes toward treatment and work rehabilitation.

CASE 3

Setting: Inpatient chronic pain treatment program

Patient Characteristics

Age: 52   Occupation: Clerical worker, on sick leave   Gender: Female

Marital Status: Divorced   Ethnicity: Hispanic

Reason for Referral

The patient experienced chronic back pain (including neck, head, and leg pain) for approximately 2 years. Within the past year she reportedly was injured while working when she bent over, hitting her head on the desk. She reported that her pain has gradually worsened and is now relatively constant. She also reported that she had injured her neck in a previous accident and that the most recent problem exaggerated these symptoms. She was unable to work since her recent injury and received wage loss payments.

Medical History

The patient, a diabetic and grossly obese woman, has had several previous medical-psychological problems including a chronic degenerative disc disease of the cervical spine and a history of chronic muscle spasms. She has also been treated for anxiety and depression in the past.

Symptoms

She reported extensive, vague physical ailments and pain, although her major pain complaints centered around her lower back, head, and neck. The patient also reported symptoms of dysphoric mood and tension, and relied extensively on medication in the past few months to relieve her pain, including, Tylenol, Naprosyn, Anaprox, and Tagamet. She also took Ludiomil for depression.

Interpretation of MMPI-2 Validity and Clinical Scales

Her approach to the MMPI-2 items, although reflecting some tendency to view herself in an overly positive light, resulted in a valid, interpretable profile. The resulting clinical profile is likely to be a good indication of her present personality functioning.

On the MMPI-2 she obtained a classic conversion V pattern with Hy and Hs extremely elevated and considerably above D. This pattern is relatively common among medical patients with psychologically based symptoms, and particularly common among chronic pain patients. Individuals with this profile pattern typically present with extensive, vague medical complaints including headaches, chest pain, back pain, numbness, and tremors. Other physical symptoms include nausea, anorexia, vomiting, and obesity. Physical symp-

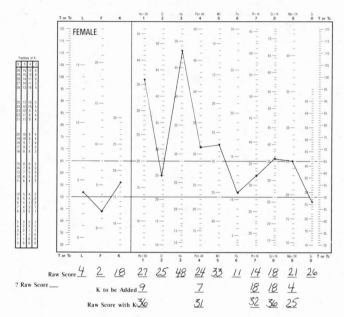

Case 3 (Occupation: Clerical Worker; Education: 13; Age: 52; Marital Status: Divorced.

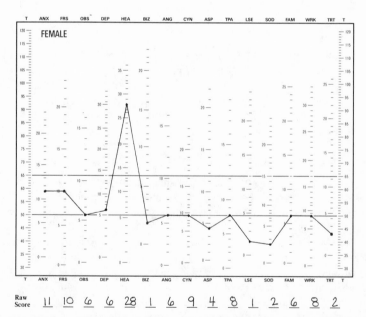

Case 3 (Occupation: Clerical Worker; Education: 13; Age: 52; Marital Status: Divorced.

toms are likely to be more intense or more extensive if the patient is experiencing stress. A patient with the 1-3/3-1 codetype is thought to harbor resentment toward others, particularly toward people who do not provide emotional support concerning their symptoms.

Individuals with this MMPI pattern may, as is the case with this patient, present the view that they are without fault or psychological weakness. Excessive denial is commonly reported for 1-3/3-1 patients. They are usually viewed as having limited psychological insight and being unaware of the psychological component in their medical complaints. They are often viewed as having a generally poor prognosis for psychological therapy since they tend to view their problems as physical and are not open to exploring psychological mechanisms underlying their problems.

Interpretation of MMPI-2 Content Scales

The Content Scales provide a strong indication that she views her problems as strictly related to physical health, reflected in her extremely high HEA score. She reported physical symptoms across several body systems. She is quite worried about her health and is preoccupied with symptoms. She also is reporting some specific fears (the FRS scale score is her second highest peak, at nearly one standard deviation above the mean). She is not presenting a generalized pattern of anxiety, but a specific pattern of fears, probably centering around health matters.

Many chronic pain patients score high on the Work Interference Scale (WRK). Keller & Butcher (1988) found that female chronic pain patients produced a mean T score of 57.8 on WRK, suggesting that these individuals possess attitudes or characteristics that make them vulnerable to work problems; for example, they have difficulty concentrating, low self-confidence, decision-making problems, and negative attitudes toward co-workers. This patient, on the other hand, obtained a WRK score below that usually found in pain patients and at the mean for the normative sample (T = 50). This suggests that she does not report many of the negative attitudes that characterize pain patients and that she is likely to be able to return to work if her physical symptoms abate.

Similarly, her response to items comprising the TRT scale was considerably below the scores obtained by chronic pain patients. In fact, her score on TRT was below the mean for the MMPI-2 normative sample, suggesting that she does not endorse those negative characteristics that work against personal change or those negative attitudes many pain patients have about health professionals. Rather, she endorsed items suggesting that she likes discussing her problems with professionals.

In sum, the MMPI-2 Content Scales suggest that she is likely to consider that her problems center strictly around health issues and she shows some fears about her health. In addition, she appears to be more open to rehabilitation efforts than pain patients frequently are.

Treatment and Discharge Information

Her treatment program centered around reducing her excessive use of medication, initiating a regular exercise program, weight reduction, stress-management procedures, and vocational planning.

The patient was considered to be fairly compliant in most aspects of her treatment plan as rated by the treatment staff in post-treatment evaluation. She actively participated in ward treatment efforts, weight control, regular exercise, and discussing her problems with the staff. However, she was less compliant (and less successful) in reducing her dependence on pain medications. Following treatment she was considered able to resume work.

The next case, Case 4, was selected to provide an example of the use of the MMPI-2 Content Scales in an outpatient mental-health setting. The case, a distressed couple, was being seen at a private-practice psychological clinic. They had participated in a study of personality factors in couples in marital therapy (Hjemboe & Butcher, 1989). The MMPI-2 Content Scales provide clearly different information about the clients than is available in their MMPI-2 clinical profile.

CASE 4

Setting: Outpatient marital therapy — independent private-practice setting.

Patient Characteristics

Husband

Age: 37   Occupation: Sales   Ethnicity: White
Marital Status: Separated (wants reconciliation)

Wife

Age: 33   Occupation: Student   Ethnicity: White
Marital Status: Separated (wants a divorce)

Referral Problems

The clients currently are separated and were being evaluated before beginning marital therapy. Their reasons for seeking help at this time were:

Husband: He views his current problem situation as "needing help for his personal problems. He would like to outline a plan of attack and get reassurance."

Wife: She views the problems as her husband's "inability to cope with life and his responsibilities in relation to the family." She indicated that she would like to get "freedom from guilt."

History and Family Characteristics

Mr. T is a 37-year-old salesman who is presently working on commission for a large wholesaler. He graduated from a two-year college and has worked in sales since his graduation. He has had job-related problems in the past and reportedly recently has been fired from his job. He is currently seeing a psychologist for his depression. He reported that he uses alcohol socially and never to excess, and has never been in alcohol or drug treatment. His mother and a sister had received psychological treatment in the past.

Ms. T is currently attending college. She is also working part-time in retail sales to defray some of the expenses. Ms. T reports that she uses alcohol, at times to excess, and has taken illegal drugs. She has never been in alcohol or drug-abuse treatment, but is currently seeing a psychotherapist for her family problems. Her mother was treated for alcoholism when she was in high school.

The Ts have been married for 11 years; this is the third marriage for Ms. T and the second marriage for Mr. T. They have two children, ages 5 and 7, together. Ms. T has custody of an older child, age 15, by a previous marriage. Mr. T has two children by his first wife (ages 13 and 15) who has custody of them. The Ts' children are currently living with Ms. T and custody, if divorce is obtained, is likely to be disputed.

Current Symptoms

The Ts are experiencing a number of severe marital problems. Both report that they have substantial problems communicating with each other, both concur that their sexual adjustment is poor, and both agree that they have substantial financial problems, including being unable to pay the mortgage on their home.

In addition, Ms. T reports that she has a great deal of trouble managing her time, she is trying to take classes, deal with the children, and work part-time.

Interpretation of the MMPI-2 Validity and Clinical Scales (Husband)

Mr. T responded to the MMPI-2 items in a frank and open manner, producing a valid MMPI-2 profile. He appears to have a strong need to admit to psychological problems and seems to feel that "letting down his defenses" will help him get attention for his problems. There may be some tendency on his part to be overly self-critical.

Mr. T appears to be experiencing a great deal of tension, physical concerns, and depression at this time. He reports feeling unhappy and is quite worried. He also appears to be indifferent to many of the activities he used to like in the past. He is no longer functioning very well on a day-to-day basis. He is overly sensitive to criticism and tends to blame himself a great deal. He seems to feel that he has not been treated well by others. He is, at present, highly sensitive to rejection, and he feels mistrustful and that he is being misunderstood. With his high clinical-scale elevations (Pa, Pt, and Sc are all above a T score of 70), there is some possibility that he is experiencing a psychotic process.

Mr. T appears to be a somewhat conventional individual who is more shy and

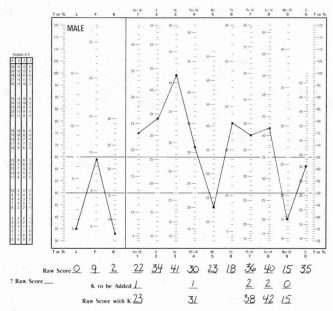

Raw Score O 9 2 22 34 41 30 23 18 36 40 15 35

? Raw Score ___

K to be Added 1

Raw Score with K 23

1

31

2 2 0

38 42 15

Case 4 (Mr. T) Occupation: Sales; Education: 14; Age: 37; Marital Status: Separated.

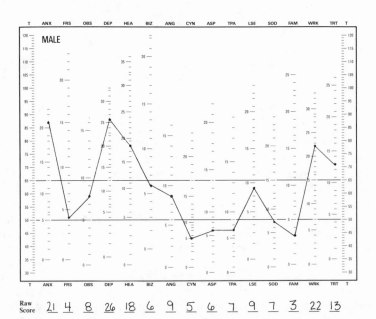

Raw Score 21 4 8 26 18 6 9 5 6 7 9 7 3 22 13

Case 4 (Mr. T) Occupation: Sales; Education: 14; Age: 37; Marital Status: Separated.

socially inhibited than others. He appears to be somewhat reticent in social situations. He is likely to be relatively nonassertive in interpersonal situations.

MMPI-2 Content Scale Interpretation (Husband)

Mr. T's performance on the MMPI-2 Content Scales reinforces the interpretation of the clinical scales. He appears to be quite anxious and depressed, and feels uncertain about the future. He appears to feel emotionally "drained" and disinterested in the things he used to like. He appears to brood and feels unhappy and hopeless. He feels tense, alone, and that other people are not a source of support to him. He seems to feel a lot of need for reassurance. His relatively low scores on the BIZ and CYN scales contraindicate psychosis that is suggested by the high scores on Pa, Pt, and Sc.

His high elevation on the MMPI-2 WRK scale suggests that he may have attributes or habits that make him vulnerable to work problems. He possesses some attitudes suggestive of poor work performance, as confirmed by his self-reported work problems. He has low self-confidence and feels tension and pressure when it comes to making decisions. He apparently feels a lack of family support about his career choice and believes that they have questioned his choice.

Although he reports a number of psychological problems, he shows low treatment potential as reflected in his high scores on the TRT scale, suggesting that he may not benefit much from a treatment program at this time.

Interpretation of the MMPI-2 Validity and Clinical Scales (Wife)

Ms. T's approach to the MMPI-2 was valid. She cooperated with the evaluation enough to provide useful information. Her clinical profile is likely to be a good indication of her present personality functioning.

Ms. T's MMPI-2 profile reflects severe personality problems. She appears to be a socially nonconforming, somewhat unconventional, and rather impulsive individual who tends to act out. She appears to be emotionally troubled and tends to behave unpredictably at times. She may have a history of unreliable behavior and may have been involved in irresponsible acts in the past. Individuals with this profile tend to be thrill seekers and may engage in hedonistic, self-serving behavior at the expense of others. She tends to enjoy parties and fun activities rather than work. A history of underachievement is characteristic of individuals with this profile. She is likely to have authority conflicts and family problems.

She may have an alcohol or drug-abuse problem at this time. Her MAC-R score (T = 63) is consistent with addictive personality features. She is probably viewed by others as pleasure oriented, manipulative, aggressive, and socially controlling.

MMPI-2 Content Scale Interpretation (Wife)

Her performance on MMPI-2 Content Scales provides a somewhat different picture of her thinking than do her clinical scale scores. Her high score on OBS suggests that she has great difficulty making decisions and that she is likely

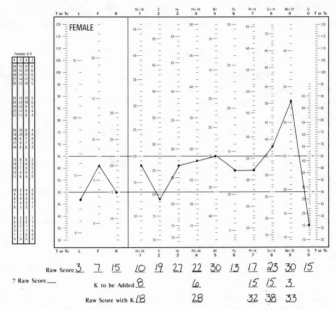

Raw Score 3 7 15 10 19 27 22 30 13 17 23 30 15
? Raw Score ___
K to be Added 8   6   15 15 3
Raw Score with K 18   28   32 38 33

Case 4 (Ms. T) Occupation: Student; Education: 13; Age: 33; Marital Status: Separated.

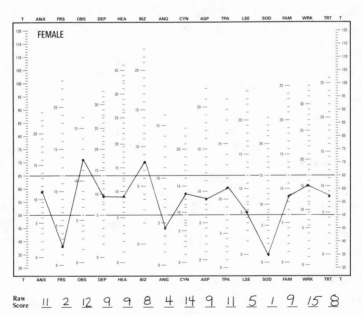

Raw Score 11 2 12 9 9 8 4 14 9 11 5 1 9 15 8

Case 4 (Ms. T) Occupation: Student; Education: 13; Age: 33; Marital Status: Separated.

to ruminate excessively about issues and problems, causing others to become impatient with her. She appears not to be very amenable to change; she may report some compulsive behaviors like counting or saving unimportant things. She is likely to be excessive in her worries and may become overwhelmed by her own thoughts. Moreover, her high score on the BIZ scale suggests unusual thinking. Individuals with this pattern may feel that they have a special mission or special powers and may have a delusional quality to their thinking. Her relatively high score on WRK suggests that she may have some attitudes and behaviors that make her vulnerable to developing problems in work adjustment.

Therapist Impressions and Outcome

The therapist viewed the T's marital problems as extreme and thought that they were not very motivated to resolve them. Verbal abuse was prominent in the sessions. The therapist judged their potential for success in therapy to be quite low. After the initial interview, the therapist viewed their problems as numerous, including communication problems that were central to their inability to deal effectively with the problems they were experiencing, lack of affection toward each other, lack of loving feelings, and a disinterest in sex. He felt that their problems were aggravated by intense power struggles, with intense anger being expressed in the sessions, each appearing to work against the other's finding solutions to problems. Extra-marital affairs were thought possible, especially with Ms. T. Ms. T appeared to have problems with alcohol. Both individuals had problems related to their previous marriages that placed pressure on their present situation.

The therapist thought that both the husband and wife had significant and essentially unresolvable differences between them. Despite this, both Mr. and Ms. T produced normal limits scores on FAM, although probably for different reasons. Mr. T, desiring reconciliation, likely denied significant family problems on the MMPI-2. However, this was not a plausible explanation for Ms. T's low FAM score since she verbalized wanting a divorce. Perhaps, Ms. T no longer considered Mr. T to be a member of her family when she answered the MMPI-2 FAM items. These hypotheses could be explored in MMPI-2 feedback sessions with Mr. and Ms. T.

After five joint sessions and one individual session for each, the marital therapy was terminated. The Ts decided to pursue divorce.

Case 5

Setting: Outpatient mental-health center

Patient Characteristics

Age: 27   Occupation: Unemployed

Gender: Male   Marital Status: Single   Ethnicity: White

Referral Problems

The client was self-referred for psychological treatment because of his intense anxiety.

Mr. D is a 27-year-old white, single male who was self-referred to an outpatient mental health clinic. Mr. D stated that he was seeking therapy for anxiety and depression, and described a nine-year history of panic attacks, dysthymic symptomatology, and numerous somatic complaints. According to Mr. D the onset of these symptoms coincided with an injury he sustained at work which left him home-bound for several months. Though he eventually recovered from the injury, he has been unable to work for the past nine years because of anxiety and panic attacks which he experiences whenever he leaves home. During this time period Mr. D has been treated with numerous medications by several psychiatrists. The medications have not alleviated any of his depressive symptoms, but they have provided some relief from his extreme anxiety, enabling Mr. D to venture outside his home for short time periods and distances.

Following a diagnostic interview at the mental health clinic Mr. D was diagnosed as suffering from a Panic Disorder with Agoraphobia and a Dysthymic Disorder. He was referred for individual psychotheraphy at the onset of which he completed an MMPI-2.

Interpretation of MMPI-2 Validity and Clinical Scales

Mr. D produced a valid MMPI-2 clinical profile, responding to the items in an open and frank manner. His clinical profile indicates that Mr. D was experiencing considerable psychological distress at the time he completed the MMPI-2. Individuals who produce this type of profile are typically quite dysphoric and pessimistic about the future, tend to have multiple somatic complaints, and numerous symptoms of anxiety. There were also indications of possible psychotic symptoms centering on persecutory delusional themes, possible antisocial tendencies, and possible familial discord.

Mr. D's extremely elevated MMPI-2 clinical profile does not convey a very clear picture of discreet problem areas, but, rather, an overall heightened state of psychological distress which appears to be manifested across a broad domain of psychological dysfunction. Examination of the Content Scale profile yields a clearer and more distinct picture of Mr. D's current psychological functioning. His scores on the Content Scales suggest that at the time he completed the MMPI-2 Mr. D was experiencing general symptoms of anxiety including tension, somatic problems, sleep difficulties, worries, poor concentration, a considerable number of specific fears, significant depressive symptoms including feeling blue and uncertain about his future, many physical symptoms across several body systems, difficulties in the area of work, and negative attitudes toward the prospect of successful treatment.

In addition to highlighting Mr. D's current condition, the MMPI-2 Content Scales served to rule out possible interpretations suggested by elevations on certain clinical scales. Thus, the possibility of some psychotic symptomatology, as suggested by elevations on clinical scales 6 and 8, is ruled out by a T score of 46 on the BIZ Content Scale. Similarly, the possibilities of antisocial

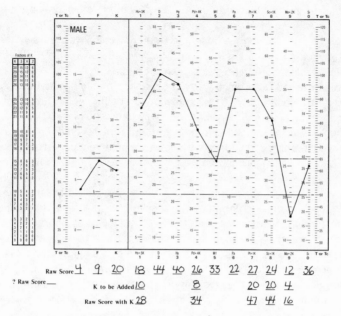

Raw Score 4 9 20 18 44 40 26 33 22 27 24 12 36

? Raw Score ___

K to be Added 10   8   20 20 4

Raw Score with K 28   34   47 44 16

Case 5 (Mr. D) Occupation: Unemployed; Age: 27; Marital Status: Single.

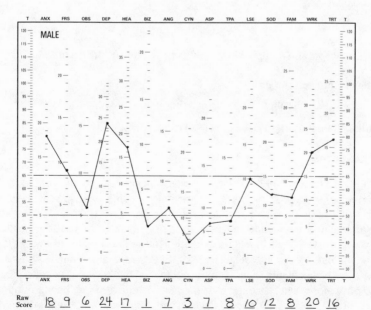

Raw Score 18 9 6 24 17 1 7 3 7 8 10 12 8 20 16

Case 5 (Mr. D) Occupation: Unemployed; Age: 27; Marital Status: Single.

tendencies and familial discord are ruled out by moderate scores on the Content Scales ASP and FAM.

Overall, the picture suggested by the Content Scales was more in keeping with his clinical presentation than that which would have been suggested by the clinical scales alone. The one somewhat surprising elevation on the Content Scales was on TRT, which was not expected in an individual who is self-referred for psychotherapy. This somewhat surprising finding was discussed with Mr. D in the course of providing feedback to him on his MMPI-2 scores in a psychotherapy session. It led to a very fruitful exploration of Mr. D's doubts and fears concerning psychotherapy following a nine-year period during which he had become disengaged from life.

Increasingly, the MMPI is being used in assessing individuals in nonclinical contexts, such as college or personnel-selection settings. The last case study was selected to illustrate how the MMPI-2 Content Scales operate in the assessment of "normal-range" individuals. This particular case was obtained from the airline-pilot applicant data set reported by Butcher (1987). It is of interest, since the applicant's clinical profile is within normal limits and the MMPI-2 Content Scales provide the most important and interpretively useful information about him.

CASE 6
Case Study: Airline Pilot Applicant

Setting Medical: Occupational health assessment program.

Patient Characteristics

Age: 29   Occupation: Former Air Force pilot   Gender: Male

Marital Status: Married   Ethnicity: White

Reason for Referral

Mr. C is a former Air Force pilot who was applying for a position as flight-crew member for a major air carrier. He participated in the psychological evaluation as part of pre-employment medical screening required of all pilot applicants for the airline. Applicants received a standard psychological test battery including: a full Wechsler Adult Intelligence Scale-Revised, Wechsler Memory Scale, Bender-Gestalt Visual Motor Test, MMPI-2, Work and Family Adjustment Scale, and clinical interview. The psychological evaluation was conducted in one day, along with an extensive medical examination. A background and reference check was conducted to verify training, work, and flying experience. Applicants were also required to pass a check ride in a 747 or DC-10 flight simulator as part of the overall evaluation.

History and Family Characteristics

Mr. C was born and grew up in a rural community in the Midwest. He had one brother and two sisters. His parents divorced when he was 13 and he lived with his father, a retail businessman, during his high-school years. His three younger siblings lived with his mother. He reported that his family relationships were "weak"—he had limited contact with his mother and siblings who moved to another state soon after the divorce. His relationship with his father was considered somewhat distant, and he rarely saw him in the past ten years. He had a few close friends in high school, but acknowledged spending much of his time with his hobbies such as building model airplanes. He did, however, enjoy participating in sports and reportedly "enjoyed competition."

Mr. C performed well in college, although he found his studies difficult. He graduated from a four-year state university with a degree in aeronautical science with a C + average. He participated in Air Force ROTC for the last two years of his undergraduate program and, upon completion of his undergraduate degree at age 22, entered the Air Force-pilot training program. After he graduated, Mr. C was assigned to fighter command after qualifying in the F-16. He flew fighters for the remaining 6 years of his enlistment. He was married to a Filipino national during one of his overseas assignments. They had one child, a boy.

Behavioral Observations

Mr. C, initially somewhat more reserved than other pilot applicants, entered the testing situation with some nervousness. He seemed tense at first and asked a number of questions about the acceptability of his performance. He was apparently highly motivated to perform well on the intellectual testing and was very persistent, continuing to work on the timed tasks even after he was told the time was up. He became visibly upset at times when the subtests became very difficult for him and made disparaging remarks about the quality of his performance.

Test Results

Mr. C performed in the average range on the Wechsler Memory Scale and obtained a Verbal IQ Score of 105; a performance IQ Score of 107; and a Full Scale IQ score of 106 on the Wechsler Adult Intelligence Scale-Revised. His reproductions of the Bender Gestalt drawings were acceptable; and he was able to recall and reproduce 6 drawings one hour later. In general, his cognitive abilities were within the acceptable range for airline-pilot applicants, although he might have to work harder than other pilots to learn complex aviation-related tasks and aircraft systems and to perform psychomotor activities in the cockpit.

Interpretation of MMPI-2 Validity and Clinical Scales

Mr. C's approach to the MMPI-2 was generally cooperative, as indicated by his performance on the MMPI-2 validity scales. His MMPI-2 profile was valid and interpretable; it was clearly within the normal range. Most of his scores were near the 50 T-score range or below. His responses to items making up

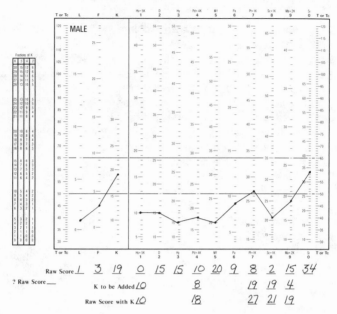

Raw Score _1_ _3_ _19_ _0_ _15_ _15_ _10_ _20_ _9_ _8_ _2_ _15_ _34_

? Raw Score ___

K to be Added _10_   8   _19_ _19_ _4_

Raw Score with K _10_   _18_   _27_ _21_ _19_

Case 6 (Mr. C) Occupation: Pilot; Education: 16; Age: 29; Marital Status: Married.

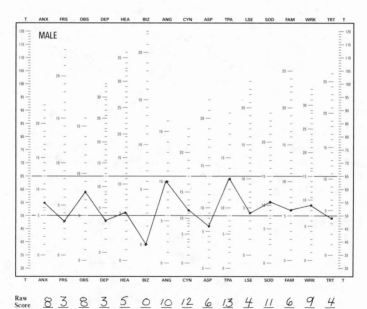

Raw Score _8_ _3_ _8_ _3_ _5_ _0_ _10_ _12_ _6_ _13_ _4_ _11_ _6_ _9_ _4_

Case 6 (Mr. C) Occupation: Pilot; Education: 16; Age: 29; Marital Status: Married.

the Mf scale were well below the MMPI-2 normative range, reflecting interests of a traditionally masculine nature. This pattern is consistent with that of individuals preferring mechanical tasks and activities over intellectual or cultural pursuits. He appeared to be somewhat more introverted on the Si scale than most pilot applicants (Si scores for pilot applicants are usually around 40 to 45 T), reflecting his generally shy, though clearly within normal limits, approach to social relationships. No serious emotional or personality problems were reflected by the clinical scales.

MMPI-2 Content Scale Interpretation

Mr. C.'s performance on the MMPI-2 Content Scale profile shows that his performance on TPA (T = 64) is clearly in the interpretable range, suggesting that he is endorsing content indicating that he is a hard-driving, work-oriented individual who tends to become impatient and irritable. He is likely to be competitive and easily annoyed. He also endorses content themes centering around anger, as reflected in his high score on ANG. He may have some problems with anger control at times.

Conclusions

Mr. C's behavior in the test situation and his performance on the MMPI-2 Content Scales suggest that he may have some problems with anger control and with controlling his impatience and irritability. The possibility exists that his competitive interpersonal style could interfere with cooperative functioning in airline crews, particularly under conditions of high stress and could reduce the level of crew coordination in the cockpit. Since he has not flown in aircraft involving a crew concept (most of his flying experience has been with single-pilot fighter aircraft), there is likely to be insufficient information about how he would function in a highly cooperative airline flight environment. Further information concerning his ability to function in a cooperative crew environment should be obtained before employment is offered.

Chapter 7

**Implications for
Clinical Assessment
and Research**

Content interpretation of objective personality instruments has gained wide acceptance in the field of personality assessment in recent years. As noted in Chapter 1, scales developed by content-oriented scale construction methods have been found to be valid (Burisch, 1984; Hase & Goldberg, 1967) and may be more easily interpreted than those developed by other methods. Content interpretation approaches to the MMPI have become an important aspect of clinical interpretation in applied settings. Changes in the MMPI item pool, especially the incorporation of new content dimensions, has required a revision of content-based MMPI interpretation. Most of the Wiggins Content Scales, one of the most widely used content interpretation approaches, are not fully scorable on the MMPI-2. Some scales were nearly entirely lost as a result of the deletion of archaic or objectionable content from the inventory.

A broad range of new items was incorporated into the MMPI-2 booklet, covering topics of particular relevance to present-day clinical practice — treatment amenability, suicidal ideation, alcohol and drug abuse, Type A behavior, to mention a few. These items expanded some content dimensions and introduced others, providing the basis for content scales unique to MMPI-2. We believe that the resulting scales broaden the MMPI content approach and provide a solid quantitative framework for understanding individuals' self-reported behavior and character. MMPI-2 data from the MMPI Restandardization Project and several other normal samples (college students and military personnel) and from clinical patients, provided a firm empirical base for the development, refinement, and critical evaluation of the MMPI-2 Content Scales. These MMPI-2 scales can provide the practitioner with a broader, more comprehensive assessment than was available in the original MMPI.

Value of Using the Content Scales

The values to the test user of employing the MMPI-2 Content Scales are several: The content dimensions underlying the MMPI-2 Content Scales contain the major themes in the MMPI-2 item pool. These include psychopathological dimensions such as anxiety, low mood, unusual mentation, and negative self-views; personality traits such as cynicism and antisocial attitudes; and important clinical problems or activities such as family problems, Type A behavior, negative work attitudes, and negative treatment attitudes.

The MMPI-2 Content Scales represent highly homogeneous dimensions that appear to assess important personality characteristics. The internal consistencies of the scales are high in comparison with other content-based scales, such as the Wiggins Scales, and provide test users with confidence about the interpretability of the underlying dimension. Most of the useful content dimensions contained in the Wiggins Content Scales are represented in the MMPI-2 Content Scales. Two notable exceptions, REL and FEM, were the least clinically useful of the scales.

Several new content dimensions available in the MMPI-2 Content Scales address problems or issues not previously available in MMPI clinical or content scales — Anger, Type A Behavior, Work Interference, and Negative Treatment Indicators. These measures should provide the clinician with additional useful clinical assessment information.

The Content Scales appear to have strong external correlates. Initial external validity studies support their use in clinical assessment. In fact, validity coefficients, using the couples' rating data as personality criteria, were at least as high as those obtained for the clinical scales of the MMPI-2 (Butcher et al., 1989).

Because the MMPI-2 Content Scales were rationally defined, interpretations of the factors assessed by the scales require little inference. Clinicians can feel confident that scale elevations on the MMPI-2 Content Scales reflect clear endorsement of the attitudes, beliefs, and symptoms that define the constructs.

The T-score transformations for the MMPI-2 Content Scales were developed following the same normative approach, uniform T scores, as the clinical scales. Consequently, scale elevation for the content scales is directly comparable to the scale-elevation ranges on the clinical scales.

The new MMPI-2 Content Scales provide the clinician with an excellent medium for providing test feedback to clients. As noted in Chapter 1, the scores from the Content Scales can be readily communicated to others. Because of the face validity of the scales, a high score on a particular scale, for example LSE, can be directly interpreted for the client in understandable terms, such as:

> Your high score on the LSE scale suggests that you have a low opinion of yourself. You are telling us that you think you are not liked by others and you do not think you are very important. Many of the items you answered indicated that you hold many negative attitudes about yourself — you seem to think that you are unattractive, awkward and clumsy, useless, and a burden to others. You certainly seem to lack self-confidence, even to the point that you find it hard to accept compliments from others. Individuals like yourself often feel overwhelmed by all the faults they see in themselves.

Of course, providing test feedback to clients needs to be based on a strong treatment or assessment relationship in order to be effective. Providing test feedback to patients should be done with considerable sensitivity and tact if it is to be readily accepted. A discussion of factors relevant to providing feedback on the MMPI-2 to therapy clients can be found in Butcher, in press.

The MMPI-2 Content Scales will be a valuable addition to MMPI test interpretation for nonclinical (normal range) subjects. In many instances, the Content Scales may be elevated if particular themes are addressed by the client, whereas the clinical scales may not be elevated in the interpretable range. (See Case 6 in Chapter 6.) High scores on a particular Content Scale reflect clear endorsement of the attitudes or problems comprising the scale. An elevated score on a scale indicates the degree to which the individual, in comparison with most people, possesses those qualities.

Possible Limitations of the MMPI-2 Content Scales

Vulnerability to Distortion as a Result of Response Sets

Content scales, probably more than empirical scales, require a cooperative test-taking attitude on the part of the subject. There is some evidence that content scales are susceptible to conscious distortion (Lachar & Alexander, 1978); however, there is also strong evidence to suggest that for most appraisals, when cooperation can be assured (Koss and Butcher, 1973; Landis & Katz, 1934), individuals present accurate self-appraisals in clinical settings. This is more likely to be the case in situations in which the client is being evaluated at his or her own request rather than when he or she is being assessed at another's behest, such as in a court-ordered evaluation or child-custody case or in personnel-screening settings.

The question of conscious distortion of the test by a subject is, of course, a concern in any self-report inventory evaluation, not just for content scales. Any careful test interpreter should attend to indicators of test validity if they are available. The original MMPI developers were sensitive to the possibility of response distortion and included specially designed validity scales to detect the presence of conscious distortion, faking, and defensiveness.

The MMPI Restandardization Committee followed a similar strategy. The traditional validity scales L, F, and K were preserved in MMPI-2, and three other validity scales (F_B, TRIN, VRIN) were developed to assess response approaches not directly measured by these traditional scales. When using the MMPI-2 Content Scales it is important to be concerned about response sets that operate toward the back of the test booklet. The Content Scales contain items that are spread throughout the booklet, whereas the clinical scales can be scored from the first 370 items. Interpretation of the MMPI-2 Content Scales, unlike interpretation of the clinical scales, requires that the subject respond to the full item pool. Ascertaining that the subject has not dissimulated responses toward the end of the booklet can be determined by evaluating the F_B score.

Meaning of Low Scores

Do low scores on the Content Scales reflect the lack of those characteristics measured by the scale? For example, does a low score on LSE indicate that the individual, in fact, has high self-esteem? The idea that low elevations on content homogeneous scales reflect the absence of the trait measured by the scale or a tendency to behave differently (i.e., opposite) to those scoring high on the scale is consistent with accepted interpretation practices for scales derived by rational strategies. However, the meaning of low scores on the Content Scales require more extensive validation before such interpretations can be confidently made. It may be correct, for example, to interpret a low score on the DEP scale as the absence of depression or a low score on FAM as reflecting an absence of family problems. However, less is known about the operation of the Content Scales in the low score ranges.

Internal Contradictions in Interpretation

Clinical interpretation of the MMPI, when both the clinical scales and content measures are used together, is sometimes complicated by the fact that different scale elevations, and consequently conflicting or contradictory interpretations, can result. For example, a patient could obtain a high score on the clinical scale Depression (Scale 2) and a low or modest score on the Wiggins DEP scale. Interpretation of these scales could result in contradictory statements in the report. This situation is possible because although the scales have the *same name* they actually measure different constructs or different facets of the same constructs. Scale 2 of the MMPI measures depression, but contains quite heterogeneous content dealing with subjective depression, psychomotor retardation, physical malfunctioning, mental dullness, and brooding. The Wiggins DEP scale, on the other hand, was defined by a more narrow item domain dealing with subjective depression.

The same situation could occur when interpreting the MMPI-2 clinical and Content Scales. The intercorrelation between the Pd and ASP scales is only .37 (see Chapter 5) in the MMPI-2 normative sample. Consequently, they appear to measure somewhat different constructs. A client could obtain a high score on Pd, for example, and a low score on ASP because the Pd scale contains item content, such as family problems, quite diverse from antisocial personality features. It is important for the test user to keep in mind the fact that some scales have similar or identical names but may, in fact, measure somewhat different constructs.

Item Overlap between Content Scales

Some of the MMPI-2 items appear on more than one Content Scale. Although efforts were made to keep item overlap to a minimum, some occurs because the scales are conceptually related and some items "belong" on both scales. Item overlap among measures, a psychometrically undesirable property, is not unique to the MMPI-2 Content Scales, it occurs on many personality scales measuring several personality dimensions. Some of the MMPI-2 Content Scales do not contain overlapping items, and item overlap was minimal on most of the other scales. Three scales, because of their more general focus (FAM, WRK, and TRT), contain items that appear on other scales because they are equally appropriate for both assessments.

Research Implications of the MMPI-2 Content Scales

Availability of New Measures

The availability of new, broad-based Content Scales for the MMPI-2 is likely to stimulate new research, as well as to contribute to ongoing clinical studies in several areas. New content-based personality measures in the MMPI-2, for example, the Anger or Low Self-Esteem scales, may provide researchers with tools for evaluating these personality characteristics in clinical populations. Similarly, several clinical problem measures, such as Type A Behavior, Family Problems, or Antisocial Practices, may provide the clinical researcher with means for evaluating the relative prominence of these problems in patient groups.

The availability of measures such as the Work Interference Scale or the Negative Treatment Indicators Scale can add new information for researchers to incorporate in studies dealing with treatment effectiveness and/or rehabilitation success. These measures may provide information for the researcher interested in exploring further the personality factors associated with various change-oriented programs.

Novel Computer Applications

Computer adaptive personality testing, that is, administering personality test items contingent upon a subject's prior responses, is an area of broadening clinical research (Butcher, Keller, & Bacon, 1985; Ben-Porath & Butcher, 1986). Programming computers to adaptively administer personality items is a somewhat more difficult task than doing so with ability or achievement items, since many personality scales do not meet the assumptions necessary to apply models that were developed for adaptive ability testing. Adaptive strategies for personality test items, particularly scales containing heterogeneous content such as the MMPI-2 clinical scales, are difficult to develop and administer. Item response theory, which has been so successful with the computer adaptation of ability items (Weiss & Vale, 1987) cannot be applied successfully with factorially complex, multidimensional scales. To adaptively administer empirically derived scales, other methods need to be employed (Clavelle & Butcher, 1977; Ben-Porath, Slutske, & Butcher, 1989).

Unidimensional personality scales such as the MMPI-2 Content Scales, however, lend themselves well to adaptive personality test administration. A recent study conducted by Ben-Porath et al. (1988) examined the possibility of applying an Item Response Theory (IRT) approach with the new MMPI-2 Content Scales. Results indicated that these scales do, in fact, meet the assumptions that are necessary for applying IRT models and that considerably fewer items need be administered by employing such models. Thus, for example, the correlation between an IRT-based 16-item short form of the DEP Scale and the full raw score on this 33-item scale was .99 in a real data simulation conducted with responses of a psychiatric sample. The correlation was essentially the same (.97) when even fewer items were used following an IRT procedure (Ben-Porath et al., 1988). Similarly, in classifying elevated versus nonelevated scores on the CYN Scale, 51% of this sample could be accurately classified following the administration of 6 of the 23 items on the CYN Scale. An attempt to apply the same model with two MMPI-2 clinical scales (Pa and D) was unsuccessful since these scales failed to meet the criteria necessary for application of IRT-based adaptive testing (Ben-Porath et al., 1988).

The feasibility of developing adaptive testing techniques for the MMPI-2 Content Scales represents a considerable breakthrough in personality assessment with the MMPI. Though other (non-IRT) techniques have been found to work well in adaptive administration of the MMPI clinical scales (Ben-Porath, Slutske, & Butcher, 1989) these alternative approaches do not offer all of the advantages available when IRT methods are employed. More specifically, while all adaptive techniques make possible a reduction in the number of items administered to obtain an interpretable score on a given scale, IRT-based techniques offer the added benefit of enabling more reliable, hence more valid, assessments of the construct in question. Thus, the amenability of the new MMPI-2 Content Scales to IRT-based adaptive testing creates the potential for further enhancement of their reliability and validity.

Future Research Directions

Future research with the MMPI-2 Content Scales could profitably be conducted in several directions. Additional research with more disturbed clinical samples would be desirable. Many of the studies employed in this developmental work included samples with a low base rate for extreme behaviors. Further research on groups with more extreme behavioral problems, such as on inpatient wards or in correctional facilities, would enable scales, such as BIZ and ASP, to be further validated against external criteria.

Several of the Content Scales could be incorporated in treatment and rehabilitation outcome studies. Research in treatment planning and rehabilitation could incorporate both the revised MMPI-2 clinical scales and the new MMPI-2 Content Scales, especially the TRT scale which may be particularly well suited to assessing compliance factors as part of personality functioning. The relationship between the new substantive dimensions in the MMPI-2 and clinical diagnosis should be explored further than was possible in the developmental research with the MMPI-2.

Personality factors in job performance are important elements to address in pre-employment screening and in job-placement research. The availability of a personality-based scale directed at personality characteristics and attitudes related to work adjustment, WRK, could be an important new variable to incorporate in work adjustment research.

The issue of test defensiveness and its impact on personality scales could be more extensively explored. The question of whether content scales are more affected by test defensiveness than empirically oriented scales could be directly studied.

The potential applicability of the MMPI-2 Content Scales in research on computer administration of personality items is great. The homogeneous content of the scales allows for the application of Item Response Theory in selecting items for administration. This procedure is promising for developing briefer screening instruments that could be incorporated in assessments for which longer personality scales are inappropriate.

This volume has presented the rationale and development of a new set of content homogeneous scales for the MMPI-2. The basic statistical analyses exploring the psychometric properties of the MMPI-2 Content Scales have been presented, along with initial validation research with the normative sample. We also attempted to show, through a number of clinical cases, how the MMPI-2 Content Scales contribute valuable clinical information that can be used, along with the traditional validity and clinical scales, to provide clues to the nature and extent of problems individuals experience. We are encouraged that these initial studies on the MMPI-2 Content Scales demonstrate strong support for their use in both research and clinical settings. We hope that making these scales available will stimulate further use and research that will add to their interpretation and usefulness.

References

American Psychological Association (1986). *American Psychological Association Guidelines for Computer-Based Tests and Interpretations.* Washington, D.C.: American Psychological Association.

Anastasi, A. (1988). *Psychological testing.* Sixth edition. New York: MacMillan.

Anthony, N. C. (1971). Comparison of clients' standard, exaggerated and matching MMPI profiles. *Journal of Consulting and Clinical Psychology*, 36, 100–103.

Ben-Porath, Y. S., and Butcher, J. N. (1986). Computers in personality assessment: A brief past, an ebullient present, and an expanding future, *Computers in Human Behavior*, 2, 167–182.

Ben-Porath, Y. S., & Butcher, J. N. (In press). Psychometric Stability of rewritten MMPI items. *Journal of Personality Assessment.*

Ben-Porath, Y. S., Slutske, W., & Butcher, J.N. (In press). A real- data simulation of computerized adaptive administration of the MMPI. *Personality Assessment: A Journal of Consulting and Clinical Psychology*, 1, 18–22.

Ben-Porath, Y. S., Waller, N. G., Slutske, W. S., & Butcher, J. N. (1988). A comparison of two methods for adaptive administration of MMPI-2 content scales. Paper presented at the *96th Annual Meeting of the American Psychological Association*, Atlanta, Georgia.

Boerger, A. R (1975). *The utility of some alternative approaches to MMPI scale construction.* Unpublished doctoral dissertation, Kent State University (See Graham, 1987).

——, Graham, J. R., & Lilly, R. S. (1974). Behavioral correlates of single scale MMPI code types. *Journal of Consulting and Clinical Psychology*, 42, 398–402.

Bogue, D. J. (Ed.) (1985). *The population of the United States: Historical trends and future projections.* New York: Free Press.

Bradley, L. A., Prokop, C. K., Margolis, R., & Gentry, W. D. (1978). Multivariate analysis of the MMPI profiles of low back pain patients. *Journal of Behavioral Medicine*, 1, 253–272.

——, & Van der Heide, L. H. (1984). Pain-related correlates of MMPI profile subgroups among back pain patients. *Health Psychology*, 3, 157–174.

Burisch, M. (1984). Approaches to personality inventory construction. *American Psychologist*, 39, 214–227.

Butcher, J. N. (1971) *Objective personality assessment.* Morristown, N.J.: General Learning Press.

——. (1972) Personality assessment: Problems and perspectives. In J. N. Butcher (Ed.), *Objective personality assessment: Changing perspectives* (pp. 1–20). New York: Academic Press.

——. (Ed.) (1979). *New developments in the use of the MMPI.* Minneapolis: University of Minnesota Press.

——. (Ed.) (1987). *Computerized psychological assessment.* New York: Basic Books.

——. (1987). Use of the MMPI in airline pilot selection. Paper given at the *22nd Annual Symposium on Recent Developments in the Use of the MMPI.* Seattle, Washington.

——. (1989). *User's Guide for the Minneseota Clinical Report (Revised Version).* Minneapolis: University of Minnesota Press.

——. (In press) *Assessing patients in psychotherapy: Use of the MMPI-2 in treatment planning.* New York: Oxford University Press.

——, Graham, J. R., Dahlstrom, W. G., & Bowman, E. (In press). Use of the MMPI-2 with college students. *Journal of Personality Assessment*, In press.

——, Jeffrey, T., Cayton, T. G., Devore, J. R., Colligan, S., & Minnegawa, R. (In press). A study of active duty military personnel with the MMPI-2. *Military Psychology*, in press.

——, Keller, L., & Bacon, S. (1985). Current developments and future directions in computerized personality assessment. *Journal of Consulting and Clinical Psychology*, 33, 803–815.

——, & Owen, P. L. (1978). Objective personality inventories: Recent research and some contemporary issues. In B. B. Wolman (Ed.), *Clinical diagnosis of mental disorders* (pp. 475–546). New York: Plenum.

——, & Tellegen, A. (1966). Objections to MMPI items. *Journal of Consulting and Clinical Psychology*, *30*, 527–534.

Caldwell, A. B. (1969). MMPI critical items. Unpublished manuscript. (Available from Clinical Psychological Services, 3122 Santa Monica Blvd., Santa Monica, California, 90404.)

Carson, R. C. (1969). Interpretative manual to the MMPI. In J. N. Butcher (Ed.), *MMPI: Research developments and clinical applications*. New York: McGraw-Hill.

Chu, C. (1966). *Object cluster analysis of the MMPI*. Unpublished doctoral dissertation, University of California, Berkeley.

Clavelle, P., & Butcher, J. N. (1977). An adaptive typological approach to psychiatric screening. *Journal of Consulting and Clinical Psychology*, 45, 851–859.

Clayton, P., & Stavig, V. (Eds.) (1983). *Minnesota guide* (2nd ed.). Minneapolis: Dorn.

Colligan, R. S., Osborne, D., Swenson, W., & Offord, K. P. (1983). *The MMPI: A contemporary normative study*. New York: Praeger.

Costello, R. M., Hulsey, T. L., Schoenfeld, L. S., & Ramamurthy, S. (1987). P-A-I-N: A four-cluster MMPI typology for chronic pain. *Pain*, 3, 199–209.

Craik, K. H. (1986). Personality research methods: An historical perspective. *Journal of Personality*, 54, 18–51.

Cronbach, L. (1951). Coefficient alpha and the internal structure of tests. *Psychometrika*, 16, 297–334.

Dahlstrom, W. G., & Dahlstrom, L. E. (1980). *Basic readings on the MMPI: a new selection on personality measurement*. Minneapolis: University of Minnesota Press.

Dahlstrom, W. G., Welsh, G. S., & Dahlstrom, L. E. (1972). *An MMPI handbook (Vol. 1): Clinical interpretation*. Minneapolis: University of Minnesota Press.

Dahlstrom, W. G., Welsh, G. S., & Dahlstrom, L. E. (1975). *An MMPI handbook: Vol. II, Research developments and applications*. Minneapolis: University of Minnesota Press.

Derogatis, L. R., Rickels, K., & Rock, A. F. (1976). The SCL-90 and the MMPI: A step in the validation of a new self-report scale. *British Journal of Psychiatry*, 128, 280–289.

Drake, L. E. (1946). A social I.E. scale for the MMPI. *Journal of Applied Psychology*, 30, 51–54.

Drake, L. E., & Oetting, E. R. (1959). *An MMPI codebook for counselors*. Minneapolis: University of Minnesota Press.

Drake, L. E., & Thiede, W. B. (1948). Further validation of the social I.E. scale for the MMPI. *Journal of Educational Research*, 41, 551–556.

Duckworth, J., & Duckworth, E. (1979). *MMPI interpretation manual for counselors and clinicians*. Muncie, Indiana: Accelerated Development, Inc.

Eyde, L., Kowal, D., & Fishburne, J. (1987). Clinical implications of validity research on computer based test interpretations of the MMPI. Paper given at the *Annual Meeting of the American Psychological Association*, New York, New York.

Fishburne, J., Eyde, L., & Kowal, D. (1988). Paper given at the *Annual Meeting of the American Psychological Association*, Atlanta, Georgia.

Foster, V. H., & Goddard, H. H. (1924). The Ohio Literacy Test. *Pedagogical Seminary*, 31, 340–351.

Gilberstadt, H., & Duker, J. (1965). *A handbook for clinical and actuarial MMPI interpretation*. Philadelphia: W. B. Saunders.

Gocka, E. F. (1965). American Lake norms for 200 MMPI scales. Unpublished materials, Veterans Administration Hospital, American Lake, Washington, 1965.

Good, Patricia K.-E., & Brantner, J. P. (1974). *A practical guide to the MMPI*. Minneapolis: University of Minnesota Press.

Gough, H. G. (1947). Simulated patterns on the MMPI. *Journal of Abnormal and Social Psychology*, 42, 215–225.

——. (1950). The F minus K dissimulation index for the MMPI. *Journal of Consulting Psychology*, 14, 408–413.

Graham, J. R. (1973). Behavioral correlates of simple MMPI code types. Paper given at the *Eighth Annual Symposium on Recent Developments in the Use of the MMPI*, New Orleans, LA.

——. (1987). *The MMPI: A practical guide*. 2nd Edition. New York: Oxford University Press.

——, & Butcher, J. N. (1988). Differentiating schizophrenic and major affective disordered inpatients with the revised form of the MMPI. Paper presented at the *23rd Annual Symposium on Recent Development in the Use of the MMPI*, St Petersburg, Florida.

——, & Lilly, R. S. (1984). *Psychological testing*. Englewood Cliffs, N.J.: Prentice-Hall.

——, Lilly, R. S., Paolino, A. F., Friedman, I., & Konick, D. S. (1973). Measuring behavior and adjustment in the community: a factor analytic scale study of the Katz Adjustment Scale (Form R1). *Journal of Community Psychology*, 1(1), 48–53.

——, & McCord, G. (1985). Interpretation of moderately elevated MMPI scores for normal subjects. *Journal of Personality Assessment*, 49 (5), 477–484.

Gray-Little, B. (1974). Attitudes toward conflict with authority as a function of DEX, I-E, and dogmatism. *Psychological Reports*, 34, 375–381.

Grayson, H. M. (1951). *Psychological admission testing program and manual*. Los Angeles: Veterans Administration Center, Neuropsychiatric Hospital.

Greene, R. L. (1980). *The MMPI: an interpretive manual*. New York: Grune & Stratton.

——. (1985). New norms, old norms, what norms for the MMPI? *Journal of Personality Assessment*, 49, 108–110.

Harris, R. E., & Lingoes, J. C. (1955, 1968). Subscales for the MMPI: An aid to profile interpretation. Unpublished manuscript. The Langley Porter Neuropsychiatric Institute.

Hase, H. D., & Goldberg, L. R. (1967). Comparative validity of different strategies of constructing personality scales. *Psychological Bulletin*, 67, 231–248.

Hathaway, S. R. (1956). Scales 5 (Masculinity-Femininity), 6 (Paranoia), and 8 (Schizophrenia). In G. S. Welsh & W. G. Dahlstrom (Eds.), *Basic readings on the MMPI in psychology and medicine* (pp. 104–111). Minneapolis: University of Minnesota Press.

Hathaway, S. R. (1965). Personality inventories. In B. Wolman (Ed.), *Handbook of clinical psychology*. New York: McGraw-Hill.

Hathaway, S. R., & Briggs, P. F. (1957). Some normative data on new MMPI scales. *Journal of Clinical Psychology*, 13, 364–368.

Hathaway, S. R., & McKinley, J. C. (1940). A multiphasic personality schedule (Minnesota): I. Construction of the schedule. *Journal of Psychology*, 10, 249–254.

Hathaway, S. R., & McKinley, J. C. (1942). A multiphasic personality schedule (Minnesota): III. The measurement of symptomatic depression. *Journal of Psychology*, 14, 73–84.

Hathaway, S. R., & Meehl, P. E. (1951). *An atlas for the clinical use of the MMPI*. Minneapolis: University of Minnesota Press.

Hjemboe, S., & Butcher, J. (1988). Use of the MMPI-2 with couples in distress. (Manuscript in preparation.)

Hoffman, H., & Jackson, D. N. (1976). Substantive dimensions of psychopathology derived from MMPI content scales and the Differential Personality Inventory. *Journal of Consulting and Clinical Psychology*, 44, 862.

Holmes, T. H., & Rahe, R. H. (1967). The social readjustment rating scale. *Journal of Psychosomatic Research*, 11, 213–218.

Hsu, L. M., & Betman, J. A. (1986). Minnesota Multiphasic Personality Inventory T Score conversion Tables, 1957–1983. *Journal of Consulting and Clinical Psychology*, 54, 497–502.

Jackson, D. (1971). The dynamics of structured personality tests: 1971. *Psychological Review*, *78*, 229–248.

——, & Carlson, K. A. (1973). Convergent and discriminant validation of the DPI. *Journal of Clinical Psychology*, 29, 214–219.

——, & Messick, S. (1958). Content and style in personality assessment. *Psychological Bulletin*, 55, 243–252.

Jarnecke, R. W., & Chambers, E. D. (1977). MMPI content scales: Dimensional structure, construct validity, and interpretive norms in a psychiatric population. *Journal of Consulting and Clinical Psychology*, 45, 1126–1131.

Johnson, J. R., Butcher, J. N., Null, C., & Johnson, K. N. (1984). Replicated item level factor analysis of the full MMPI. *Journal of Personality and Social Psychology*, 47, 105–114.

Kammeier, M. L., Hoffman, H., & Loper, R. G. (1973). Personality characteristics of alcoholics as college freshmen and at time of treatment. *Quarterly Journal of Studies on Alcohol*, *34*, 390–399.

Katz, M. M. and Lyerly, S. B. (1963). Methods for measuring adjustment and social behavior in the community. *Psychological Reports*, *13*, 503–535.

Keller, L. S., & Butcher, J. N. (1990). *Assessment of chronic pain patients with the MMPI-2*. Minneapolis: University of Minnesota Press, forthcoming.

Koss, M. P. (1979) MMPI item content:Recurring issues. In J. N. Butcher (Ed.), *New developments in the use of the MMPI*. (pp 3–38). Minneapolis: University of Minnesota Press.

——, & Butcher, J. N. (1973). A comparison of psychiatric patients' self report with other sources of clinical information. *Journal of Research in Personality*, 7, 225–236.

——, Butcher, J. N., & Hoffman, N. G. (1976). The MMPI critical items: How well do they work? *Journal of Consulting and Clinical Psychology*, 44, 921–928.

Lachar, D. (1974). *The MMPI: Clinical assessment and automated Interpretation*. Los Angeles: Western Psychological Services.

——, & Alexander, R. S. (1978). Veridicality of self-report: Replicated correlates of the Wiggins MMPI content scales. *Journal of Consulting and Clinical Psychology*, 46, 1349–1356.

Lachar, D., Dahlstrom, W. G., and Moreland, K. (1986). Relationship of ethnic background and other demographic characteristics to MMPI patterns in psychiatric samples. In W. G. Dahlstrom, D. Lachar, & L. E. Dahlstrom (Eds.) *MMPI patterns of American minorities*. Minneapolis: University of Minnesota Press.

——, & Wrobel, T. A. (1979). Validating clinicians' hunches: Construction of a new MMPI critical item set. *Journal of Consulting and Clinical Psychology*, 47, 277–284.

Landis, C., & Katz, S. E. (1934). The validity of certain questions which purport to measure neurotic tendencies. *Journal of Applied Psychology*, 18, 343–356.

Lanyon, R. I. (1968). *A handbook of MMPI group profiles*. Minneapolis: University of Minnesota Press.

Leary, T. (1957). *Interpersonal diagnosis of personality*. New York: Ronald.

Lewandowski, D., & Graham, J. R. (1972). Empirical correlates of frequently occurring two-point MMPI code types: A replicated study. *Journal of Consulting and Clinical Psychology*, 39, 467–472.

Loper, R. G., Kammeier, M. L., & Hoffman, H. (1973). MMPI characteristics of college freshmen males who later become alcoholic. *Journal of Abnormal Psychology*, 82, 159–162.

Lubin, B., Larsen, R. M., & Matarazzo, J. (1984). Patterns of psychological test usage in the United States 1935–1982. *American Psychologist*, 39, 451–454.

McCreary, C. (1985). Empirically derived MMPI profile clusters and characteristics of low back pain patients. *Journal of Consulting and Clinical Psychology*, 53, 558–560.

McGill, J., Lawlis, G. F., Selby, D., Mooney, V., & McCoy, C. E. (1983). Relationship of MMPI profile clusters to pain behaviors. *Journal of Behavioral Medicine*, 6, 77–92.

McKenna, T., & Butcher, J. N. (1987). Continuity of the MMPI with alcoholics. Paper given at the 22nd *Annual Symposium on Recent Developments in the Use of the MMPI*. Seattle, Washington, April, 1987.

Meehl, P. E., (1945). The dynamics of "structured" personality tests. *Journal of Clinical Psychology*, 1, 296–303.

——. (1972). Reactions, reflections, projections. In J. N. Butcher (Ed.), *Objective personality assessment: Changing perspectives*. New York: Academic Press.

Mezzich, J. E., Damarin, F. L., & Erickson, J. R. (1974). Comparative validity of strategies and indices for differential diagnosis of depressive states from other psychiatric conditions using the MMPI. *Journal of Consulting and Clinical Psychology*, 42, 691–698.

McKinley, J. C., & Hathaway, S. R. (1940). A multiphasic personality schedule (Minnesota): II. A differential study of hypochondriasis. *Journal of Psychology*, 10, 255–268.

McKinley, J. C., & Hathaway, S. R. (1942). A multiphasic personality schedule (Minnesota): IV. Psychasthenia. *Journal of Applied Psychology*, 26, 614–624.

McKinley, J. C., & Hathaway, S. R. (1943). The identification and measurement of the psychoneuroses in medical practice: The MMPI. *Journal of the American Medical Association*, 122, 161–167.

McKinley, J. C., & Hathaway, S. R. (1944). The MMPI: V. Hysteria, hypomania, and psychopathic deviate. *Journal of Applied Psychology*, 28, 153–174.

McKinley, J. C., Hathaway, S. R., & Meehl, P. E. (1948). The MMPI: VI. The K scale. *Journal of Consulting Psychology*, 12, 20–31.

Marks, P. A., Seeman, W., & Haller, D. L. (1974). *The actuarial use of the MMPI with adolescents and adults*. New York: Oxford University Press.

Masuda, M., & Holmes, T. H. (1967). Magnitude estimations of social readjustments. *Journal of Psychosomatic Research*, 11, 221–226.

Meehl, P. E. (1971). Prefatory comment. In L. D. Goodstein & R. I. Lanyon (Eds.), *Readings in personality assessment* (pp. 245–246). New York: Wiley.

Meehl, P. E., & Hathaway, S. R. (1946). The K factor as a suppressor variable in the MMPI. *Journal of Applied Psychology*, 30, 525–564.

MMPI-2: *Manual for Administration and Scoring*. Minneapolis: University of Minnesota Press.

Norman, W. T. (1963). Relative importance of test item content. *Journal of Consulting Psychology*, 27, 166–174.

O'Neil, H. F., Teague, M., Lushene, R. E., & Davenport, S. (1975). Personality characteristics of women's liberation activists as measured by the MMPI. *Psychological Reports*, 37, 355–361.

Payne, F. D., & Wiggins, J. S. (1972). MMPI profile types and the self-report of psychiatric patients. *Journal of Abnormal Psychology*, 79, 1–8.

Potter, C. S. (1950). A method of using the MMPI with the blind. In Donahue, Wilma, & Dabelstein, D. (Eds.), *Psychological diagnosis and counseling of the adult blind: Selected papers from the proceedings of the University of Michigan Conference for the Blind, 1947*. New York: American Foundation for the Blind.

Prokop, C. K., Bradley, L. A., Margolis, R., & Gentry, W. D. (1980). Multivariate analyses of the MMPI profiles of low back pain patients. *Journal of Personality Assessment*, 44, 246–252.

Rahe, R. H., & Arthur, R. J. (1978). Life change and illness studies: Past history and future directions. *Journal of Human Stress*, 3–13.

Regier, D. A., Myers, J. K., Kramer, L., Robins, L. N., Blazer, D. G., Hough, R. L., Eaton, W. W., & Locke, B. Z. (1984). The NIMH Epidemiologic Catchment Area Program: Historical context, major objectives, and study population characteristics. *Archives of General Psychiatry*, 41, 934–941.

Rosen, A. (1966). Stability of new MMPI scales and statistical procedures for evaluating changes and differences in psychiatric patients. *Journal of Consulting Psychology*, 30, 142–145.

Rosenman, R. H., Brand, R. J., Jenkins, C. D., Friedman, M., & Straus, R. (1975). Coronary heart disease in the Western Collaborative Group Study: Final follow-up experience of 8 1/2 years. *Journal of the American Medical Association*, 233, 872–877.

SAS/STAT Guide for personal computers version. Sixth Edition (1985). Cary, N.C.: SAS Institute, Inc.

Serkownek, K. (1975). Subscales for Scales 5 and O of the Minnesota Multiphasic Personality Inventory. Unpublished materials. (Available from 3134 Whitehorn Rd., Cleveland Hths., Ohio.)

Spanier, G. B. (1976). Measuring dyadic adjustment: New scales for assessing the quality of marriage and similar dyads. *Journal of Marriage and the Family*, 38, 15–28.

——, & Filsinger, E. E. (1983). The dyadic adjustment scale. In E. E. Filsinger (Ed.), *Marriage and family assessment* (pp. 155–168). Beverly Hills: Sage.

SPSS Inc. (1986). *SPSS-X User's Guide* (2nd Edition). New York: McGraw-Hill.

Stein, K. B. (1968). The TSC Scales: The outcome of a cluster analysis of the 550 MMPI items. In P. McReynolds (Ed.) *Advances in psychological assessment*. Volume 1. Palo Alto, Ca.: Science and Behavior Books.

Taylor, J. B., Ptacek, M., Carithers, M., Griffin, C., & Coyne, L. (1972). Rating scales as measures of clinical judgement. III: Judgements of the self on personality inventory scales and direct ratings. *Educational and Psychological Measurement*, 32, 543–557.

Tellegen, A. (1988). Uniform T scores for the MMPI-2. Paper given at the *96th Annual Convention of the American Psychological Association*. Atlanta, Georgia.

Tryon, R. C. (1966). Unrestricted cluster and factor analysis with application to the MMPI and Holzinger-Harmon problems. *Multivariate Behavioral Research*, 1, 229–244.

——, & Bailey, D. (Eds.) (1965). *User's manual of the BC Try system of cluster and factor analysis*. (Taped version). Berkeley: University of California Computer Center.

Weiss, D., & Vale, C. D. (1987). Computerized adaptive testing for measuring abilities and other psychological variables. In J. N. Butcher (Ed) *Computerized psychological assessment*. New York: Basic Books, Inc.

Welsh, G. S. (1948). An extension of Hathaway's MMPI profile coding system. *Journal of Consulting Psychology*, 12, 343–344.

——. (1951). Some practical uses of MMPI profile coding. *Journal of Consulting Psychology*, 15, 82–84.

——. (1956). Factor dimensions A and R. In G. S. Welsh and W. G. Dahlstrom (Eds.), *Basic readings on the MMPI in psychology and medicine*. Minneapolis: University of Minnesota Press.

——, & Dahlstrom, W. G. (Eds.), (1956). *Basic readings on the MMPI in psychology and medicine*. Minneapolis: University of Minnesota Press.

Wiggins, J. S. (1966). Substantive dimensions of self-report in the MMPI item pool. *Psychological Monographs*, 80, (22 Whole No. 630).

——. (1969). Content dimensions in the MMPI. In J. N. Butcher (Ed.), *MMPI: Research developments and clinical applications*. New York: McGraw-Hill.

——. (1972). *Content scales: Basic data for scoring and interpretation*. Unpublished materials (See Graham, 1977).

——. (1973). *Personality and prediction: Principles of personality assessment*. Reading, Ma: Addison-Wesley.

——, Goldberg, L., & Appelbaum, M. (1971). MMPI Content Scales: Interpretive norms and correlations with other scales. *Journal of Consulting and Clinical Psychology*, 37, 403–410.

——, & Vollmar, J. (1959). The content of the MMPI. *Journal of Clinical Psychology*, 15, 45–47.

Woodworth, R. S. (1920). *Personal data sheet*. Chicago: Stoelting.

Wrobel, T. A., & Lachar, D. (1982). Validity of the Wiener Subtle and Obvious scales for the MMPI: Another example of the importance of inventory item content. *Journal of Consulting and Clinical Psychology*, 50, 469–470.

Appendixes

Appendix A
MMPI-2 Booklet

DO NOT MAKE ANY MARKS ON THIS BOOKLET.

1. I like mechanics magazines.

2. I have a good appetite.

3. I wake up fresh and rested most mornings.

4. I think I would like the work of a librarian.

5. I am easily awakened by noise.

6. My father is a good man, or (if your father is dead) my father was a good man.

7. I like to read newspaper articles on crime.

8. My hands and feet are usually warm enough.

9. My daily life is full of things that keep me interested.

10. I am about as able to work as I ever was.

11. There seems to be a lump in my throat much of the time.

12. My sex life is satisfactory.

13. People should try to understand their dreams and be guided by or take warning from them.

14. I enjoy detective or mystery stories.

15. I work under a great deal of tension.

16. Once in a while I think of things too bad to talk about.

17. I am sure I get a raw deal from life.

18. I am troubled by attacks of nausea and vomiting.

19. When I take a new job, I like to find out who it is important to be nice to.

20. I am very seldom troubled by constipation.

21. At times I have very much wanted to leave home.

22. No one seems to understand me.

23. At times I have fits of laughing and crying that I cannot control.

24. Evil spirits possess me at times.

25. I would like to be a singer.

26. I feel that it is certainly best to keep my mouth shut when I'm in trouble.

27. When people do me a wrong, I feel I should pay them back if I can, just for the principle of the thing.

28. I am bothered by an upset stomach several times a week.

29. At times I feel like swearing.

30. I have nightmares every few nights.

31. I find it hard to keep my mind on a task or job.

32. I have had very peculiar and strange experiences.

33. I seldom worry about my health.

34. I have never been in trouble because of my sex behavior.

35. Sometimes when I was young I stole things.

36. I have a cough most of the time.

37. At times I feel like smashing things.

38. I have had periods of days, weeks, or months when I couldn't take care of things because I couldn't "get going."

39. My sleep is fitful and disturbed.

40. Much of the time my head seems to hurt all over.

GO ON TO THE NEXT PAGE

41. I do not always tell the truth.

42. If people had not had it in for me, I would have been much more successful.

43. My judgment is better than it ever was.

44. Once a week or oftener I suddenly feel hot all over, for no real reason.

45. I am in just as good physical health as most of my friends.

46. I prefer to pass by school friends, or people I know but have not seen for a long time, unless they speak to me first.

47. I am almost never bothered by pains over my heart or in my chest.

48. Most anytime I would rather sit and daydream than do anything else.

49. I am a very sociable person.

50. I have often had to take orders from someone who did not know as much as I did.

51. I do not read every editorial in the newspaper every day.

52. I have not lived the right kind of life.

53. Parts of my body often have feelings like burning, tingling, crawling, or like "going to sleep."

54. My family does not like the work I have chosen (or the work I intend to choose for my lifework).

55. I sometimes keep on at a thing until others lose their patience with me.

56. I wish I could be as happy as others seem to be.

57. I hardly ever feel pain in the back of my neck.

58. I think a great many people exaggerate their misfortunes in order to gain the sympathy and help of others.

59. I am troubled by discomfort in the pit of my stomach every few days or oftener.

60. When I am with people, I am bothered by hearing very strange things.

61. I am an important person.

62. I have often wished I were a girl. (Or if you are a girl) I have never been sorry that I am a girl.

63. My feelings are not easily hurt.

64. I enjoy reading love stories.

65. Most of the time I feel blue.

66. It would be better if almost all laws were thrown away.

67. I like poetry.

68. I sometimes tease animals.

69. I think I would like the kind of work a forest ranger does.

70. I am easily downed in an argument.

71. These days I find it hard not to give up hope of amounting to something.

72. My soul sometimes leaves my body.

73. I am certainly lacking in self-confidence.

74. I would like to be a florist.

75. I usually feel that life is worthwhile.

76. It takes a lot of argument to convince most people of the truth.

77. Once in a while I put off until tomorrow what I ought to do today.

78. I am liked by most people who know me.

79. I do not mind being made fun of.

80. I would like to be a nurse.

GO ON TO THE NEXT PAGE

81. I think most people would lie to get ahead.

82. I do many things which I regret afterwards (I regret things more than others seem to).

83. I have very few quarrels with members of my family.

84. I was suspended from school one or more times for bad behavior.

85. At times I have a strong urge to do something harmful or shocking.

86. I like to go to parties and other affairs where there is lots of loud fun.

87. I have met problems so full of possibilities that I have been unable to make up my mind about them.

88. I believe women ought to have as much sexual freedom as men.

89. My hardest battles are with myself.

90. I love my father, or (if your father is dead) I loved my father.

91. I have little or no trouble with my muscles twitching or jumping.

92. I don't seem to care what happens to me.

93. Sometimes when I am not feeling well I am irritable.

94. Much of the time I feel as if I have done something wrong or evil.

95. I am happy most of the time.

96. I see things or animals or people around me that others do not see.

97. There seems to be a fullness in my head or nose most of the time.

98. Some people are so bossy that I feel like doing the opposite of what they request, even though I know they are right.

99. Someone has it in for me.

100. I have never done anything dangerous for the thrill of it.

101. Often I feel as if there is a tight band around my head.

102. I get angry sometimes.

103. I enjoy a race or game more when I bet on it.

104. Most people are honest chiefly because they are afraid of being caught.

105. In school I was sometimes sent to the principal for bad behavior.

106. My speech is the same as always (not faster or slower, no slurring or hoarseness).

107. My table manners are not quite as good at home as when I am out in company.

108. Anyone who is able and willing to work hard has a good chance of succeeding.

109. I seem to be about as capable and smart as most others around me.

110. Most people will use somewhat unfair means to gain profit or an advantage rather than to lose it.

111. I have a great deal of stomach trouble.

112. I like dramatics.

113. I know who is responsible for most of my troubles.

114. Sometimes I am so strongly attracted by the personal articles of others, such as shoes, gloves, etc., that I want to handle or steal them, though I have no use for them.

115. The sight of blood doesn't frighten me or make me sick.

116. Often I can't understand why I have been so irritable and grouchy.

117. I have never vomited blood or coughed up blood.

GO ON TO THE NEXT PAGE

118. I do not worry about catching diseases.

119. I like collecting flowers or growing house plants.

120. I frequently find it necessary to stand up for what I think is right.

121. I have never indulged in any unusual sex practices.

122. At times my thoughts have raced ahead faster than I could speak them.

123. If I could get into a movie without paying and be sure I was not seen I would probably do it.

124. I often wonder what hidden reason another person may have for doing something nice for me.

125. I believe that my home life is as pleasant as that of most people I know.

126. I believe in law enforcement.

127. Criticism or scolding hurts me terribly.

128. I like to cook.

129. My conduct is largely controlled by the behavior of those around me.

130. I certainly feel useless at times.

131. When I was a child, I belonged to a group of friends that tried to be loyal through all kinds of trouble.

132. I believe in a life hereafter.

133. I would like to be a soldier.

134. At times I feel like picking a fist fight with someone.

135. I have often lost out on things because I couldn't make up my mind soon enough.

136. It makes me impatient to have people ask my advice or otherwise interrupt me when I am working on something important.

137. I used to keep a diary.

138. I believe I am being plotted against.

139. I would rather win than lose in a game.

140. Most nights I go to sleep without thoughts or ideas bothering me.

141. During the past few years I have been well most of the time.

142. I have never had a fit or convulsion.

143. I am neither gaining nor losing weight.

144. I believe I am being followed.

145. I feel that I have often been punished without cause.

146. I cry easily.

147. I cannot understand what I read as well as I used to.

148. I have never felt better in my life than I do now.

149. The top of my head sometimes feels tender.

150. Sometimes I feel as if I must injure either myself or someone else.

151. I resent having anyone trick me so cleverly that I have to admit I was fooled.

152. I do not tire quickly.

153. I like to know some important people because it makes me feel important.

154. I am afraid when I look down from a high place.

155. It wouldn't make me nervous if any members of my family got into trouble with the law.

156. I am never happy unless I am roaming or traveling around.

157. What others think of me does not bother me.

GO ON TO THE NEXT PAGE

158. It makes me uncomfortable to put on a stunt at a party even when others are doing the same sort of things.

159. I have never had a fainting spell.

160. I liked school.

161. I frequently have to fight against showing that I am bashful.

162. Someone has been trying to poison me.

163. I do not have a great fear of snakes.

164. I seldom or never have dizzy spells.

165. My memory seems to be all right.

166. I am worried about sex.

167. I find it hard to make talk when I meet new people.

168. I have had periods in which I carried on activities without knowing later what I had been doing.

169. When I get bored I like to stir up some excitement.

170. I am afraid of losing my mind.

171. I am against giving money to beggars.

172. I frequently notice my hand shakes when I try to do something.

173. I can read a long while without tiring my eyes.

174. I like to study and read about things that I am working at.

175. I feel weak all over much of the time.

176. I have very few headaches.

177. My hands have not become clumsy or awkward.

178. Sometimes, when embarrassed, I break out in a sweat which annoys me greatly.

179. I have had no difficulty in keeping my balance in walking.

180. There is something wrong with my mind.

181. I do not have spells of hay fever or asthma.

182. I have had attacks in which I could not control my movements or speech but in which I knew what was going on around me.

183. I do not like everyone I know.

184. I daydream very little.

185. I wish I were not so shy.

186. I am not afraid to handle money.

187. If I were a reporter I would very much like to report news of the theater.

188. I enjoy many different kinds of play and recreation.

189. I like to flirt.

190. My people treat me more like a child than a grown-up.

191. I would like to be a journalist.

192. My mother is a good woman, or (if your mother is dead) my mother was a good woman.

193. In walking I am very careful to step over sidewalk cracks.

194. I have never had any breaking out on my skin that has worried me.

195. There is very little love and companionship in my family as compared to other homes.

196. I frequently find myself worrying about something.

197. I think I would like the work of a building contractor.

198. I often hear voices without knowing where they come from.

GO ON TO THE NEXT PAGE

199. I like science.

200. It is not hard for me to ask help from my friends even though I cannot return the favor.

201. I very much like hunting.

202. My parents often objected to the kind of people I went around with.

203. I gossip a little at times.

204. My hearing is apparently as good as that of most people.

205. Some of my family have habits that bother and annoy me very much.

206. At times I feel that I can make up my mind with unusually great ease.

207. I would like to belong to several clubs.

208. I hardly ever notice my heart pounding and I am seldom short of breath.

209. I like to talk about sex.

210. I like to visit places where I have never been before.

211. I have been inspired to a program of life based on duty which I have since carefully followed.

212. I have at times stood in the way of people who were trying to do something, not because it amounted to much but because of the principle of the thing.

213. I get mad easily and then get over it soon.

214. I have been quite independent and free from family rule.

215. I brood a great deal.

216. Someone has been trying to rob me.

217. My relatives are nearly all in sympathy with me.

218. I have periods of such great restlessness that I cannot sit long in a chair.

219. I have been disappointed in love.

220. I never worry about my looks.

221. I dream frequently about things that are best kept to myself.

222. Children should be taught all the main facts of sex.

223. I believe I am no more nervous than most others.

224. I have few or no pains.

225. My way of doing things is apt to be misunderstood by others.

226. Sometimes without any reason or even when things are going wrong I feel excitedly happy, "on top of the world."

227. I don't blame people for trying to grab everything they can get in this world.

228. There are persons who are trying to steal my thoughts and ideas.

229. I have had blank spells in which my activities were interrupted and I did not know what was going on around me.

230. I can be friendly with people who do things which I consider wrong.

231. I like to be with a crowd who play jokes on one another.

232. Sometimes in elections I vote for people about whom I know very little.

233. I have difficulty in starting to do things.

234. I believe I am a condemned person.

235. I was a slow learner in school.

236. If I were an artist I would like to draw flowers.

237. It does not bother me that I am not better looking.

GO ON TO THE NEXT PAGE

238. I sweat very easily even on cool days.

239. I am entirely self-confident.

240. At times it has been impossible for me to keep from stealing or shoplifting something.

241. It is safer to trust nobody.

242. Once a week or oftener I become very excited.

243. When in a group of people I have trouble thinking of the right things to talk about.

244. Something exciting will almost always pull me out of it when I am feeling low.

245. When I leave home I do not worry about whether the door is locked and the windows closed.

246. I believe my sins are unpardonable.

247. I have numbness in one or more places on my skin.

248. I do not blame a person for taking advantage of people who leave themselves open to it.

249. My eyesight is as good as it has been for years.

250. At times I have been so entertained by the cleverness of some criminals that I have hoped they would get away with it.

251. I have often felt that strangers were looking at me critically.

252. Everything tastes the same.

253. I drink an unusually large amount of water every day.

254. Most people make friends because friends are likely to be useful to them.

255. I do not often notice my ears ringing or buzzing.

256. Once in a while I feel hate toward members of my family whom I usually love.

257. If I were a reporter I would very much like to report sporting news.

258. I can sleep during the day but not at night.

259. I am sure I am being talked about.

260. Once in a while I laugh at a dirty joke.

261. I have very few fears compared to my friends.

262. In a group of people I would not be embarrassed to be called upon to start a discussion or give an opinion about something I know well.

263. I am always disgusted with the law when a criminal is freed through the arguments of a smart lawyer.

264. I have used alcohol excessively.

265. I am likely not to speak to people until they speak to me.

266. I have never been in trouble with the law.

267. I have periods in which I feel unusually cheerful without any special reason.

268. I wish I were not bothered by thoughts about sex.

269. If several people find themselves in trouble, the best thing for them to do is to agree upon a story and stick to it.

270. It does not bother me particularly to see animals suffer.

271. I think that I feel more intensely than most people do.

272. There never was a time in my life when I liked to play with dolls.

273. Life is a strain for me much of the time.

GO ON TO THE NEXT PAGE

274. I am so touchy on some subjects that I can't talk about them.

275. In school I found it very hard to talk in front of the class.

276. I love my mother, or (if your mother is dead) I loved my mother.

277. Even when I am with people I feel lonely much of the time.

278. I get all the sympathy I should.

279. I refuse to play some games because I am not good at them.

280. I seem to make friends about as quickly as others do.

281. I dislike having people around me.

282. I have been told that I walk during sleep.

283. The person who provides temptation by leaving valuable property unprotected is about as much to blame for its theft as the one who steals it.

284. I think nearly anyone would tell a lie to keep out of trouble.

285. I am more sensitive than most other people.

286. Most people inwardly dislike putting themselves out to help other people.

287. Many of my dreams are about sex.

288. My parents and family find more fault with me than they should.

289. I am easily embarrassed.

290. I worry over money and business.

291. I have never been in love with anyone.

292. The things that some of my family have done have frightened me.

293. I almost never dream.

294. My neck spots with red often.

295. I have never been paralyzed or had any unusual weakness of any of my muscles.

296. Sometimes my voice leaves me or changes even though I have no cold.

297. My mother or father often made me obey even when I thought that it was unreasonable.

298. Peculiar odors come to me at times.

299. I cannot keep my mind on one thing.

300. I have reason for feeling jealous of one or more members of my family.

301. I feel anxiety about something or someone almost all the time.

302. I easily become impatient with people.

303. Most of the time I wish I were dead.

304. Sometimes I become so excited that I find it hard to get to sleep.

305. I have certainly had more than my share of things to worry about.

306. No one cares much what happens to you.

307. At times I hear so well it bothers me.

308. I forget right away what people say to me.

309. I usually have to stop and think before I act even in small matters.

310. Often I cross the street in order not to meet someone I see.

311. I often feel as if things are not real.

312. The only interesting part of newspapers is the comic strips.

313. I have a habit of counting things that are not important such as bulbs on electric signs, and so forth.

314. I have no enemies who really wish to harm me.

GO ON TO THE NEXT PAGE

315. I tend to be on my guard with people who are somewhat more friendly than I had expected.

316. I have strange and peculiar thoughts.

317. I get anxious and upset when I have to make a short trip away from home.

318. I usually expect to succeed in things I do.

319. I hear strange things when I am alone.

320. I have been afraid of things or people that I knew could not hurt me.

321. I have no dread of going into a room by myself where other people have already gathered and are talking.

322. I am afraid of using a knife or anything very sharp or pointed.

323. Sometimes I enjoy hurting persons I love.

324. I can easily make other people afraid of me, and sometimes do for the fun of it.

325. I have more trouble concentrating than others seem to have.

326. I have several times given up doing a thing because I thought too little of my ability.

327. Bad words, often terrible words, come into my mind and I cannot get rid of them.

328. Sometimes some unimportant thought will run through my mind and bother me for days.

329. Almost every day something happens to frighten me.

330. At times I am all full of energy.

331. I am inclined to take things hard.

332. At times I have enjoyed being hurt by someone I loved.

333. People say insulting and vulgar things about me.

334. I feel uneasy indoors.

335. I am not unusually self-conscious.

336. Someone has control over my mind.

337. At parties I am more likely to sit by myself or with just one other person than to join in with the crowd.

338. People often disappoint me.

339. I have sometimes felt that difficulties were piling up so high that I could not overcome them.

340. I love to go to dances.

341. At periods my mind seems to work more slowly than usual.

342. While in trains, busses, etc., I often talk to strangers.

343. I enjoy children.

344. I enjoy gambling for small stakes.

345. If given the chance I could do some things that would be of great benefit to the world.

346. I have often met people who were supposed to be experts who were no better than I.

347. It makes me feel like a failure when I hear of the success of someone I know well.

348. I often think, "I wish I were a child again."

349. I am never happier than when alone.

350. If given the chance I would make a good leader of people.

351. I am embarrassed by dirty stories.

352. People generally demand more respect for their own rights than they are willing to allow for others.

353. I enjoy social gatherings just to be with people.

GO ON TO THE NEXT PAGE

354. I try to remember good stories to pass them on to other people.

355. At one or more times in my life I felt that someone was making me do things by hypnotizing me.

356. I find it hard to set aside a task that I have undertaken, even for a short time.

357. I am quite often not in on the gossip and talk of the group I belong to.

358. I have often found people jealous of my good ideas, just because they had not thought of them first.

359. I enjoy the excitement of a crowd.

360. I do not mind meeting strangers.

361. Someone has been trying to influence my mind.

362. I can remember "playing sick" to get out of something.

363. My worries seem to disappear when I get into a crowd of lively friends.

364. I feel like giving up quickly when things go wrong.

365. I like to let people know where I stand on things.

366. I have had periods when I felt so full of pep that sleep did not seem necessary for days at a time.

367. Whenever possible I avoid being in a crowd.

368. I shrink from facing a crisis or difficulty.

369. I am apt to pass up something I want to do when others feel that it isn't worth doing.

370. I like parties and socials.

371. I have often wished I were a member of the opposite sex.

372. I am not easily angered.

373. I have done some bad things in the past that I never tell anybody about.

374. Most people will use somewhat unfair means to get ahead in life.

375. It makes me nervous when people ask me personal questions.

376. I do not feel I can plan my own future.

377. I am not happy with myself the way I am.

378. I get angry when my friends or family give me advice on how to live my life.

379. I got many beatings when I was a child.

380. It bothers me when people say nice things about me.

381. I don't like hearing other people give their opinions about life.

382. I often have serious disagreements with people who are close to me.

383. When things get really bad, I know I can count on my family for help.

384. I liked playing "house" when I was a child.

385. I am not afraid of fire.

386. I have sometimes stayed away from another person because I feared doing or saying something that I might regret afterwards.

387. I can express my true feelings only when I drink.

388. I very seldom have spells of the blues.

389. I am often said to be hotheaded.

390. I wish I could get over worrying about things I have said that may have injured other people's feelings.

GO ON TO THE NEXT PAGE

391. I feel unable to tell anyone all about myself.

392. Lightning is one of my fears.

393. I like to keep people guessing what I'm going to do next.

394. My plans have frequently seemed so full of difficulties that I have had to give them up.

395. I am afraid to be alone in the dark.

396. I have often felt bad about being misunderstood when trying to keep someone from making a mistake.

397. A windstorm terrifies me.

398. I frequently ask people for advice.

399. The future is too uncertain for a person to make serious plans.

400. Often, even though everything is going fine for me, I feel that I don't care about anything.

401. I have no fear of water.

402. I often must sleep over a matter before I decide what to do.

403. People have often misunderstood my intentions when I was trying to put them right and be helpful.

404. I have no trouble swallowing.

405. I am usually calm and not easily upset.

406. I would certainly enjoy beating criminals at their own game.

407. I deserve severe punishment for my sins.

408. I am apt to take disappointments so keenly that I can't put them out of my mind.

409. It bothers me to have someone watch me at work even though I know I can do it well.

410. I am often so annoyed when someone tries to get ahead of me in a line of people that I speak to that person about it.

411. At times I think I am no good at all.

412. When I was young I often did not go to school even when I should have gone.

413. One or more members of my family are very nervous.

414. I have at times had to be rough with people who were rude or annoying.

415. I worry quite a bit over possible misfortunes.

416. I have strong political opinions.

417. I would like to be an auto racer.

418. It is all right to get around the law if you don't actually break it.

419. There are certain people whom I dislike so much that I am inwardly pleased when they are catching it for something they have done.

420. It makes me nervous to have to wait.

421. I am apt to pass up something I want to do because others feel that I am not going about it in the right way.

422. I was fond of excitement when I was young.

423. I am often inclined to go out of my way to win a point with someone who has opposed me.

424. I am bothered by people outside, on the streets, in stores, etc., watching me.

425. The man who had most to do with me when I was a child (such as my father, stepfather, etc.) was very strict with me.

426. I used to like to play hopscotch and jump rope.

427. I have never seen a vision.

428. I have several times had a change of heart about my lifework.

GO ON TO THE NEXT PAGE

429. Except by doctor's orders I never take drugs or sleeping pills.

430. I am often sorry because I am so irritable and grouchy.

431. In school my marks in classroom behavior were quite regularly bad.

432. I am fascinated by fire.

433. When I am cornered I tell that portion of the truth which is not likely to hurt me.

434. If I was in trouble with several friends who were as guilty as I was, I would rather take the whole blame than give them away.

435. I am often afraid of the dark.

436. When a man is with a woman he is usually thinking about things related to her sex.

437. I am usually very direct with people I am trying to correct or improve.

438. I dread the thought of an earthquake.

439. I readily become one hundred percent sold on a good idea.

440. I usually work things out for myself rather than get someone to show me how.

441. I am afraid of finding myself in a closet or small closed place.

442. I must admit that I have at times been worried beyond reason over something that really did not matter.

443. I do not try to cover up my poor opinion or pity of people so that they won't know how I feel.

444. I am a high-strung person.

445. I have frequently worked under people who seem to have things arranged so that they get credit for good work but are able to pass off mistakes onto those under them.

446. I sometimes find it hard to stick up for my rights because I am so reserved.

447. Dirt frightens or disgusts me.

448. I have a daydream life about which I do not tell other people.

449. Some of my family have quick tempers.

450. I cannot do anything well.

451. I often feel guilty because I pretend to feel more sorry about something than I really do.

452. I strongly defend my own opinions as a rule.

453. I have no fear of spiders.

454. The future seems hopeless to me.

455. The members of my family and my close relatives get along quite well.

456. I would like to wear expensive clothes.

457. People can pretty easily change my mind even when I have made a decision about something.

458. I am made nervous by certain animals.

459. I can stand as much pain as others can.

460. Several times I have been the last to give up trying to do a thing.

461. It makes me angry to have people hurry me.

462. I am not afraid of mice.

463. Several times a week I feel as if something dreadful is about to happen.

464. I feel tired a good deal of the time.

465. I like repairing a door latch.

466. Sometimes I am sure that other people can tell what I am thinking.

467. I like to read about science.

468. I am afraid of being alone in a wide-open place.

GO ON TO THE NEXT PAGE

469. I sometimes feel that I am about to go to pieces.

470. A large number of people are guilty of bad sexual conduct.

471. I have often been frightened in the middle of the night.

472. I am greatly bothered by forgetting where I put things.

473. The one to whom I was most attached and whom I most admired as a child was a woman (mother, sister, aunt, or other woman).

474. I like adventure stories better than romantic stories.

475. Often I get confused and forget what I want to say.

476. I am very awkward and clumsy.

477. I really like playing rough sports (such as football or soccer).

478. I hate my whole family.

479. Some people think it's hard to get to know me.

480. I spend most of my spare time by myself.

481. When people do something that makes me angry, I let them know how I feel about it.

482. I usually have a hard time deciding what to do.

483. People do not find me attractive.

484. People are not very kind to me.

485. I often feel that I'm not as good as other people.

486. I am very stubborn.

487. I have enjoyed using marijuana.

488. Mental illness is a sign of weakness.

489. I have a drug or alcohol problem.

490. Ghosts or spirits can influence people for good or bad.

491. I feel helpless when I have to make some important decisions.

492. I always try to be pleasant even when others are upset or critical.

493. When I have a problem it helps to talk it over with someone.

494. My main goals in life are within my reach.

495. I believe that people should keep personal problems to themselves.

496. I am not feeling much pressure or stress these days.

497. It bothers me greatly to think of making changes in my life.

498. My greatest problems are caused by the behavior of someone close to me.

499. I hate going to doctors even when I'm sick.

500. Although I am not happy with my life, there is nothing I can do about it now.

501. Talking over problems and worries with someone is often more helpful than taking drugs or medicine.

502. I have some habits that are really harmful.

503. When problems need to be solved, I usually let other people take charge.

504. I recognize several faults in myself that I will not be able to change.

505. I am so sick of what I have to do every day that I just want to get out of it all.

506. I have recently considered killing myself.

507. I often become very irritable when people interrupt my work.

508. I often feel I can read other people's minds.

GO ON TO THE NEXT PAGE

509. Having to make important decisions makes me nervous.

510. Others tell me I eat too fast.

511. Once a week or more I get high or drunk.

512. I have had a tragic loss in my life that I know I'll never get over.

513. Sometimes I get so angry and upset I don't know what comes over me.

514. When people ask me to do something I have a hard time saying no.

515. I am never happier than when I am by myself.

516. My life is empty and meaningless.

517. I find it difficult to hold down a job.

518. I have made lots of bad mistakes in my life.

519. I get angry with myself for giving in to other people so much.

520. Lately I have thought a lot about killing myself.

521. I like making decisions and assigning jobs to others.

522. Even without my family I know there will always be someone there to take care of me.

523. At movies, restaurants, or sporting events, I hate to have to stand in line.

524. No one knows it but I have tried to kill myself.

525. Everything is going on too fast around me.

526. I know I am a burden to others.

527. After a bad day, I usually need a few drinks to relax.

528. Much of the trouble I'm having is due to bad luck.

529. At times I can't seem to stop talking.

530. Sometimes I cut or injure myself on purpose without knowing why.

531. I work very long hours even though my job doesn't require this.

532. I usually feel better after a good cry.

533. I forget where I leave things.

534. If I could live my life over again, I would not change much.

535. I get very irritable when people I depend on don't get their work done on time.

536. If I get upset I'm sure to get a headache.

537. I like to drive a hard bargain.

538. Most men are unfaithful to their wives now and then.

539. Lately I have lost my desire to work out my problems.

540. I have gotten angry and broken furniture or dishes when I was drinking.

541. I work best when I have a definite deadline.

542. I have become so angry with someone that I have felt as if I would explode.

543. Terrible thoughts about my family come to me at times.

544. People tell me I have a problem with alcohol but I disagree.

545. I always have too little time to get things done.

546. My thoughts these days turn more and more to death and the life hereafter.

547. I often keep and save things that I will probably never use.

548. I've been so angry at times that I've hurt someone in a physical fight.

549. In everything I do lately I feel that I am being tested.

GO ON TO THE NEXT PAGE

550. I have very little to do with my relatives now.

551. I sometimes seem to hear my thoughts being spoken out loud.

552. When I am sad, visiting with friends can always pull me out of it.

553. Much of what is happening to me now seems to have happened to me before.

554. When my life gets difficult, it makes me want to just give up.

555. I can't go into a dark room alone even in my own home.

556. I worry a great deal over money.

557. The man should be the head of the family.

558. The only place where I feel relaxed is in my own home.

559. The people I work with are not sympathetic with my problems.

560. I am satisfied with the amount of money I make.

561. I usually have enough energy to do my work.

562. It is hard for me to accept compliments.

563. In most marriages one or both partners are unhappy.

564. I almost never lose self-control.

565. It takes a greal deal of effort for me to remember what people tell me these days.

566. When I am sad or blue, it is my work that suffers.

567. Most married couples don't show much affection for each other.

Appendix B
Koss-Butcher-Revised
and Lachar-Wrobel
Critical Items

Koss-Butcher Critical Items, Revised

Acute Anxiety State			
2F	28T	208F	463T
3F	39T	218T	469T
5T	59T	223F	
10F	140F	301T	
15T	172T	444T	

Depressed Suicidal Ideation				
9F	92T	23 3T	411T	520T
38T	95F	273T	454T	524T
65T	130T	303T	485T	
71T	146T	306T	506T	
75F	215T	388F	518T	

Threatened Assault
37T
85T
134T
213T
389T

Situational Stress Due to Alcoholism	
125F	511T
264T	518T
487T	
489T	
502T	

Mental Confusion		
24T	180T	325T
31T	198T	
32T	299T	
72T	311T	
96T	316T	

Persecutory Ideas			
17T	144T	241T	361T
42T	145T	251T	
99T	162T	259T	
124T	216T	314F	
138T	228T	333T	

Lacher-Wrobel Critical Item Sets

Anxiety and Tension		
15T	261F	463T
17T	299T	
172T	301T	
218T	320T	
223F	405F	

Depression and Worry			
2F	75F	273T	454T
3F	130T	303T	
10F	150T	339T	
65T	165F	411T	
73T	180T	415T	

Sleep Disturbance	
5T	471T
30T	
39T	
140F	
328T	

Deviant Beliefs		
42T	162T	333T
99T	216T	336T
106F	228T	355T
138T	259T	361T
144T	314F	466T

Deviant Thinking and Experience	
32T	298T
60T	307T
96T	316T
122T	319T
198T	427F

Substance Abuse
168T
264T
429F

Antisocial Attitude	
27T	240T
35T	254T
84T	266F
105T	324T
227T	

Family Conflict
21T
83F
125F
288T

Problematic Anger
85T
134T
213T
389T

Sexual Concern and Deviation	
12F	268T
34F	
62T (men)/F (women)	
121F	
166T	

Somatic Symptoms				
18T	47F	111T	176F	255F
28T	53T	142F	182T	295F
33F	57F	159F	224F	464T
40T	59T	164F	229T	
44T	101T	175T	247T	

Appendix C
Harris-Lingoes
Subscales (Scoring
Direction of Items)

Harris-Lingoes Subscales

D_1 — Subjective Depression (32 items)

True
  31   38   39   46   56   73   92   127   130   146   147   170   175   215
  233

False
  2   9   43   49   75   95   109   118   140   148   178   188   189   223
  260   267   330
Males: Mean 6.86; S.D. 3.79.   Females: Mean 7.65; S.D. 4.21.

D_2 — Psychomotor Retardation (14 items)

True
  38   46   170   233

False
  9   29   37   49   55   76   134   188   189   212
Males: Mean 5.34; S.D. 1.82.   Females: Mean 5.74; S.D. 1.83.

D_3 — Physical Malfunctioning (11 items)

True
  18   117   175   181

False
  2   20   45   141   142   143   148
Males: Mean 2.89; S.D. 1.23.   Females: Mean 3.22; S.D. 1.36.

D_4 — Mental Dullness (15 items)

True
  15   31   38   73   92   147   170   233

False
  9   10   43   75   109   165   188
Males: Mean 2.42; S.D.2.09.   Females: Mean 2.55; S.D. 2.21.

D_5 — Brooding (20 items)

True
  38   56   92   127   130   146   170   215

False
  75   95
Males: Mean 1.83; S.D. 1.77.   Females: Mean 2.50; S.D. 1.95

Hy_1 — Denial of Social Anxiety (6 items)

True
none

False
129   161   167   185   243   265
Males: Mean 3.89; S.D. 1.86.   Females: Mean 3.85; S.D. 1.87.

Hy_2 — Need for Affection (12 items)

True
230

False
26   58   76   81   98   110   124   151   213   241   263
Males: Mean 6.69; S.D. 2.58.   Females: Mean 6.88; S.D. 2.44.

Hy_3 — Lassitude-malaise (15 items)

True
31   39   65   175   218

False
2   3   9   10   45   95   125   141   148   152
Males: Mean 2.55; S.D. 2.20.   Females: Mean 2.73; S.D. 2.48.

Hy_4 — Somatic Complaints (17 items)

True
11   18   40   44   101   172

False
8   47   91   159   164   173   176   179   208   224   249
Males: Mean 2.50; S.D. 2.06.   Females: Mean 3.22; S.D. 2.53.

Hy_5 — Inhibition of Aggression (7 items)

True
none

False
7   14   29   115   116   135   157
Males: Mean 3.29; S.D. 1.32.   Females: Mean 3.46; S.D. 1.29.

Pd_1 — Familial Discord (9 items)

True
  21   54   195   202   288

False
  83   125   214   217
Males: Mean 1.78; S.D. 1.52.   Females: Mean 2.05; S.D. 1.65.

Pd_2 — Authority Problems (8 items)

True
  35   105

False
  34   70   129   160   263   266
Males: Mean 3.29; S.D. 1.52.   Females: Mean 2.35; S.D. 1.34.

Pd_3 — Social Imperturbability (6 items)

True
none

False
  70   129   158   167   185   243
Males: Mean 3.64; S.D. 171.   Females: Mean 3.37; S.D. 1.73.

Pd_4 — Social Alienation (13 items)

True
  17   22   42   56   82   99   113   219   225   259

False
  12   129   157
Males: Mean 3.74; S.D. 1.89.   Females: Mean 3.98; S.D. 1.93.

Pd_5 — Self-Alienation (12 items)

True
  31   32   52   56   71   82   89   94   113   264

False
  9   95
Males: Mean 3.39; S.D. 2.08.   Females: Mean 3.35; S.D. 2.07.

Pa_1 — Persecutory Ideas (17 items)

True
17	22	42	99	113	138	144	145	162	234	259	305	333	336
355	361												

False
314
Males: Mean 1.74; S.D. 1.66.   Females: Mean 1.79; S.D. 1.67.

Pa_2 — Poignancy (9 items)

True
22   146   271   277   285   307   334

False
100   244
Males: Mean 2.36; S.D. 1.43.   Females: Mean 2.57; S.D. 1.58.

Pa_3 — Naivete (9 items)

True
16

False
81   98   104   110   283   284   286   315
Males: Mean 4.84; S.D. 2.09.   Females: Mean 4.95; S.D. 2.09.

Sc_1 — Social Alienation (21 items)

True
17	21	22	42	46	138	145	190	221	256	277	281	291	292
320	333												

False
90   276   278   280   343
Males: Mean 2.72; S.D. 2.42.   Females: Mean 3.11; S.D. 2.59.

Sc_2 — Emotional Alienation (11 items)

True
65   92   234   273   303   323   329   332

False
9   210   290
Males: Mean 1.05; S.D. 1.04.   Females: Mean 1.12; S.D. 1.09.

Sc_3 — Lack of Ego Mastery, Cognitive (10 items)

True
31   32   147   170   180   299   311   316   325

False
165
Males: Mean 1.31; S.D. 1.66.   Females: Mean 1.18; S.D. 1.62.

Sc_4 — Lack of Ego Mastery, Conative (14 items)

True
31   38   48   65   92   233   234   273   299   303   325

False
9   210   290
Males: Mean 2.13; S.D. 1.85.   Females: Mean 2.17; S.D. 1.95.

Sc_5 — Lack of Ego Mastery, Defecftive Inhibition (11 items)

True
23   85   168   182   218   242   274   320   322   329   355

False
none
Males: Mean 1.42; S.D. 1.43.   Females: Mean 1.57; S.D. 1.57.

Sc_6 — Bizarre Sensory Experiences (20 items)

True
23   32   44   168   182   229   247   252   296   298   307   311   319   355

False
91   106   177   179   255   295
Males: Mean 1.90; S.D. 2.04.   Females: Mean 2.07; S.D. 2.20.

Ma_1 — Amorality (6 items)

True
131   227   248   250   269

False
263
Males: Mean 1.97; S.D. 1.29.   Females: Mean 1.56; S.D. 1.20.

Ma_2 — Psychomotor Acceleration (11 items)

True
15　85　87　122　169　206　218　242　244

False
100　106

Males: Mean 5.29; S.D. 2.07.　　Females: Mean 5.07; S.D. 1.99.

Ma_3 — Imperturbability (8 items)

True
155　200　220

False
93　136　158　167　243

Males: Mean 3.51; S.D. 1.66.　　Females: Mean 3.06; S.D. 1.56.

Ma_4 — Ego Inflation (9 items)

True
13　50　55　61　98　145　190　211　212

False
none

Males: Mean 3.04; S.D. 1.53.　　Females: Mean 3.09; S.D. 1.64.

Appendix D
Biographical
Information Form

MMPI RESTANDARDIZATION PROJECT

DIRECTIONS: Use black lead pencil (No. 2) only. Make a heavy dark mark that completely fills the circle you have selected (see Example below).

Example: Wrong

Right

If you make a mistake, or change your mind, please erase carefully and thoroughly.

This sheet will be processed by automatic equipment. Please keep it free from wrinkles and stray marks.

SUBJECT NUMBER	SEX	BIRTHDATE	LOCATION	TODAY'S DATE

I. BIOGRAPHICAL INFORMATION

1. Current marital status:
- O Married
- O Widowed
- O Divorced (or had marriage annulled)
- O Separated
- O Never Married

If you have never been married, please skip to question #7. Otherwise, please continue with question #2.

2. How many years has your current marital status (married, divorced, annulled, widowed, or separated) lasted?

Number of Years

3. If now married or widowed, have you ever been divorced, separated, or had a marriage annulled?
- O Yes
- O No

4. How many times have you been married?
- O 1
- O 2
- O 3
- O 4
- O 5
- O 6
- O 7
- O 8
- O 9 or more

If you have been married only once, please skip to question #7. Otherwise, please continue with question #5.

5. If you have been married more than once, how many years ago did your previous marriage (the one just before your most recent one) end?

Number of Years

6. How did this previous marriage end?
- O Divorce (or annulment)
- O Death of Spouse

7. Are you currently enrolled in or attending school?
- O Yes
- O No

If Yes,
- O Full Time
- O Part Time

8. What is the highest grade (year of education) completed?
- O 1 O 2 O 3 O 4 O 5 O 6
- O 7 O 8 O 9 O 10 O 11 O 12
- O Or High School Equivalency
- O 13 O 14 O 15 O 16 O 17 O 18
- O 19 O 20+ O Business College or Technical School

9. Degrees earned:
- O B.A.
- O B.S.
- O A.A.
- O M.A.
- O M.S.
- O Doctorate

Go on to next page

DO NOT WRITE IN THIS AREA

DO
NOT
WRITE
IN
THIS
AREA

10. Complete the categories that apply to you.

- O Presently employed
- O Unemployed
- O Retired
- O Student
- O Housewife
- O Self-employed
- O Part-time employment
- O On leave
- O Disabled
- O None of the above

11. What is your usual occupation? (If now retired, disabled, unemployed, or on leave, what was your previous occupation?)

- O Laborer
- O Clerical Worker
- O Skilled Craftsperson
- O Manager
- O Professional
- O None of the above

12. If not now employed, have you ever held a regular full-time job?

- O Yes
- O No

If Yes, in what year did you last work?

0	0
1	1
2	2
3	3
4	4
5	5
6	6
7	7
8	8
9	9

Are you looking for work now?

- O Yes
- O No

13. How are you paid?

- O Salaried
- O Hourly pay
- O Commission
- O Disability Pay
- O Welfare
- O Tips
- O Self-employed
- O Pension
- O Unemployment
- O None of the above

14. Total family income:

- O Under $3,000
- O $3,000-3,999
- O $4,000-4,999
- O $5,000-5,999
- O $6,000-7,999
- O $8,000-9,999
- O $10,000-11,999
- O $12,000-14,999
- O $15,000-19,999
- O $20,000-24,999
- O $25,000-29,999
- O $30,000-34,999
- O $35,000-44,999
- O $45,000-54,999
- O $55,000-64,999
- O $65,000-74,999
- O $75,000+

15. Father's usual occupation or work:

- O Laborer
- O Manager
- O Clerical Worker
- O Professional
- O Skilled Craftsperson
- O None of the above

Father's education (grade completed):

O 1	O 5	O 9	O 13	O 17
O 2	O 6	O 10	O 14	O 18
O 3	O 7	O 11	O 15	O 19
O 4	O 8	O 12	O 16	O 20

Mother's usual occupation or work:

- O Laborer
- O Manager
- O Clerical Worker
- O Professional
- O Skilled Craftsperson
- O None of the above

Mother's education (grade completed):

O 1	O 5	O 9	O 13	O 17
O 2	O 6	O 10	O 14	O 18
O 3	O 7	O 11	O 15	O 19
O 4	O 8	O 12	O 16	O 20

16. Number of older brothers:

O 1	O 4	O 7	O 10	O 13
O 2	O 5	O 8	O 11	O 14
O 3	O 6	O 9	O 12	

Number of older sisters:

O 1	O 4	O 7	O 10	O 13
O 2	O 5	O 8	O 11	O 14
O 3	O 6	O 9	O 12	

Go on to next page

Number of younger brothers:

○ 1 ○ 4 ○ 7 ○ 10 ○ 13
○ 2 ○ 5 ○ 8 ○ 11 ○ 14
○ 3 ○ 6 ○ 9 ○ 12

Number of younger sisters:

○ 1 ○ 4 ○ 7 ○ 10 ○ 13
○ 2 ○ 5 ○ 8 ○ 11 ○ 14
○ 3 ○ 6 ○ 9 ○ 12

17. What is your ethnic origin?
○ Asian   ○ Native American
○ Black   ○ White
○ Hispanic   ○ Other

18. What is your native language?
○ English
○ Spanish
○ Other

19. Where have you lived most of your life?
○ City
○ Town
○ Rural Area

20. What is your present dwelling?
○ Own home   ○ Rooming house
○ Condominium   ○ Dormitory
○ Rented apartment or house ○ Other

21. From what part of the world did your ancestors come? Fill in the circles that apply to you.
○ A. Native American (Indian, Eskimo, Aleut)
○ B. Canada (French, English, native)
○ C. Mexico
○ D. Australia/New Zealand
○ E. Central America
○ F. Caribbean Islands
○ G. South America
○ H. Europe
○ I. Middle East
○ J. Africa
○ K. Asia
○ L. Pacific Islands

If you completed an item lettered, E, F, G, H, I, J, K, or L, please write country name in box.

[   ]

22. What is your religion?
Christian: ○ Roman Catholic
             ○ Eastern Orthodox
             ○ Mormon
             ○ Protestant

If Protestant, which denomination? Please write in box.

[   ]

○ Jewish   ○ Buddhist
○ Muslim   ○ Baha'i
○ Hindu   ○ None

II. GENERAL INFORMATION

Yes	No	
Ⓨ	Ⓝ	1. Have you ever been given a ticket for speeding?
Ⓨ	Ⓝ	2. Have you ever been arrested for anything other than a motor vehicle violation?
Ⓨ	Ⓝ	3. Are you now taking any medicine prescribed by a doctor?
Ⓨ	Ⓝ	4. Have you ever been treated by a psychologist or psychiatrist for an emotional problem?
Ⓨ	Ⓝ	5. Are you now in psychological or psychiatric treatment?
Ⓨ	Ⓝ	6. Have you ever been hospitalized for emotional problems?
Ⓨ	Ⓝ	7. Have you ever been in treatment for drug or alcohol abuse?
Ⓨ	Ⓝ	8. Have you had an operation or major physical illness in the last year?
Ⓨ	Ⓝ	9. Do you have a physical handicap?

10. When was the last time that you went to a physician?
○ last week   ○ 7-12 months ago
○ 2-4 weeks ago   ○ 2-3 years ago
○ 2-6 months ago   ○ more than 3 years ago

11. Please complete the statement that describes your alcohol use?
○ I have never used alcohol.
○ I used to drink but do not drink now.
○ I drink socially but never to excess.
○ I sometimes drink to the point of feeling "high."
○ I usually drink moderately but will often drink more than I should.
○ I often use alcohol to excess.
○ I have had serious problems with my drinking.
○ I consider myself an alcoholic.
○ I have been in treatment for alcohol abuse.

12. Please complete the statement that best describes your use of drugs:
○ I have never used drugs such as marijuana, cocaine, or barbiturates.
○ I have used such drugs but they are not a problem for me.
○ I now have or in the past have had a problem with such drugs.

13. Have any members of your family had emotional problems that required treatment?

Yes	No		Yes	No	
Ⓨ	Ⓝ	Mother	Ⓨ	Ⓝ	Grandparent
Ⓨ	Ⓝ	Father	Ⓨ	Ⓝ	Aunt or Uncle
Ⓨ	Ⓝ	Son or Daughter	Ⓨ	Ⓝ	Niece or Nephew
Ⓨ	Ⓝ	Sister or Brother			

14. Have any members of your family been treated for alcohol or drug problems?

Yes	No		Yes	No	
Ⓨ	Ⓝ	Mother	Ⓨ	Ⓝ	Grandparent
Ⓨ	Ⓝ	Father	Ⓨ	Ⓝ	Aunt or Uncle
Ⓨ	Ⓝ	Son or Daughter	Ⓨ	Ⓝ	Niece or Nephew
Ⓨ	Ⓝ	Sister or Brother			

Appendix E
Life Events Form

NCS Trans-Optic® MP15-18028: 54

MMPI RESTANDARDIZATION PROJECT

Directions

1. Use black lead (No. 2) only. Make a heavy dark mark that completely fills the circle you have selected (See Example below).

   Example:

   Wrong ⊘⊗⊙◑

   Right ⓨ●

   ●ⓝ

2. If you make a mistake, or change your mind, please erase carefully and thoroughly.

3. This sheet will be processed by automatic equipment. Please keep it free from wrinkles and stray marks.

SUBJECT NUMBER	SEX	BIRTHDATE	LOCATION	TODAY'S DATE

LIFE EVENTS (ADULT)

Please indicate by completing the yes or no circle if any of the events listed below have happened to you **within the last six months.**

YES NO		YES NO		YES NO	
ⓨ ⓝ	1. Death of spouse	ⓨ ⓝ	15. Business difficulties or loss	ⓨ ⓝ	29. Change of personal habits
ⓨ ⓝ	2. Divorce	ⓨ ⓝ	16. Change in financial status	ⓨ ⓝ	30. Trouble with boss
ⓨ ⓝ	3. Marital separation	ⓨ ⓝ	17. Death of close friend	ⓨ ⓝ	31. Change in work hours or conditions
ⓨ ⓝ	4. Jail term	ⓨ ⓝ	18. Change to different line of work	ⓨ ⓝ	32. Change in residence
ⓨ ⓝ	5. Death of close family member	ⓨ ⓝ	19. Change in number of arguments with family members	ⓨ ⓝ	33. Change in schools
ⓨ ⓝ	6. Personal injury or illness			ⓨ ⓝ	34. Change in recreation
		ⓨ ⓝ	20. Assume high mortgage		
ⓨ ⓝ	7. Marriage			ⓨ ⓝ	35. Change in church activities
		ⓨ ⓝ	21. Unable to pay mortgage or loan		
ⓨ ⓝ	8. Fired from job			ⓨ ⓝ	36. Change in social activities
		ⓨ ⓝ	22. Change in work responsibilities		
ⓨ ⓝ	9. Got back together after marital separation			ⓨ ⓝ	37. Take out small loan
		ⓨ ⓝ	23. Son or daughter leaving home		
ⓨ ⓝ	10. Retirement			ⓨ ⓝ	38. Change in sleeping habits
		ⓨ ⓝ	24. Trouble with in-laws		
ⓨ ⓝ	11. Change in health of family member			ⓨ ⓝ	39. Change in number of family outings and holidays
		ⓨ ⓝ	25. Outstanding personal achievement		
ⓨ ⓝ	12. Pregnancy				
		ⓨ ⓝ	26. Wife or husband begins or stops work	ⓨ ⓝ	40. Change in eating habits
ⓨ ⓝ	13. Sexual difficulties				
		ⓨ ⓝ	27. Begin or end school	ⓨ ⓝ	41. Minor violations of the law
ⓨ ⓝ	14. Addition of new member to family				
		ⓨ ⓝ	28. Change in living conditions		

■○○○○○○○○○○○○○○○○○○○○■■■■■

DO NOT WRITE IN THIS AREA

Appendix F
Relationship Form

MMPI RESTANDARDIZATION PROJECT

Directions: Use black lead pencil (no. 2) only. Make a heavy dark mark that completely fills the circle you have selected (see Example below).

Example: Wrong   ⊘⊗⊘⊙

Right   ●Ⓝ

      Ⓨ●

If you make a mistake, or change your mind, please erase carefully and thoroughly.

This sheet will be processed by automatic equipment. Please keep it free from wrinkles and stray marks.

SUBJECT NUMBER	SEX	BIRTHDATE	LOCATION	TODAY'S DATE

RELATIONSHIP

Please describe how you view the relationship you now have with your marital/living partner.

1. **In each item listed indicate the extent of agreement or disagreement between you and your partner.**

1. Always Agree	2. Almost Always Agree	3. Usually Agree	4. Usually Disagree	5. Almost Always Disagree	6. Always Disagree	
①	②	③	④	⑤	⑥	Handling finances
①	②	③	④	⑤	⑥	Religious matters
①	②	③	④	⑤	⑥	Affection
①	②	③	④	⑤	⑥	Friends
①	②	③	④	⑤	⑥	Sexual relations
①	②	③	④	⑤	⑥	Parents or in-laws
①	②	③	④	⑤	⑥	Aims and goals in life
①	②	③	④	⑤	⑥	Amount of time together
①	②	③	④	⑤	⑥	Major decisions (career, purchase)
①	②	③	④	⑤	⑥	Household tasks
①	②	③	④	⑤	⑥	Leisure-time activities
①	②	③	④	⑤	⑥	Social obligations

DO NOT WRITE IN THIS AREA

Go on to next page

DO
NOT
WRITE
IN
THIS
AREA

2. In each item below indicate how often you experience or perceive this to be true in your present relationship.

1. All the time	2. Most of the time	3. More often than not	4. Occasionally	5. Only rarely	6. Virtually never	
①	②	③	④	⑤	⑥	Consider separation or divorce
①	②	③	④	⑤	⑥	One or other leaves the house after a quarrel
①	②	③	④	⑤	⑥	Think things are going well between you
①	②	③	④	⑤	⑥	Confide in your partner
①	②	③	④	⑤	⑥	Regret that you ever lived together or married
①	②	③	④	⑤	⑥	You and your partner quarrel
①	②	③	④	⑤	⑥	You and your partner get on each other's nerves
①	②	③	④	⑤	⑥	Kiss your partner
①	②	③	④	⑤	⑥	Engage in outside interests together

Go on to next page

3. **How often do the following events occur between you and your partner?**

1. Never	2. Less than once a month	3. Once or twice a month	4. Once or twice a week	5. Once a day	6. More Often	
①	②	③	④	⑤	⑥	Stimulating exchange of ideas
①	②	③	④	⑤	⑥	Laugh together
①	②	③	④	⑤	⑥	Calm discussion
①	②	③	④	⑤	⑥	Work on project together

4. **Couples sometimes agree and sometimes disagree about the two items below. Indicate if either item caused differences of opinion or were problems in your relationship during the past few weeks.**

   Yes   No
   ⓨ   Ⓝ   Being too tired for sex

   ⓨ   Ⓝ   Not showing love

5. **Which <u>one</u> of the following best describes your marital satisfaction:**

   ○ Extremely dissatisfied   ○ Somewhat satisfied
   ○ Very dissatisfied   ○ Very satisfied
   ○ Somewhat dissatisfied   ○ Extremely satisfied

6. **Select the <u>one</u> statement below that best describes how you feel about the future of your relationship.**

   ○ I want desperately for my relationship to succeed and <u>would go to almost any length</u> to see that it does.

   ○ I want very much for my relationship to succeed and <u>will do all I can</u> to see that it does.

   ○ I want very much for my relationship to succeed and <u>will do my fair share</u> to see that it does.

   ○ It would be nice if my relationship succeeded, but <u>I can't do much more than I am doing now</u> to help it succeed.

   ○ It would be nice if my relationship succeeded, but <u>I refuse to do any more than I am doing now</u> to keep it going.

   ○ My relationship can never succeed, and <u>there is no more that I can do</u> to keep it going.

Appendix G
Couple's Rating Form

MMPI RESTANDARDIZATION PROJECT

SUBJECT NUMBER	S E X	BIRTHDATE	LOCATION	RATER NUMBER	TODAY'S DATE

Directions: Use black lead pencil (no. 2) only. Make a heavy dark mark that completely fills the circle you have selected (see Example below).

Example: Wrong ⊘⊗⊙⊚
Right ⊙●

If you make a mistake, or change your mind, please erase carefully and thoroughly.

This sheet will be processed by automatic equipment. Please keep it free from wrinkles and stray marks.

RATER INFORMATION

PART I. Please provide the following information about yourself:

1. **Education:**
   What is the <u>highest</u> grade (year) completed?
   Grade School ○1 ○2 ○3 ○4
   ○5 ○6 ○7 ○8

   High School ○9 ○10 ○11 ○12

   College ○13 ○14 ○15 ○16

   ○ Business or Technical School

2. **Marital Status:**
   ○ Married
   ○ Separated
   ○ Divorced
   ○ Widowed
   ○ Never married

3. **Ethnic Origin:**
   ○ Asian
   ○ Black
   ○ Hispanic
   ○ Native American
   ○ White
   ○ Other

4. **Relationship to the person you are rating:**
   ○ Husband/wife/living partner
   ○ Steady boyfriend/girlfriend
   ○ Best friend
   ○ Parent
   ○ Child
   ○ Brother/Sister
   ○ Other relative
   ○ Casual acquaintance
   ○ Employee
   ○ Therapist

5. **How long have you known the person you are rating?**

   Number of Years:

6. **Please fill in the circle that indicates the closeness of the relationship:**
   ○ Not very close
   ○ Somewhat close
   ○ Very close
   ○ Extremely close

DO NOT WRITE IN THIS AREA

DO NOT WRITE IN THIS AREA

PART II Information about the Person Being Rated.

The statements in the following list describe different kinds of activities, moods, and behaviors that may be observed in people at various times. Some are positive, others are negative. Please describe the person by filling in the circle in the appropriate column opposite each statement to indicate how often you have observed that characteristic or know that it occurs. Please be sure that you respond to each of the statements.

1. Almost Never	2. Sometimes	3. Often	4. Almost Always	
①	②	③	④	1. Has good sense of humour
①	②	③	④	2. Has trouble sleeping at night
①	②	③	④	3. Blames self for things that go wrong
①	②	③	④	4. Is unrealistic about own abilities
①	②	③	④	5. Worries about health a great deal
①	②	③	④	6. Prefers to do things just right
①	②	③	④	7. Lacks an interest in things
①	②	③	④	8. Is restless
①	②	③	④	9. Has difficulty remembering things
①	②	③	④	10. Is affectionate
①	②	③	④	11. Lacks energy
①	②	③	④	12. Appears worn out
①	②	③	④	13. Feelings get hurt easily by little things
①	②	③	④	14. Is self-confident
①	②	③	④	15. Feels people do not care about him/her
①	②	③	④	16. Gets very sad or blue and is slow to come out of it
①	②	③	④	17. Tries too hard
①	②	③	④	18. Has many fears
①	②	③	④	19. Is creative in solving problems and meeting challenges
①	②	③	④	20. Gets nervous and jittery
①	②	③	④	21. Does some strange things for no reason
①	②	③	④	22. Has temper tantrums
①	②	③	④	23. Gets annoyed easily
①	②	③	④	24. Has bad dreams
①	②	③	④	25. Worries and frets over little things
①	②	③	④	26. Is cheerful
①	②	③	④	27. Is undependable
①	②	③	④	28. Talks about committing suicide
①	②	③	④	29. Gets angry and actually breaks things
①	②	③	④	30. Talks to self

Go on to next page

1. Almost Never	2. Some-times	3. Often	4. Almost Always	
①	②	③	④	31. Lacks control over emotions
①	②	③	④	32. Resents being told what to do
①	②	③	④	33. Is moody
①	②	③	④	34. Acts stubborn
①	②	③	④	35. Gets very excited or happy for little or no reason
①	②	③	④	36. Does not seem to care about other people's feelings
①	②	③	④	37. Worries about the future
①	②	③	④	38. Shows feelings easily
①	②	③	④	39. Is generous to others
①	②	③	④	40. Thinks others are talking about him/her
①	②	③	④	41. Is suspicious of others
①	②	③	④	42. Complains of headaches, stomach trouble, or other ailments
①	②	③	④	43. Acts very bossy
①	②	③	④	44. Is friendly
①	②	③	④	45. Argues about minor things
①	②	③	④	46. Gets into fights and hits people
①	②	③	④	47. Is cooperative
①	②	③	④	48. Does just the opposite of what is asked
①	②	③	④	49. Gets very angry and yells
①	②	③	④	50. Doesn't answer when spoken to
①	②	③	④	51. Swears and curses
①	②	③	④	52. Upsets routine of others for no good reason
①	②	③	④	53. Is pleasant and relaxed
①	②	③	④	54. Is resentful
①	②	③	④	55. Is very upset by small but unexpected events
①	②	③	④	56. Takes drugs other than those prescribed by a doctor
①	②	③	④	57. Is envious or jealous of others
①	②	③	④	58. Is critical of other people
①	②	③	④	59. Tells lies for no apparent reason
①	②	③	④	60. Gets along well with others
①	②	③	④	61. Drinks alcohol to excess (gets sick or passes out)
①	②	③	④	62. Is ambitious
①	②	③	④	63. Talks back to others
①	②	③	④	64. Has been arrested or in trouble with the law
①	②	③	④	65. Is overly responsible
①	②	③	④	66. Avoids contact with people for no reason
①	②	③	④	67. Acts very shy
①	②	③	④	68. Is constructive and helpful
①	②	③	④	69. Starts many projects but does not complete them
①	②	③	④	70. Likes to flirt
①	②	③	④	71. Acts without thinking
①	②	③	④	72. Has a very hard time making any decisions
①	②	③	④	73. Is overly sensitive to any rejection
①	②	③	④	74. Is sought out by others for advice or help
①	②	③	④	75. Nags a lot

Go on to next page

1. Almost Never	2. Some-times	3. Often	4. Almost Always	
①	②	③	④	76. Acts hostile and unfriendly
①	②	③	④	77. Is willing to try new things
①	②	③	④	78. Is passive and obedient to superiors
①	②	③	④	79. Talks too much
①	②	③	④	80. Goes to religious services and functions
①	②	③	④	81. Acts bored and restless
①	②	③	④	82. Craves attention
①	②	③	④	83. Is distractible
①	②	③	④	84. Shows sound judgment
①	②	③	④	85. Eats too much for own good
①	②	③	④	86. Stirs up excitement
①	②	③	④	87. Expresses belief in strange things
①	②	③	④	88. Acts to keep people at a distance
①	②	③	④	89. Brags too much about own successes
①	②	③	④	90. Takes too many risks
①	②	③	④	91. Whines and demands special attention
①	②	③	④	92. Drives fast and recklessly
①	②	③	④	93. Puts own self down
①	②	③	④	94. Is thoughtful of others
①	②	③	④	95. Is irritable and grouchy over even minor things
①	②	③	④	96. Has problems or conflicts over sex
①	②	③	④	97. Breaks down and cries easily
①	②	③	④	98. Is very concerned about death
①	②	③	④	99. Gives advice too freely
①	②	③	④	100. Threatens to harm people who disagree with him/her
①	②	③	④	101. Makes big plans
①	②	③	④	102. Wears strange or unusual clothes
①	②	③	④	103. Laughs and jokes with people
①	②	③	④	104. Acts helpless
①	②	③	④	105. Volunteers for projects
①	②	③	④	106. Takes advantage of others who cannot fight back
①	②	③	④	107. Gives up too easily
①	②	③	④	108. Tells people off about their faults and mistakes
①	②	③	④	109. Seems convinced that something dreadful is about to happen
①	②	③	④	110. Enjoys parties, entertainments, or having friends over

DO NOT WRITE IN THIS AREA

NCS Trans-Optic® MB15-18026-6543

Appendix H
Item-Scale
Membership and
Scoring Direction for
the MMPI-2 Content
Scales

ANX — Anxiety (23 items)

True

15	30	31	39	170	196	273	290	299	301	305	339	408	415	463
469	509	556												

False

140 208 223 405 496

Males: Mean 5.53; S.D. 4.17.   Females: Mean 6.53; S.D. 4.51.

FRS — Fears (23 items)

True

154	317	322	329	334	392	395	397	435	438	441	447	458	468	471
555														

False

115 163 186 385 401 453 462

Males: Mean 3.80; S.D. 2.96.   Females: Mean 6.59; S.D. 3.60.

OBS — Obsessiveness (16 items)

True

55	87	135	196	309	313	327	328	394	442	482	491	497	509	547
553														

False

Males: Mean 4.93; S.D. 3.06.   Females: Mean 5.50; S.D. 3.32.

DEP — Depression (33 items)

True

38	52	56	65	71	82	92	130	146	215	234	246	277	303	306
331	377	399	400	411	454	506	512	516	520	539	546	554		

False

3   9   75   95   388

Males: Mean 4.79; S.D. 4.62.   Females: Mean 5.86; S.D. 5.02.

HEA — Health Concerns (36 items)

True

11	18	28	36	40	44	53	59	97	101	111	149	175	247

False

20	33	45	47	57	91	117	118	141	142	159	164	176	179	181
194	204	224	249	255	295	404								

Males: Mean 5.29; S.D. 3.91.   Females: Mean 6.16; S.D. 4.47.

BIZ—Bizarre Mentation (23 items)

True

24	32	60	96	138	162	198	228	259	298	311	316	319	333	336
355	361	466	490	508	543	551								

False
427
Males: Mean 2.30; S.D. 2.50.   Females: Mean 2.21; S.D. 2.49.

ANG — Anger (16 items)

True

29	37	116	134	302	389	410	414	430	461	486	513	540	542	548

False
564
Males: Mean 5.63; S.D. 3.31.   Females: Mean 5.68; S.D. 3.08.

CYN — Cynicism (23 items)

True

50	58	76	81	104	110	124	225	241	254	283	284	286	315	346
352	358	374	399	403	445	470	538							

False
none
Males: Mean 9.50; S.D. 5.35.   Females: Mean 8.73; S.D. 5.16.

ASP — Antisocial Practices (22 items)

True

26	35	66	81	84	104	105	110	123	227	240	248	250	254	269
283	284	374	412	418	419									

False
266
Males: Mean 7.91; S.D. 4.19.   Females: Mean 6.17; S.D. 3.70.

TPA — Type A (19 items)

True

27	136	151	212	302	358	414	419	420	423	430	437	507	510	523
531	535	541	545											

False
none
Males: Mean 8.08; S.D. 3.68.   Females: Mean 7.41; S.D. 3.34.

LSE — Low Self-Esteem (24 items)

True

| 70 | 73 | 130 | 235 | 326 | 369 | 376 | 380 | 411 | 421 | 450 | 457 | 475 | 476 | 483 |
| 485 | 503 | 504 | 519 | 526 | 562 | | | | | | | | | |

False

61   78   109

Males: Mean 4.25; S.D. 3.69.   Females: Mean 5.16; S.D. 4.24.

SOD — Social Discomfort (24 items)

True

46   158   167   185   265   275   281   337   349   367   479   480   515

False

49   86   262   280   321   340   353   359   360   363   370

Males: Mean 7.65; S.D. 4.77.   Females: Mean 7.53; S.D. 4.80.

FAM — Family Problems (25 items)

True

| 21 | 54 | 145 | 190 | 195 | 205 | 256 | 292 | 300 | 323 | 378 | 379 | 382 | 413 | 449 |
| 478 | 543 | 550 | 563 | 567 | | | | | | | | | | |

False

83   125   217   383   455

Males: Mean 5.32; S.D. 3.52.   Females: Mean 6.14; S.D. 3.77.

WRK — Work Interference (33 items)

True

| 15 | 17 | 31 | 54 | 73 | 98 | 135 | 233 | 243 | 299 | 302 | 339 | 364 | 368 | 394 |
| 409 | 428 | 445 | 464 | 491 | 505 | 509 | 517 | 525 | 545 | 554 | 559 | 566 | | |

False

10   108   318   521   561

Males: Mean 7.30; S.D. 4.98.   Females: Mean 8.51; S.D. 5.45.

TRT — Negative Treatment Indicators (26 items)

True

| 22 | 92 | 274 | 306 | 364 | 368 | 373 | 375 | 376 | 377 | 391 | 399 | 482 | 488 | 491 |
| 495 | 497 | 499 | 500 | 504 | 528 | 539 | 554 | | | | | | | |

False

493   494   501

Males: Mean 4.70; S.D. 3.71.   Females: Mean 5.02; S.D. 3.98.

Appendix I
Item Composition of
the Content Scales

ANX (Anxiety)

15. (T) I work under a great deal of tension.
30. (T) I have nightmares every few nights.
31. (T) I find it hard to keep my mind on a task or job.
39. (T) My sleep is fitful and disturbed.
140. (F) Most nights I go to sleep without thoughts or ideas bothering me.
170. (T) I am afraid of losing my mind.
196. (T) I frequently find myself worrying about something.
208. (F) I hardly ever notice my heart pounding and I am seldom short of breath.
223. (F) I believe I am no more nervous than most others.
273. (T) Life is a strain for me much of the time.
290. (T) I worry over money and business.
299. (T) I cannot keep my mind on one thing.
301. (T) I feel anxiety about something or someone almost all the time.
305. (T) I have certainly had more than my share of things to worry about.
339. (T) I have sometimes felt that difficulties were piling up so high that I could not overcome them.
405. (F) I am usually calm and not easily upset.
408. (T) I am apt to take disappointments so keenly that I can't put them out of my mind.
415. (T) I worry quite a bit over possible misfortunes.
463. (T) Several times a week I feel as if something dreadful is about to happen.
469. (T) I sometimes feel that I am about to go to pieces.
496. (F) I am not feeling much pressure or stress these days.
509. (T) Having to make important decisions makes me nervous.
556. (T) I worry a great deal over money.

FRS (Fears)

115. (F) The sight of blood doesn't frighten me or make me sick.
154. (T) I am afraid when I look down from a high place.
163. (F) I do not have a great fear of snakes.
186. (F) I am not afraid to handle money.
317. (T) I get anxious and upset when I have to make a short trip away from home.
322. (T) I am afraid of using a knife or anything very sharp or pointed.
329. (T) Almost every day something happens to frighten me.
334. (T) I feel uneasy indoors.
385. (F) I am not afraid of fire.
392. (T) Lightning is one of my fears.
395. (T) I am afraid to be alone in the dark.
397. (T) A windstorm terrifies me.
401. (F) I have no fear of water.
435. (T) I am often afraid of the dark.
438. (T) I dread the thought of an earthquake.
441. (T) I am afraid of finding myself in a closet or small closed place.
447. (T) Dirt frightens or disgusts me.
453. (F) I have no fear of spiders.
458. (T) I am made nervous by certain animals.
462. (F) I am not afraid of mice.
468. (T) I am afraid of being alone in a wide-open place.
471. (T) I have often been frightened in the middle of the night.
555. (T) I can't go into a dark room alone even in my own home.

OBS (Obsessiveness)

55. (T) I sometimes keep on at a thing until others lose their patience with me.
87. (T) I have met problems so full of possibilities that I have been unable to make up my mind about them.
135. (T) I have often lost out on things because I couldn't make up my mind soon enough.

196. (T) I frequently find myself worrying about something.
309. (T) I usually have to stop and think before I act even in small matters.
313. (T) I have a habit of counting things that are not important such as bulbs on electric signs, and so forth.
327. (T) Bad words, often terible words, come into my mind and I cannot get rid of them.
328. (T) Sometimes some unimportant thought will run through my mind and bother me for days.
394. (T) My plans have frequently seemed so full of difficulties that I have had to give them up.
442. (T) I must admit that I have at times been worried beyond reason over something that really did not matter.
482. (T) I usually have a hard time deciding what to do.
491. (T) I feel helpless when I have to make some important decisions.
497. (T) It bothers me greatly to think of making changes in my life.
509. (T) Having to make important decisions makes me nervous.
547. (T) I often keep and save things that I will probably never use.
553. (T) Much of what is happening to me now seems to have happened to me before.

DEP (Depression)

3. (F) I wake up fresh and rested most mornings.
9. (F) My daily life is full of things that keep me interested.
38. (T) I have had periods of days, weeks, or months when I couldn't take care of things because I couldn't "get going".
52. (T) I have not lived the right kind of life.
56. (T) I wish I could be as happy as others seem to be.
65. (T) Most of the time I feel blue.
71. (T) These days I find it hard not to give up hope of amounting to something.
75. (F) I usually feel that life is worthwhile.
82. (T) I do many things which I regret afterwards (I regret things more than others seem to).
92. (T) I don't seem to care what happens to me.
95. (F) I am happy most of the time.
130. (T) I certainly feel useless at times.
146. (T) I cry easily.
215. (T) I brood a great deal.
234. (T) I believe I am a condemned person.
246. (T) I believe my sins are unpardonable.
277. (T) Even when I am with people I feel lonely much of the time.
303. (T) Most of the time I wish I were dead.
306. (T) No one cares much what happens to you.
331. (T) I am inclined to take things hard.
377. (T) I am not happy with myself the way I am.
388. (F) I very seldom have spells of the blues.
399. (T) The future is too uncertain for a person to make serious plans.
400. (T) Often, even though everything is going fine for me, I feel that I don't care about anything.
411. (T) At times I think I am no good at all.
454. (T) The future seems hopeless to me.
506. (T) I have recently considered killing myself.
512. (T) I have had a tragic loss in my life that I know I'll never get over.
516. (T) My life is empty and meaningless.
520. (T) Lately I have thought a lot about killing myself.
539. (T) Lately I have lost my desire to work out my problems.
546. (T) My thoughts these days turn more and more to death and the life herafter.
554. (T) When my life gets difficult, it makes me want to just give up.

HEA (Health Concerns)

11. (T) There seems to be a lump in my throat much of the time.
18. (T) I am troubled by attacks of nausea and vomiting.
20. (F) I am very seldom troubled by constipation.
28. (T) I am bothered by an upset stomach several times a week.
33. (F) I seldom worry about my health.
36. (T) I have a cough most of the time.
40. (T) Much of the time my head seems to hurt all over.
44. (T) Once a week or oftener I suddenly feel hot all over, for no real reason.
45. (F) I am in just as good physical health as most of my friends.
47. (F) I am almost never bothered by pains over my heart or in my chest.
53. (T) Parts of my body often have feelings like burning, tingling, crawling, or like "going to sleep".
57. (T) I hardly ever feel pain in the back of my neck.
59. (T) I am troubled by discomfort in the pit of my stomach every few days or oftener.
91. (F) I have little or no trouble with my muscles twitching or jumping.
97. (T) There seems to be a fullness in my head or nose most of the time.
101. (T) Often I feel as if there is a tight band around by head.
111. (T) I have a great deal of stomach trouble.
117. (F) I have never vomited blood or coughed up blood.
118. (F) I do not worry about catching diseases.
141. (F) During the past few years I have been well most of the time.
142. (F) I have never had a fit or convulsion.
149. (T) The top of my head sometimes feels tender.
159. (F) I have never had a fainting spell.
164. (F) I seldom or never have dizzy spells.
175. (T) I feel weak all over much of the time.
176. (F) I have very few headaches.
179. (F) I have had no difficulty in keeping my balance in walking.
181. (F) I do not have spells of hay fever or asthma.
194. (F) I have never had any breaking out on my skin that has worried me.
204. (F) My hearing is apparently as good as that of most people.
224. (F) I have few or no pains.
247. (T) I have numbness in one or more places on my skin.
249. (F) My eyesight is as good as it has been for years.
255. (F) I do not often notice my ears ringing or buzzing.
295. (F) I have never been paralyzed or had any unusual weakness of any of my muscles.
404. (F) I have no trouble swallowing.

BIZ (Bizarre Mentation)

24. (T) Evil spirits possess me at times.
32. (T) I have had very peculiar and strange experiences.
60. (T) When I am with people, I am bothered by hearing very strange things.
96. (T) I see things or animals or people around me that others do not see.
138. (T) I believe I am being plotted against.
162. (T) Someone has been trying to poison me.
198. (T) I often hear voices without knowing where they come from.
228. (T) There are persons who are trying to steal my thoughts and ideas.
259. (T) I am sure I am being talked about.
298. (T) Peculiar odors come to me at times.
311. (T) I often feel as if things are not real.
316. (T) I have strange and peculiar thoughts.
319. (T) I hear strange things when I am alone.
333. (T) People say insulting and vulgar things about me.
336. (T) Someone has control over my mind.
355. (T) At one or more times in my life I felt that someone was making me do things by hypnotizing me.

361. (T) Someone has been trying to influence my mind.
427. (F) I have never seen a vision.
466. (T) Sometimes I am sure that other people can tell what I am thinking.
490. (T) Ghosts or spirits can influence people for good or bad.
508. (T) I often feel I can read other people's minds.
543. (T) Terrible thoughts about my family come to me at times.
551. (T) I sometimes seem to hear my thoughts being spoken out loud.

ANG (Anger)

 29. (T) At times I feel like swearing.
 37. (T) At times I feel like smashing things.
116. (T) Often I can't understand why I have been so irritable and grouchy.
134. (T) At times I feel like picking a fist fight with someone.
302. (T) I easily become impatient with people.
389. (T) I am often said to be hotheaded.
410. (T) I am often so annoyed when someone tries to get ahead of me in a line of people that I speak to that person about it.
414. (T) I have at times had to be rough with people who were rude or annoying.
430. (T) I am often sorry because I am so irritable and grouchy.
461. (T) It makes me angry to have people hurry me.
486. (T) I am very stubborn.
513. (T) Sometimes I get so angry and upset I don't know what comes over me.
540. (T) I have gotten angry and broken furniture or dishes when I was drinking.
542. (T) I have become so angry with someone that I have felt as if I would explode.
548. (T) I've been so angry at times that I've hurt someone in a physical fight.
564. (F) I almost never lose self-control.

CYN (Cynicism)

 50. (T) I have often had to take orders from someone who did not know as much as I did.
 58. (T) I think a great many people exaggerate their misfortunes in order to gain the sympathy and help of others.
 76. (T) It takes a lot of argument to convince most people of the truth.
 81. (T) I think most people would lie to get ahead.
104. (T) Most people are honest chiefly because they are afraid of being caught.
110. (T) Most people will use somewhat unfair means to gain profit or an advantage rather than to lose it.
124. (T) I often wonder what hidden reason another person may have for doing something nice for me.
225. (T) My way of doing things is apt to be misunderstood by others.
241. (T) It is safer to trust nobody.
254. (T) Most people make friends because friends are likely to be useful to them.
283. (T) The person who provides temptation by leaving valuable property unprotected is about as much to blame for its theft as the one who steals it.
284. (T) I think nearly anyone would tell a lie to keep out of trouble.
286. (T) Most people inwardly dislike putting themselves out to help other people.
315. (T) I tend to be on my guard with people who are somewhat more friendly than I had expected.
346. (T) I have often met people who were supposed to be experts who were no better than I.
352. (T) People generally demand more respect for their own rights than they are willing to allow for others.
358. (T) I have often found people jealous of my good ideas, just because they had not thought of them first.
374. (T) Most people will use somewhat unfair means to get ahead in life.
399. (T) The future is too uncertain for a person to make serious plans.
403. (T) People have often misunderstood my intentions when I was trying to put them right and be helpful.

445. (T) I have frequently worked under people who seem to have things arranged so that they get credit for good work but are able to pass off mistakes onto those under them.
470. (T) A large number of people are guilty of bad sexual conduct.
538. (T) Most men are unfaithful to their wives now and then.

ASP (Antisocial Practices)

26. (T) I feel that it is certainly best to keep my mouth shut when I'm in touble.
35. (T) Sometimes when I was young I stole things.
66. (T) It would be better if almost all laws were thrown away.
81. (T) I think most people would lie to get ahead.
84. (T) I was suspended from school one or more times for bad behavior.
104. (T) Most people are honest chiefly because they are afraid of being caught.
105. (T) In school I was sometimes sent to the principal for bad behavior.
110. (T) Most people will use somewhat unfair means to gain profit or an advantage rather than to lose it.
123. (T) If I could get into a movie without paying and be sure I was not seen I would probably do it.
227. (T) I don't blame people for trying to grab everything they can get in this world.
240. (T) At times it has been impossible for me to keep from stealing or shoplifting something.
248. (T) I do not blame a person for taking advantage of people who leave themselves open to it.
250. (T) At times I have been so entertained by the cleverness of some criminals that I have hoped they would get away with it.
254. (T) Most people make friends because friends are likely to be useful to them.
266. (F) I have never been trouble with the law.
269. (T) If several people find themselves in trouble, the best thing for them to do is to agree upon a story and stick to it.
283. (T) The person who provides temptation by leaving valuable property unprotected is about as much to blame for its theft as the one who steals it.
284. (T) I think nearly anyone would tell a lie to keep out of trouble.
374. (T) Most people will use somewhat unfair means to get ahead in life.
412. (T) When I was young I often did not go to school even when I should have gone.
418. (T) It is all right to get around the law if you don't actually break it.
419. (T) There are certain people whom I dislike so much that I am inwardly pleased when they are catching it for something they have done.

TPA (Type A)

27. (T) When people do me a wrong, I feel I should pay them back if I can, just for the principle of the thing.
136. (T) It makes me impatient to have people ask my advice or otherwise interrupt me when I am working on something important.
151. (T) I resent having anyone trick me so cleverly that I have to admit I was fooled.
212. (T) I have at times stood in the way of people who were trying to do something, not because it amounted to much but because of the principle of the thing.
302. (T) I easily become impatient with people.
358. (T) I have often found people jealous of my good ideas, just because they had not thought of them first.
414. (T) I have at times had to be rough with people who were rude or annoying.
419. (T) There are certain people whom I dislike so much that I am inwardly pleased when they are catching it for something they have done.
420. (T) It makes me nervous to have to wait.
423. (T) I am often inclined to go out of my way to win a point with someone who has opposed me .
430. (T) I am often sorry because I am so irritable and grouchy.
437. (T) I am usually very direct with people I am trying to correct or improve.

507. (T) I often become very irritable when people interrupt my work.
510. (T) Others tell me I eat too fast.
523. (T) At movies, restaurants, or sporting events, I hate to have to stand in line.
531. (T) I work very long hours even though my job doesn't require this.
535. (T) I get very irritable when people I depend on don't get their work done on time.
541. (T) I work best when I have a definite deadline.
545. (T) I always have too little time to get things done.

LSE (Low Self-Esteem)

61. (F) I am an important person.
70. (T) I am easily downed in an argument.
73. (T) I am certainly lacking in self-confidence.
78. (F) I am liked by most people who know me.
109. (F) I seem to be about as capable and smart as most others around me.
130. (T) I certainly feel useless at times.
235. (T) I was a slow learner in school.
326. (T) I have several times given up doing a thing because I thought too little of my ability.
369. (T) I am apt to pass up something I want to do when others feel that it isn't worth doing.
376. (T) I do not feel I can plan my own future.
380. (T) It bothers me when people say nice things about me.
411. (T) At times I think I am no good at all.
421. (T) I am apt to pass up something I want to do because others feel that I am not going about it in the right way.
450. (T) I cannot do anything well.
457. (T) People can pretty easily change my mind even when I have made a decision about something.
475. (T) Often I get confused and forget what I want to say.
476. (T) I am very awkward and clumsy.
483. (T) People do not find me attractive.
485. (T) I often feel that I'm not as good as other people.
503. (T) When problems need to be solved, I usually let other people take charge.
504. (T) I recognize several faults in myself that I will not be able to change.
519. (T) I get angry with myself for giving in to other people so much.
526. (T) I know I am a burden to others.
562. (T) It is hard for me to accept compliments.

SOD (Social Discomfort)

46. (T) I prefer to pass by school friends, or people I know but have not seen for a long time, unless they speak to me first.
49. (F) I am a very sociable person.
86. (F) I like to go to parties and other affairs where there is lots of loud fun.
158. (T) It makes me uncomfortable to put on a stunt at a party even when others are doing the same sort of things.
167. (T) I find it hard to make talk when I meet new people.
185. (T) I wish I were not so shy.
262. (F) In a group of people I would not be embarrassed to be called upon to start a discussion or give an opinion about something I know well.
265. (T) I am likely not to speak to people until they speak to me.
275. (T) In school I found it very hard to talk in front of the class.
280. (F) I seem to make friends about as quickly as others do.
281. (T) I dislike having people around me.
321. (F) I have no dread of going into a room by myself where other people have already gathered and are talking.
337. (T) At parties I am more likely to sit by myself or with just one other person than to join in with the crowd.
340. (F) I love to go to dances.
349. (T) I am never happier than when alone.

353. (F) I enjoy social gatherings just to be with people.
359. (F) I enjoy the excitement of a crowd.
360. (F) I do not mind meeting strangers.
363. (F) My worries seem to disappear when I get into a crowd of lively friends.
367. (T) Whenever possible I avoid being in a crowd.
370. (F) I like parties and socials.
479. (T) Some people think it's hard to get to know me.
480. (T) I spend most of my spare time by myself.
515. (T) I am never happier than when I am by myself.

FAM (Family Problems)

21. (T) At times I have very much wanted to leave home.
54. (T) My family does not like the work I have chosen (or the work I intend to choose for my lifework).
83. (F) I have very few quarrels with members of my family.
125. (F) I believe that my home life is as pleasant as that of most people I know.
145. (T) I feel that I have often been punished without cause.
190. (T) My people treat me more like a child than a grown-up.
195. (T) There is very little love and companionship in my family as compared to other homes.
205. (T) Some of my family have habits that bother and annoy me very much.
217. (F) My relatives are nearly all in sympathy with me.
256. (T) Once in a while I feel hate towards members of my family whom I usually love.
292. (T) The things that some of my family have done have frightened me.
300. (T) I have reason for feeling jealous of one or more members of my family.
323. (T) Sometimes I enjoy hurting persons I love.
378. (T) I get angry when my friends or family give me advice on how to live my life.
379. (T) I got many beatings when I was a child.
382. (T) I often have serious disagreements with people who are close to me.
383. (F) When things get really bad, I know I can count on my family for help.
413. (T) One or more members of my family are very nervous.
449. (T) Some of my family have quick tempers.
455. (F) The members of my family and my close relatives get along quite well.
478. (T) I hate my whole family.
543. (T) Terrible thoughts about my family come to me at times.
550. (T) I have very little to do with my relatives now.
563. (T) In most marriages one or both partners are unhappy.
567. (T) Most married couples don't show much affection for each other.

WRK (Work Interference)

10. (F) I am about as able to work as I ever was.
15. (T) I work under a great deal of tension.
17. (T) I am sure I get a raw deal from life.
31. (T) I find it hard to keep my mind on a task or job.
54. (T) My family does not like the work I have chosen (or the work I intend to choose for my lifework).
73. (T) I am certainly lacking in self-confidence.
98. (T) Some people are so bossy that I feel like doing the opposite of what they request, even though I know they are right.
108. (F) Anyone who is able and willing to work hard has a good chance of succeeding.
135. (T) I have often lost out on things because I couldn't make up my mind soon enough.
233. (T) I have difficulty in starting to do things.
243. (T) When in a group of people I have trouble thinking of the right things to talk about.
299. (T) I cannot keep my mind on one thing.
302. (T) I easily become impatient with people.
318. (F) I usually expect to succeed in things I do.

339. (T) I have sometimes felt that difficulties were piling up so high that I could not overcome them.
364. (T) I feel like giving up quickly when things go wrong.
368. (T) I shrink from facing a crisis or difficulty.
394. (T) My plans have frequently seemed so full of difficulties that I have had to give them up.
409. (T) It bothers me to have someone watch me at work even though I know I can do it well.
428. (T) I have several times had a change of heart about my lifework.
445. (T) I have frequently worked under people who seem to have things arranged so that they get credit for good work but are able to pass off mistakes onto those under them.
464. (T) I feel tired a good deal of the time.
491. (T) I feel helpless when I have to make some important decisions.
505. (T) I am so sick of what I have to do every day that I just want to get out of it all.
509. (T) Having to make important decisions makes me nervous.
517. (T) I find it difficult to hold down a job.
521. (F) I like making decisions and assigning jobs to others.
525. (T) Everything is going on too fast around me.
545. (T) I always have too little time to get things done.
554. (T) When my life gets difficult, it makes me want to just give up.
559. (T) The people I work with are not sympathetic with my problems.
561. (F) I usually have enough energy to do my work.
566. (T) When I am sad or blue, it is my work that suffers.

TRT (Negative Treatment Indicators)

 22. (T) No one seems to understand me.
 92. (T) I don't seem to care what happens to me.
274. (T) I am so touchy on some subjects that I can't talk about them.
306. (T) No one cares much what happens to you.
364. (T) I feel like giving up quickly when things go wrong.
368. (T) I shrink from facing a crisis or difficulty.
373. (T) I have done some bad things in the past that I never tell anybody about.
375. (T) It makes me nervous when people ask me personal questions.
376. (T) I do not feel I can plan my own future.
377. (F) I am not happy with myself the way I am.
391. (T) I feel unable to tell anyone all about myself.
399. (T) The future is too uncertain for a person to make serious plans.
482. (T) I usually have a hard time deciding what to do.
488. (T) Mental illness is a sign of weakness.
491. (T) I feel helpless when I have to make some important decisions.
493. (F) When I have a problem it helps to talk it over with someone.
494. (F) My main goals in life are within my reach.
495. (T) I believe that people should keep personal problems to themselves.
497. (T) It bothers me greatly to think of making changes in my life.
499. (T) I hate going to doctors even when I'm sick.
500. (T) Although I am not happy with my life, there is nothing I can do about it now.
501. (F) Talking over problems and worries with someone is often more helpful than taking drugs or medicine.
504. (T) I recognize several faults in myself that I will not be able to change.
528. (T) Much of the trouble I'm having is due to bad luck.
539. (T) Lately I have lost my desire to work out my problems.
554. (T) When my life gets difficult, it makes me want to just give up.

Appendix J
Converting MMPI-2 Content Scales Raw Scores into Uniform T Scores

Males

RAW SCORE	ANX	FRS	OBS	DEP	HEA	BIZ	ANG	CYN	ASP	TPA	LSE	SOD	FAM	WRK	TRT
36					112										
35					110										
34					108										
33				100	106									98	
32				99	105									96	
31				97	103									94	
30				95	101									92	
29				94	99									90	
28				92	97									89	
27				90	95									87	
26				88	93									85	104
25				87	91								105	83	101
24				85	89						101	89	102	81	99
23	92	113		83	87	120		83			98	86	99	79	96
22	90	119		82	85	119		80	94		96	84	97	78	94
21	87	107		80	83	115		77	90		93	81	94	76	91
20	85	103		78	81	112		74	87		91	78	91	74	89
19	82	100		77	80	108		71	83	89	88	76	88	72	86
18	80	97		75	78	105		68	79	85	85	73	85	70	84
17	77	93		73	76	101		65	76	81	83	71	82	68	81
16	75	90	87	71	74	98	86	62	72	77	80	68	80	67	79
15	72	87	84	70	72	94	82	59	69	72	77	65	77	65	76
14	70	84	80	68	70	91	78	56	65	68	75	63	74	63	74
13	67	80	77	66	68	88	74	54	62	64	72	60	71	61	71
12	65	77	73	65	66	84	70	52	58	60	70	58	68	59	69
11	62	74	70	63	64	81	67	51	55	56	67	55	66	57	66
10	60	70	66	61	62	77	63	49	53	53	64	54	63	56	64
9	57	67	63	59	60	74	59	48	51	50	62	52	60	54	61
8	55	64	59	58	58	70	56	47	49	48	59	50	57	52	59
7	53	60	56	56	56	67	53	46	47	46	57	49	55	50	56
6	52	57	53	55	53	63	50	44	46	44	55	47	52	48	54
5	50	54	50	53	51	60	48	43	44	43	53	45	50	46	52
4	47	51	47	51	48	57	46	41	42	41	51	43	47	44	49
3	45	48	44	48	44	54	43	40	40	38	48	41	44	41	47
2	42	45	41	45	41	51	40	38	37	36	45	39	41	39	43
1	39	41	37	41	37	46	36	35	34	32	41	35	37	36	39
0	35	35	33	36	33	39	32	32	30	30	35	32	33	33	35
RAW SCORE	ANX	FRS	OBS	DEP	HEA	BIZ	ANG	CYN	ASP	TPA	LSE	SOD	FAM	WRK	TRT

Females

ANX	FRS	OBS	DEP	HEA	BIZ	ANG	CYN	ASP	TPA	LSE	SOD	FAM	WRK	TRT	RAW SCORE
				107											36
				105											35
				103											34
			97	101									99		33
			95	100									97		32
			93	98									95		31
			92	96									92		30
			90	94									90		29
			88	92									88		28
			87	90									86		27
			85	89									84	102	26
			83	87								99	82	100	25
			82	85						97	87	96	80	97	24
89	101		80	83	113		83			94	84	94	78	95	23
86	98		78	81	110		80	98		92	82	91	76	92	22
84	94		77	79	108		77	94		89	80	89	73	89	21
81	91		75	77	105		75	91		86	77	86	71	87	20
79	88		73	76	102		72	88	94	84	75	83	69	84	19
76	85		72	74	99		69	85	90	81	72	81	67	82	18
74	81		70	72	96		67	82	86	78	70	78	65	79	17
71	78	87	68	70	93	88	64	79	81	76	68	75	63	77	16
69	75	83	67	68	90	84	61	75	77	73	65	73	61	74	15
66	72	79	65	66	87	80	58	72	73	70	63	70	59	72	14
64	68	75	63	64	84	76	56	69	69	68	60	68	57	69	13
61	65	71	62	63	81	72	54	66	64	65	58	65	55	67	12
59	62	67	60	61	79	68	53	63	60	62	56	62	54	64	11
56	59	63	58	59	76	64	51	59	56	60	54	60	52	61	10
55	56	59	57	57	73	60	50	56	53	57	52	57	51	59	9
53	53	56	55	55	70	56	48	54	50	55	51	55	50	57	8
51	51	53	54	53	67	53	47	52	48	54	49	52	48	55	7
49	48	50	52	51	64	50	46	49	45	52	48	50	46	53	6
47	46	48	50	49	61	47	44	47	43	51	46	47	45	51	5
45	43	46	48	46	58	45	42	45	41	49	44	45	43	49	4
43	41	44	45	43	56	42	40	42	38	47	41	42	40	46	3
40	38	41	42	40	52	39	38	39	36	44	39	39	37	43	2
37	35	37	39	36	47	36	35	36	33	40	35	36	34	39	1
34	31	32	34	32	39	31	32	33	30	35	32	32	31	35	0

ANX FRS OBS DEP HEA BIZ ANG CYN ASP TPA LSE SOD FAM WRK TRT RAW SCORE

Index

Index

James N. Butcher is a professor of psychology at the University of Minnesota. He is author of numerous books, including *A Handbook of Cross-National MMPI Research*, with Paolo Pancheri (Minnesota, 1976), *New Developments in the Use of the MMPI* (Minnesota, 1979), and *Abnormal Psychology and Modern Life* (1988). Butcher contributes to the *Journal of Consulting and Clinical Psychology*.

John R. Graham is a professor of psychology and director of clinical training at Kent State University. His books include *The MMPI: A Practical Guide*, now in a second edition and *MMPI-2: Assessing Personality and Psychopathology* (forthcoming).

Carolyn L. Williams is an assistant professor of epidemiology in the School of Public Health, University of Minnesota, and co-editor, with Joseph Westermeyer, of *Refugee Mental Health in Resettlement Countries*.

Yossef S. Ben-Porath is a postdoctoral fellow in psychology at the University of Minnesota. His articles on the MMPI-2 have appeared in *Psychological Assessment: A Journal of Consulting and Clinical Psychology* and the *Journal of Personality Assessment*.